W9-AXK-807

To Cormac & Moira

from all the farwoods
with thanks for a
memorable weekend
— the first of many
if you'll have us.

Gerry   Vicky

CLIVE ASLET
AND ALAN POWERS

THE NATIONAL TRUST
BOOK OF
THE ENGLISH HOUSE

VIKING
in association with the
NATIONAL TRUST

VIKING

Penguin Books Ltd, Harmondsworth, Middlesex, England
Viking Penguin Inc., 40 West 23rd Street, New York, New York 10010, U.S.A.
Penguin Books Australia Ltd, Ringwood, Victoria, Australia
Penguin Books Canada Ltd, 2801 John Street, Markham, Ontario, Canada L3R 1B4
Penguin Books (N.Z.) Ltd, 182–190 Wairau Road, Auckland 10, New Zealand

First published 1985

Copyright © Clive Aslet and Alan Powers, 1985

All rights reserved.
No part of this publication may be reproduced,
stored in a retrieval system, or transmitted in any form
or by any means, electronic, mechanical, photocopying,
recording or otherwise, without the prior
permission of the copyright owner.

Set in Clowes Dante
Typeset by CCC, printed and bound in Great Britain by
William Clowes Limited, Beccles and London

Designed by Judith Gordon

BRITISH LIBRARY CATALOGUING IN PUBLICATION DATA

Aslet, Clive
The National Trust book of the English House.
1. Architecture, Domestic—England—History
2. Country homes—England—History
I. Title   II. Powers, Alan
728.8′3′0942   NA7620

ISBN 0–670–80175–5

CONTENTS

PREFACE

*There are few things so good – and therefore
so well worth describing – as a
good English house.*

Robert Kerr, *The Gentleman's House*, 1864

What is there to say in another book on the English house? The subject may seem to have been pretty thoroughly treated from most points of view – large houses, small houses, regional houses, houses of different periods. Many people's image of the English house is of a palatial house on a big estate in the country. Everyone now has a clear idea of how a duke used to live. But there have always been comparatively few dukes; a much larger number of owners were rich merchants, successful businessmen, younger sons of the aristocracy, farmers, churchmen, retired admirals and clever lawyers. Theirs were houses of the middling size. Since English society has always had a special respect for land ownership, they often built in the country, or what looked like the country, although they may have had a town house instead or as well. Whether or not they farmed on a big scale, they were probably able to grow their own vegetables and cultivate their own orchards, and perhaps keep their own hens and milch cows. There were of course no shops for these commodities until the twentieth century. The few acres immediately around the house also formed an agreeable setting which ensured the privacy that is so highly regarded by English people. These gentlemanly but not over-grand houses form an unbroken and typically English line from the manor houses of the Saxons to the present. These are the houses that we wanted to write about.

The subject had a great fascination and emotional appeal in the early part of this century. This was reflected in the nature of the National Trust's early houses, which tended to be the smaller, vernacular type. They then seemed the ones most at risk. But as the century progressed, and especially since the Second World War, the great houses that looked as though they would stand for ever have come increasingly under threat. Those that came to the Trust have become show-places of unsurpassed splendour. They are household names. The less glamorous houses of the middling size have, by contrast, attracted less attention from scholars, media and public – although happily they still have a special if less vaunted place in the Trust. Unlike the great houses they still serve the needs of modern life as well as they served the needs of their builders. Their appeal is that they can be lived in; they remain essentially private even when they are open to visitors.

While the middling-sized house has a continuous history, we have chosen to treat it as a series of themes rather than in strict chronological succession. Thus the first chapter, which defines and explains the growth of the vernacular house from Saxon times, continues the story through the traditionally built cottages and farmhouses of the eighteenth century and even into the vernacular revival of the twentieth century. The second chapter begins with the intrusion of the Classical ideas of the Renaissance into the national English style of the Tudor period. Classicism is a theme which encompasses the majority of houses built from then until the early nineteenth century. But concurrently there developed an increasingly romantic and backward-looking tendency in style, which was the basis of Victorian stylistic diversity. This is the subject of the third chapter. But then the English house is not all a question of building methods and architectural style: the look of a house, not to mention the comfort, convenience and health of those who live in it, was also determined by how it was run. The domestic arrangements, which reached a high point of complexity in the mid-Victorian period, are described in Chapter 4. The fifth chapter begins by examining the Edwardian house – the summation of much that went before – as it was seen by the celebrated German observer Hermann Muthesius. It traces the history of the architect-designed middling-sized house into our own day. One of the important achievements of the twentieth century has been to transfer the standards of the middle-class house to mass housing, particularly through the Garden Suburb ideal. This is the subject of the last section of the book. It takes us away from the genus of the prosperous middle-class house, but takes up the theme of the cottage which has been an undercurrent throughout. Because many of the leading ideas introduced into the middling-sized house were carried over into mass housing – often by the same architects – the history of the English house has a direct bearing on the lives of millions of people in England today.

The book is principally about English houses, but we have from time to time ventured over the Borders to touch on the national traditions of Scotland and Wales. We have also tried to describe the principal characteristics of middle-class town houses of each period. However, we have not confined ourselves rigidly to middling-sized houses but have mentioned large houses where their influence down the scale made it imperative. While incorporating as much original research as we could, we have where possible concentrated on buildings that can be visited or at least still seen. As one travels round the country one inevitably sees far more buildings of the nineteenth and twentieth centuries than from the previous thousand years. So much more was built, so much more survives. We have therefore given more weight to the last two centuries than previous books, and we have brought our account right into the present day.

The scheme of the book was worked out in collaboration. Alan Powers wrote Chapters 1 and 2, Clive Aslet Chapters 3 and 4. Having been thinking along similar lines from the time we studied together in Cambridge, we discovered no problem in writing the fifth and sixth chapters over one typewriter in a middling-sized house of the early twentieth century in the Green Belt in Surrey.

We wish to thank Peter Davidson, FSA (Scot.), for information on Scottish houses for Chapter 1; Marcus Binney for an advance proof copy of the chapter on villas from his book on Sir Robert Taylor; Andrew Saint for the loan of an unpublished lecture, 'Heat, Light and Drains'; and Catriona Luckhurst for her care and skill in editing.

ACKNOWLEDGEMENTS

Photographs: Aerofilms Ltd, 19; *Architectural Review*, 131, 132 (Martin Charles) 136; Austin, James, 36, 51, 141, 142; Avoncroft Museum of Buildings, Bromsgrove, 13, 130; Bryant, Richard (Arcaid), 18; Burns, Howard (Conway Library), 49; Peter Burton, 33; *Country Life*, 8, 12, 22, 38, 39, 40, 41, 42, 43, 45, 47, 52, 53, 54, 58, 62, 71, 73, 74, 78, 82, 83, 91, 105, 107, 111, 118, 122; Davis, Norman, 132; Einzig, Richard (Arcaid), 133; Erith and Terry, 44, 135; Fawcett, David, 11; Fiennes, Mark, 127; First Garden City Museum, Letchworth, 144; Giraudon (with permission from the town of Bayeux), 7; GLC, 50, 94, 96, 102, 103, 137; Guildhall Library, London, 80; Hall, George H., 76; Harris Museum and Art Gallery, Preston, 95; Haywood, Trevor, 10, Howard, Geoff, 90, 120; Judges Postcards Ltd, Hastings, 9; Kersting, A. F., 6, 14, 20, 23, 32, 37, 64, 68, 72, 86, 89, 92, 104; Nairn, Ian, 130; National Monuments Record, 5, 28, 29, 66, 77, 88 (Gordon Barnes); National Trust, 1, 2, 16, 21, 31, 34, 35, 56, 59, 84; National Trust for Scotland, 4; New, Godfrey, 53, 80; Oxfordshire County Libraries, 65; Picturepoint Ltd, 57; Powers, Alan, 121, 139; RIBA Drawings Collection, 85, 108, 115, 116, 119, 124, 125, 128, 129; Rogue Images, 63, 93; Royal Commission on Ancient and Historical Monuments of Scotland, 79; Science Museum, London, 100; Smith, Edwin, 24, 25, 26, 27, 69, 138; Suffolk Archaeological Unit, 3; Whitaker, Jeremy, 17; Widdicombe, Derek, 15, 30; Winstone, Reece, 46.

Text figures redrawn or adapted by Richard Andrews and John Sandham based on illustrations published by: Heinemann Educational in *Homes Fit for Heroes* by Mark Swenarton, fig. 17; HMSO, figs. 1, 4; Penguin Books in the Buildings of England series, fig. 5, in *Architecture in Britain 1530–1830* by John Summerson, fig. 11 in *Georgian London* by John Summerson, fig. 12; Society for Medieval Archaeology, University College, London, in *Mediaeval Cruck-building and its Derivatives* by F. W. B. Charles, figs. 2, 3. Figs. 10 and 13 are based on original plans held by the National Trust. Figs. 6 and 7 were drawn by Richard Harris and are reproduced courtesy of the Weald and Downland Open Air Museum.

1. The Old Clergy House, Alfriston, East Sussex, late fourteenth century.
Shown here shortly before its acquisition and restoration by
the National Trust in 1896.

▣ ONE ▣

THE MEDIEVAL
AND VERNACULAR HOUSE

A time there was – as one may guess
And as, indeed, earth's testimonies tell
Before the birth of consciousness,
When all went well

Thomas Hardy, *Before Life and After*

In 1896, a year after its foundation, the National Trust acquired its first building. A nominal sum of ten pounds was paid for the Clergy House at Alfriston, in the chalk country of the South Downs. Until the early nineteenth century, the house had sheltered successive parish priests, and in 1888 a new vicar began to campaign for the restoration of the sadly neglected building.

The repairs were carried out between 1896 and 1897. They had momentous consequences for the future of England's historic houses. The Clergy House was typical of the early buildings – small medieval structures which needed immediate attention to save them from collapse – acquired by the Trust and restored as habitable dwellings. In its early years, the Trust shared many aims with the Society for the Protection of Ancient Buildings, tracing a common ancestry from the artistic and social writings of John Ruskin. The Clergy House was restored for £350 by one of the Society's enthusiastic young architects, Alfred Powell, using authentic materials like rammed chalk for the floor, and making as few alterations to the building as possible. Within a few years, other collaborations between the Society and the Trust helped to preserve the Old Post Office at Tintagel (supervised by Detmar Blow, 1904) and the Priest's House at Muchelney, Somerset (supervised by Sidney Barnsley, 1911, at a cost of £65).

Thus the late nineteenth century realized, none too soon, the value of the smaller domestic buildings of the Middle Ages and after, which we now call vernacular.

One immediately recognizable vernacular quality of the Clergy House is use of local building materials – oak for the timber frame and chalk for the

2. The Old Post Office, Tintagel, fourteenth century. A small manor-house of rough stone,
saved from destruction in 1895 and restored by the National Trust in 1904.

floor. The Horsham stone which formed the original roof came from further
afield, and there may even have been roofing stones from Devon, which were
carried all round the coast of England.

Another way of identifying vernacular buildings is through their conformity
to type. They are part of folk art, in which originality is not sought or valued.
Thus the Clergy House is an example of the commonest type of house in the
south-east between 1400 and 1500, the Wealden house. The typical features of

a Wealden house are the projecting ends – in this case only one – where the upper storey is 'jettied' out over the ground floor. In between, the central section, which is the open hall common to all medieval houses, appears to be recessed under the eaves of the hipped roof.

Although one might now think of the Clergy House as a cottage, it represents the size and standard of house which was generally found not far below the ranks of the nobility. Status was not expressed in the number of rooms, but in the size of the timbers and the quality of their ornamentation. There was a finely moulded and carved cross-beam behind the priest as he sat to take his meals at the upper end of the hall. The ogee-headed service doors (with a double curve) which he looked down to at the other end were signs that the wrights (or house carpenters) had been asked to build a house as good as any yeoman farmer's.

No builder's name is recorded, as is usual with vernacular buildings. Even the date would be uncertain if outside evidence did not suggest a time around 1400. Indeed, similar houses were built for over a hundred years, as the late Wealden house at Bignor, Sussex, demonstrates.

It is uncertainties like these which make the study of vernacular buildings so attractive. The Clergy House serves well to illustrate the architectural meaning of 'vernacular', a term borrowed from the study of language.

The vernacular exists in a clearly defined historical period between the twelfth and nineteenth centuries. Within that period, it constitutes a middle band in the complete range of building activity. To one side is 'polite' architecture, the work of professional masons and architects who aimed at a degree of artistic expression through building, and worked in a national or international context. To the other side is the building work of untutored amateurs. The Clergy House was built by professionals, otherwise its timber frame would not have survived intact through so many years of decay and neglect.

To quote Nikolaus Pevsner, 'A bicycle shed is a building; Lincoln Cathedral is a piece of architecture.'[1] Vernacular architecture, or building, is not quite like either, and needs a separate category of its own. Being folk art rather than 'High Art', it evolved differently in different regions, although the same approach to the problems of building existed everywhere.

As already mentioned, a fundamental part of vernacular character is the use of local materials, giving rise to the development of regional schools of building. There were also differences resulting from farming practice, since most vernacular buildings were associated with the life of the land. In Wales and the north-west, for instance, farming was based on cattle raising, and so the long-house, in which men and animals lived under the same roof and sometimes almost in the same room, was a long-lasting tradition.

Vernacular building was very conservative. Plans and types of construction evolved slowly, and ways of making joints or fitting roof timbers together were passed down through the generations. The changes that did take place were partly the result of demands for space and light in houses; for example, the aisled hall with its low sweeping roof and posts standing in the middle of the floor gave way to single-span roofs with higher walls. Cross wings were built in order to have larger rooms at each end of the hall. Changes were also linked to the availability of timbers. When the great oaks had been used up for building, ships or firewood, smaller trees and other types of wood had to take their place. In some areas only poor wood was available, but stone gradually took its place.

It would be a mistake, though, to attribute every feature of vernacular building to such material causes. We cannot suppose that the choice of great timbers for the cruck halls of the West Midlands was entirely the result of structural calculations. They were evidently designed to delight the eye and to impress. They have the same type of aesthetic effect as more sophisticated architecture of later periods. At the same time, vernacular buildings are distinguishable from polite architecture by a lack of self-consciousness. They seem to speak of a lost world of innocence when buildings satisfied simple human needs. Vernacular buildings do not strive to be beautiful, clever or original, and as a consequence they avoid being ugly, mean-spirited or vulgar.

The poet and artist William Blake was a pioneer of vernacular appreciation. As he wrote to John Flaxman from the cottage at Felpham, Sussex, which he had been lent in 1800:

> We are safe arrived at our Cottage, which is more beautiful than I thought it, & more convenient. It is a perfect Model for Cottages &, I think, for Palaces of Magnificence, only Enlarging, not altering its proportions, & adding ornaments & not principals. Nothing can be more grand in its Simplicity and Usefulness. Simple without Intricacy, it seems to be the Spontaneous Effusion of Humanity, congenial to the wants of Man. No other formed House can ever please me so well; nor shall I ever be perswaded, I believe, that it can be improved either in Beauty or Use.[2]

At this date there was a sentimental appreciation of old cottages, but it was not until the end of the nineteenth century that vernacular buildings were studied methodically.

Are all medieval houses vernacular? We should perhaps exclude houses built by expert stonemasons, the medieval equivalent of architects. There are also houses which should more properly be considered as castles. Nevertheless, the majority of surviving medieval houses fall clearly within the definition of vernacular that we have established.

By the sixteenth century, the majority of houses of wealthy persons and of the court were 'polite' in outline, following the new fashion for symmetry and flat roofs. There was still a considerable vernacular influence, however, in the choice of building materials and the design of structural details.

Montacute, Somerset, 1588–c. 1600, a grand and courtly house, still has in its hall a distinctly 'folk-art' plaster relief of the unfaithful husband 'riding the Skimmington'.

In the seventeenth and eighteenth centuries, the 'polite threshold', that is the boundary between polite and vernacular architecture, moved further down the social scale, so that middle-class houses in the south east of England reflected some architectural ideas ultimately derived from the Italian Renaissance. By the time that William Blake was lauding his Felpham cottage, traditional vernacular only survived for cottages and farm buildings, although the growing industries had achieved a new vernacular of their own.

By the time the National Trust bought the Clergy House, it would be safe to say that genuine vernacular was dead, and a large and sympathetic body of experts, backed by the sentiments of the public, was already mourning its demise.

There is a direct continuity from the Middle Ages to the end of the vernacular. These houses have a common sense of breadth and simplicity and other more detailed qualities which will become apparent as we look at them more closely.

THE EARLIEST HOUSES

Knowledge of pre-vernacular houses is very fragmentary. We may begin with the settlements at the extreme ends of the British Isles, in the Penwith peninsula, Cornwall, and in the Orkney Islands, where stone-built houses have been excavated which are usually round in form, suggesting a roof supported by a central post.

At Skara Brae, in the Orkneys, the neolithic settlement of six to eight houses is extraordinarily complete. The houses were built of well-coursed stone, and include built-in stone furniture which would be perfectly serviceable today, yet the period of settlement was between 3100 and 2450 BC. A sandstorm finally covered them until excavations began in 1850.

These houses were rather more advanced than the windowless 'black houses' which survived in recent times in the Outer Hebrides, built of loose stone with a turf roof which needed the heat of the fire to keep it from dissolution.

Of English houses before the Roman occupation, very little direct evidence has survived. The houses of the Romans themselves were an isolated interlude of sophistication, although it is interesting to note that they adapted to local circumstances by using wood framing for the upper floors, to contrast with brick and tile below.

The succession leading to the English vernacular really begins with the Saxons. Their halls were rectangular in plan and entirely built of wood. They were arranged in apparently random clusters in villages in the eastern parts of England. It may be assumed that they brought their building skills with them from the Continent, for Anglo-Saxon houses closely resemble the description given by the Roman historian Tacitus:

It is sufficiently well-known that none of the Germanic people dwell in cities, and that they do not even tolerate houses which are built in rows. They dwell apart and at a distance from one another, according to the preference which they may have for the stream, the plain or the grove. They do not lay out their village after our fashion, with the buildings contiguous to each other and in close contact. Every man surrounds his house with a space, either for protection against the accident of fire, or from ignorance of the art of building. They do not make use of stone cut from the quarry, or of tiles; for every kind of building they make use of unshapely wood, which falls short of beauty and attractiveness. They carefully colour some parts of their building with earth which is so clear and bright as to resemble painting and coloured designs.

The appearance of Saxon houses may be seen in an archaeological reconstruction at West Stow, near Bury St Edmunds in Suffolk. There were some eighty buildings on a hill-top site, occupied between AD 400 and 650. The windowless thatched buildings were up to 30 ft (9 m) long, with walls of wooden staves. They had a clay hearth opposite the door, and were probably floored with planks over a pit. A common Saxon form was the long house, which provided accommodation for cattle at one end and for humans at the other. An example with stone walls and a turf roof has been excavated at Mawgan Porth in Cornwall far from the main area of Saxon settlement. The long house continued to be used in remote regions like Wales and the Lake District for many centuries. A superstition existed that the cattle should be able to see the fire and, more practically, the heat from their bodies added to the general warmth. In later examples, the shippon or byre is separated from the house by a cross passage, but is still built under the same roof-line.

Saxon houses made skilful use of a limited range of woodworking techniques and established a generous scale of construction which remained a pattern for

3. A reconstructed Anglo-Saxon settlement at West Stow, Suffolk, based on archaeological evidence from the period 400 to 600 AD.

the Middle Ages. The hall, with its hearth and high roof, was the main room of the house – other rooms were hardly considered.

THE NORMAN CONQUEST

The date of the Norman Conquest, 1066, is not of immediate importance in the history of the English house. Nevertheless, at some time during the early Norman period changes took place in the use of timber which contributed to the establishment of the vernacular building techniques.

Saxon houses were built with posts set into holes dug into the soil. At some date, perhaps even before the Conquest, wooden beams, called sill-plates, were laid on the ground instead, and the upright members were jointed into them. A house built like this naturally leaves little evidence for the archaeologist, so not much is known of timber houses before the earliest surviving examples from the twelfth century.

The Conquest led to a transformation of the complicated Anglo-Saxon system of property rights into the more rigid feudal system of France, the monument to which is the Domesday Book of 1086. The classic pattern of the English village was established, with church, manor-house and lesser houses in an informal grouping. The manor was an important piece of property, which was granted by the king, but could be inherited or bought and sold. The manor-house provided a residence for the lord of the manor or his representative, and was sometimes the site of the manorial court, the bottom layer of the pyramid of local authority. At this early period, it is likely to have been the only substantial house in the village, although not necessarily very large, particularly in remote parts of the country.

The castles of the Norman barons provided more domestic accommodation than did most houses; in their keeps rooms were piled on top of each other and topped off with a flat roof. The aisled stone hall at Oakham Castle, Rutland, c. 1180–90, is closer to the traditional manor-house in form, but is built with the sophistication of cathedral masons. The form of the tower house became part of the vernacular of the Border counties of England, where defence was necessary. The towers had three or four floors and stood at the corner of a pele, or barmkin – the enclosure in which cattle were herded in times of alarm. Some villages had a 'vicar's pele', which was meant to provide communal protection. The tower houses would not have resisted a serious siege, but presumably deterred the casual marauder. They were necessarily built of stone, with features like arrow-loops and battlements.

The tower house is only of marginal importance in England, but in Scotland it was the main form of dwelling for the gentleman and the yeoman farmer. In the social structure of Scotland, the class differences were not as great as in England, so that anyone could style himself a laird who owned a small farm and a house which, in theory at least, was defensible. In R. L. Stevenson's *Kidnapped*, David Balfour describes himself as being 'of Shaws', to be accused by Alan Breck of 'tagging a midden-yard to his name'.

Tower houses continued to be built when the need for defence had largely vanished. The early-seventeenth-century Scotstarvit Tower in Fife was over a hundred years out of date compared to the Renaissance novelties of Falkland Palace.

4 and 5. Scotstarvit Tower, Fife. A seventeenth-century survivor of the tower-house form, contrasted with the more domestic bastle house of the borders, at Glassonby, Cumbria, of the sixteenth century.

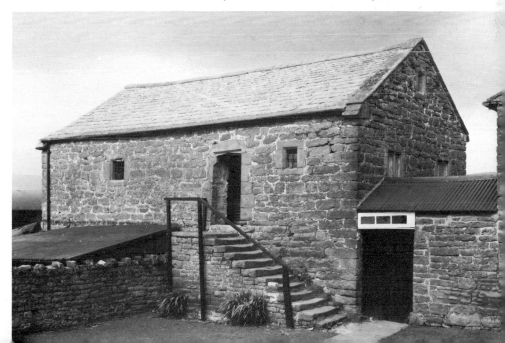

A later, more domestic variant of the tower house was the bastle house, which is only found in a restricted area of England close to the Border. It was a response to the severe Border troubles of the Tudor period, consisting of a two-storey building in which the livestock was housed at ground level, and people on the upper floor, reached by an outside stone stair.

The outside stair persisted in the burghs (or towns) of lowland Scotland into the nineteenth century, and many examples can be seen at Culross and other ports of Fife. The lower floor is used for storage, or as a separate tenement.

The bastle house resembles the two-storey domestic buildings of the Norman period which were built of stone and are the earliest English houses to survive in continuous use. Among them are the Manor House, Hemingford Gray, Cambridgeshire, 1150, and Boothby Pagnell, Lincolnshire, 1180. Many

6. The interior of the Manor House, Hemingford Grey, Cambridgeshire. An upper room of c. 1150 with original stonework and fireplace.

apparently similar houses exist in fragmentary form or can be traced from records, but there is much more that one would like to know about them. They are massive and simple in shape, with few touches of ornament.

It has usually been assumed that the upper storeys of these buildings were used as halls. In the Bayeux Tapestry (*c.* 1077), a house at Bosham, Sussex, is depicted. It is one of the best pictures of a house from such an early period. King Harold is shown dining in the upper room before crossing the Channel. Another document showing the way upper rooms were used is the record of a building failure in the *Anglo-Saxon Chronicle* for 978. The floor of an upper chamber at Calne, Wiltshire, collapsed during a meeting of the Witenagemot, or council, leaving the holy Dunstan who 'stood alone upon a beam'.

These examples do not necessarily prove that the upper rooms were used as halls. In fact, there is strong evidence that they were chamber blocks associated with, but separate from, wooden halls of a conventional kind, which have disappeared. Excavations near surviving stone buildings at Netherne, Surrey,

7. The Bayeux Tapestry shows King Harold feasting in the upper room of a house at Bosham, West Sussex. There is still very little evidence about the way early houses were used.

and Wharram Percy, Yorkshire, have revealed traces of such timber buildings.

Domestic buildings before the thirteenth century are surprisingly variable in form compared to the uniformity of the later Middle Ages. A royal palace, like Henry II's Clarendon, might be a random group of buildings strung out in a line and linked by lean-to roofed passages and covered ways. The bishops' palaces at Hereford, Old Sarum and Wolvesey (Winchester) were more enclosed, anticipating the later courtyard form, possibly through the example of the monastic cloister.

Stone town houses like the so-called Jew's House at Lincoln and Moyses Hall, Bury St Edmunds, both *c.* 1160, have substantial upper rooms, presumably because of the need to make the best use of the land and to provide protection in times of civil disturbance. Both houses have two-light windows under round arched heads, and fireplaces on each floor. They were never a common type

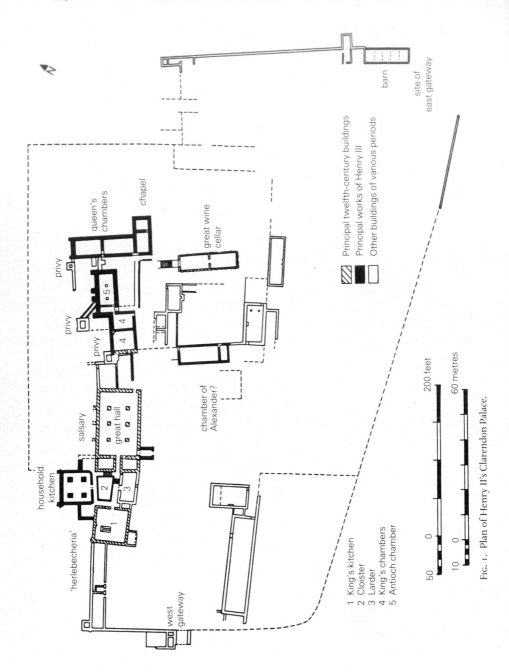

FIG. 1. Plan of Henry II's Clarendon Palace.

1 King's kitchen
2 Cloister
3 Larder
4 King's chambers
5 Antioch chamber

Principal twelfth-century buildings
Principal works of Henry III
Other buildings of various periods

barn
site of east gateway
queen's chambers
chapel
great wine cellar
privy
privy
privy
chamber of Alexander?
salsary
great hall
household kitchen
'herlebecheria'
west gateway

and nearly all English towns up to the seventeenth century were built mostly of timber.

The lack of sufficient numbers of surviving buildings makes the history of the English house before the 1250s a more than usually speculative study. One of the best-preserved examples at the end of this period, Little Wenham Hall, Suffolk, c. 1260, is exceptional in many ways. It is the earliest brick building in

8. Little Wenham Hall, Suffolk c. 1260. An exceptional house using castle forms and the earliest English brickwork.

England after the Roman period and has a unique plan with rooms on three floors; it is well integrated, in the castle manner, yet it is not a fully defensible building. By contrast, Old Soar, Plaxtol, Kent, *c.* 1290, built of Kentish ragstone, shows the classic medieval pattern of a large upper chamber, or solar, at the end of the hall, which in this case no longer survives.

THE TIMBER-FRAMED HOUSE

By the beginning of the fourteenth century the integrated plan of the house as a hall with two end sections for service and for private living was beginning its three-hundred-year domination. Other plan types that existed before seem to have died out.

The standardization of planning was contemporary with advances in the technique of timber construction. Although timber was never the only material employed, it dominated English vernacular building until the fifteenth century, and remained important in many areas for much longer. We must therefore look in some detail at the way in which it was used.

Since the hall was the principal element in a house, it is not surprising that the efforts of medieval house-builders were directed to making the wooden structure enclosing it as impressive as possible. The advance in the technique of carpentry which made new forms possible was the mortice and tenon joint, held by wooden pegs. With this technique, a house could be put together as an assembly of wooden members forming a frame that rested flat on the ground on the sill-plate, which served instead of foundations. These joints operated equally well in compression or tension, which was fortunate as they were subjected to different stresses during the building of the house and in its finished state. They also permitted the use of unseasoned oak, which was likely to change shape as it dried out.

The medieval house was usually a long rectangle in plan, one room in depth from front to back. At certain points, spaced about 16 ft (4.9 m) apart, were heavy timber trusses which crossed the house from front to back and, joined by lighter timbers, formed the structural framework for the walls and roof; these trusses were hardly visible from the outside. The space between trusses is called a bay. The system of designing in bays is similar to the method of stone construction in Gothic churches.

When we look at a medieval timber house, it is most important to examine the design of the truss. This is the key to understanding the date of the house and its place in the regional style. In an open hall, it also provides the climax of architectural effect, whether with the massive crucks of the West Country or the delicately carved crown-posts of the south-east. When looking at a Stuart or Georgian house, we would be chiefly concerned with the plan and the elevation. With a medieval house it is the cross-section, hidden from immediate view, which really matters. The plan is likely to follow the common pattern and the elevation to be a reflection of the system of bays inside, although perhaps substantially altered through the years. The truss is the centre of the structure, however, and cannot be altered without physical danger. The tie-beam may be built into the floor, and the crown-post may only be visible with a torch in the attic, but if the house is old enough, such features are almost sure to be found.

The temptation when writing the history of these houses is to look for patterns of evolution. For many years an engagingly eccentric building in Lincolnshire called Tea-Pot Hall led historians astray into believing that it was the 'missing link' between a sort of primitive hut and the English form of cruck construction. After it had been accidentally set on fire in a VJ Day celebration, however, it was discovered that it was of early-nineteenth-century date.

In fact, no timber buildings datable to any time before the thirteenth century have survived. By then the techniques of house building were already well developed in different areas.

Dates are less important than location in tracing a picture of influences and development. The principal regions of timber building, where money was plentiful and houses have survived, are the Weald of Kent and Sussex, Essex and Suffolk, and the midland and marcher counties of Warwickshire, Worcestershire, Hereford, Shropshire and Cheshire. The south-eastern regions are characterized by lighter and more economical forms of construction, compared to the massive timbers of the west. Even here, there are distinctions between the sophisticated and fashionable tendencies of the lowland areas and the rugged conservatism of the 'highland' houses.

The Cruck House

The intentions of the medieval house-carpenter can best be understood by looking at cruck buildings. On philological evidence, this technique goes back at least to the tenth century, when *furcae*, or forks, are first mentioned in connection with building. It may have an earlier history as a variant of Saxon practice.

The simplest cruck construction consists of two posts rising from the ground to form a triangle, linked at the top by a ridge pole to another similar triangle.

Curved timbers were usually selected from the forest to make a matching pair of cruck-blades. The main members of the frame were all pre-shaped and jointed so that the house was delivered to the site as a kit of parts.

The cruck trusses were then apparently assembled on the ground; evidence for this can be found in the notched numbers on the principal timbers which indicate how they should be put together. Next they were raised, or 'reared' by the house-owner with the assistance of servants and neighbours. It is remarkable to think of such great weights of timber being handled in this way.

The rearing technique helps to explain the form of the cruck frame; it was also a reflection of the plan of the house, which followed the seldom-varied formula. Every house had an upper and a lower end, the upper end usually on the left as the house was entered. The houses which survive from the twelfth century had, in addition to a hall, a two-storey bay at the upper end with a parlour below and solar above, both reserved for private use by the owner, in contrast to the semi-public character of the hall.

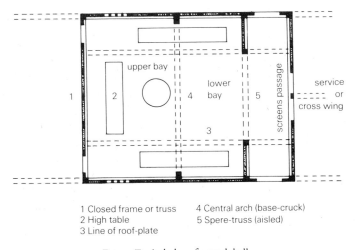

1 Closed frame or truss   4 Central arch (base-cruck)
2 High table   5 Spere-truss (aisled)
3 Line of roof-plate

FIG. 2. Typical plan of a cruck hall.

At the lower end, a corresponding bay contained a pantry and buttery on the ground floor (for storing dry goods and drink) and a room over.

According to F. W. B. Charles,[3] the upper end frame of the house was always reared first. This would make the external wall at the end of the house, complete with all its subsidiary framing, which would be difficult to joint in at a later stage. A rope at the apex of the cruck-blades and levers at the feet (running through 'blind' mortice holes which survive in many cases) were the means of raising the timbers, whose massive size and special jointing were adapted to this method. If the frame was twisted out of shape, the joints became stronger.

A second truss would be reared parallel to this, leaving the space for the parlour in between. On the ground, the trusses were connected by the sill-plate, and other sill-plates ran across the house on the line of each truss. The second truss had to be connected straight away to the first, in order to make it stable. A post was raised on the second truss sill-plate, supported laterally with curved braces; in the top of this post lapped joints were cut so that the tie-beam and collar of the second truss fitted securely into the post when the

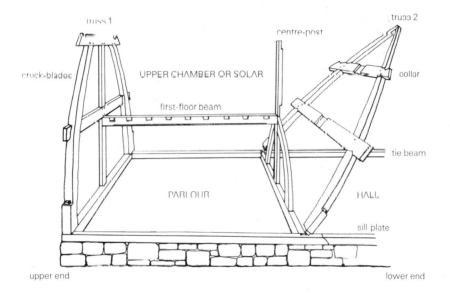

FIG. 3. Rearing a cruck hall.

second 'rearing' took place. The post was also connected to the first truss by the first-floor beam.

The purlins, running horizontally along the roof-slope from truss to truss, were inserted at an early stage to make the structure more rigid. They would be extended out in mid-air to connect with the third truss, situated in the middle of the hall. This third truss was more elegant and open in design than the others, as it would be seen in the upper part of the hall. It would have a high collar rather than a tie-beam. The truss at the lower end of the hall would then be reared, held steady by the purlins as before, and finally a truss for the lower end wall was added.

By the end of this process, the main elements of the frame would be in place. There would be no clear distinction between roof and walls, but a wall plate was inserted running the full length on each side of the house, carried *over* the tie-beam ends. This was a unique feature of the cruck form, resembling a modern 'curtain wall' structure more than a building with load-bearing walls.

The central truss in the hall did not have a tie-beam, and the wall plate would be attached to the crucks by a cruck-spur – a short piece of wood which was jointed in. A wall-post ran vertically from the foot of the cruck to the cruck-spur, providing a rectangular appearance from the outside.

The medieval carpenter-architect had to rely on a visual appreciation of mechanics and some of the elements of the cruck frame were overstructured once it had been reared. The scale of timbers is very impressive, specially as seen in isolation in the frame of Plas Cadwgan from Wrexham, re-erected at the Avoncroft Museum of Building at Bromsgrove.

In this example, the middle truss of the hall is a 'raised cruck', standing on the side walls, but extending with continuous pieces of timber up to the apex of the roof. The collar-beam is 'cambered' upwards and supports a king-post which rises the full height of the upper triangle, with struts branching from it. Below the collar, the shape of the arch is filled with knee-braces which add visual and mechanical strength. Plas Cadwgan also has a 'spere-truss' at the lower end of the hall. A survival from the aisled hall, this was particularly suitable as a framework for the screens passage which ran through the house between the only two doors. The spere-posts which stood out in the middle of the floor were not an impediment in this position, and provided interesting visual variety. The whole construction is roughly hewn but beautifully proportioned.

For the larger houses of the fourteenth century, the commonest form was the base-cruck, in which the cruck framework rose from the ground but

9. Plas Cadwgan (originally from Wrexham), the frame of a fourteenth-century cruck hall re-erected at the Avoncroft Museum, Bromsgrove. The nearer truss is a raised cruck, the further one is an aisled spere-truss with service doors. Both have knee-braced collars with king-posts.

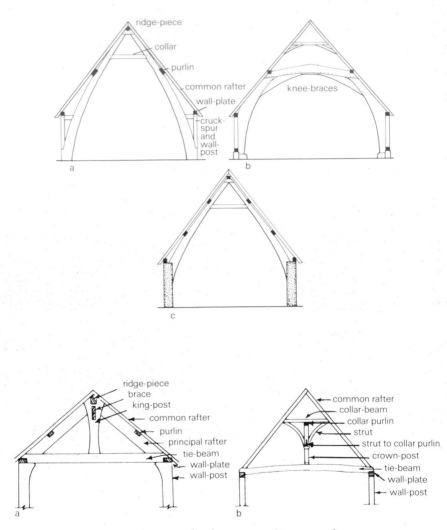

FIG. 5. Sections of roof structures: (a) king-post roof,
(b) crown-post roof.

stopped short at the tie-beam or collar. Above this, a much lighter construction held the upper part of the roof in place. This was a more rational response to the demands of structure than the full cruck, but sometimes the upper part was continued on the same scale with an invisible joint. The central hall truss

10. Weobley, Herefordshire, preserves a multitude
of timber-framed buildings from the fourteenth to sixteenth centuries. They all show
the heavy framing of the west-midland style.

at Lower Brockhampton, Herefordshire, with its bold quatrefoil filling of the
upper section, is constructed in this way.

Although one expects the full cruck to be the earliest form, the surviving
examples are usually later in date than the more sophisticated cruck forms.
They are also used for humbler buildings, with less skill in construction.

According to F. W. B. Charles, there was an early peak of excellence:

> Every subsequent alteration, whether made to the building itself or to the technique of timber-framing, has proved a step down from the heights of medieval carpentry. In sheer architectural quality, sophistication of design and immaculate detail, the craft . . . reached its peak about 1400. For structural adventure, and more imposing scale, the few buildings left from about 1300 should be sought.[4]

Evidence of the earlier type can be found at Martley Vicarage, Worcestershire, a pre-cruck form. The later period could well be represented by the solar cross-wing at Shell Manor, Himbleton, Worcestershire, of c. 1450, with a noble tie-beam truss roof. The method of reared construction meant that a cross-wing was effectively a separate structure, although attached to the hall. It could thus survive, as in this case, when the hall was demolished. Across the road from Shell Manor is Shell Cottage, a diminutive but complete hall-house in miniature of c. 1500. The service and solar bays are treated as 'outshuts' – single-storey extensions under the main roof slope.

Later examples of the cruck form can be seen in profusion in the Herefordshire village of Weobley, but it was gradually superseded by the post-and-truss form which can be seen in the reconstructed Merchant's House from Bromsgrove at the Avoncroft Museum (c. 1500). The heavy timbers retain the regional character, which extended through into Wales. Crucks are known to have been used for farmhouses in the north of England beyond 1700, but for most purposes this remarkable type of structure, described by C. F. Innocent as being 'as peculiarly British as the bulldog or the red grouse',[5] gradually faded away like the grin of the Cheshire Cat.

The South-East Region and the Wealden House

The earliest type of house which can be identified in the south-east is the aisled hall. Only a few examples, like St Clere's Hall at St Osyth's, Essex, survive in any complete form, but numerous examples show evidence of being aisled halls before later alterations.

One such is the hall at Wingfield College, Suffolk (c. 1300), an establishment for priests, linked to the parish church. Here the posts of the central truss – which would have stood in the middle of the floor – have been sawn off and now rest on a tie-beam, which has cracked under the weight of the heavy superstructure.

After the aisled hall, the most widespread type of house to develop was the Wealden house, which we have already encountered at Alfriston. These houses continued to be built into the late sixteenth century. They were the typical houses of the prosperous tradesman and yeoman farmer, and a large number are still inhabited.

The Weald of Kent was a particularly prosperous area in the fourteenth century, the first in which a predominance of houses of the middle size can be noted. It was an area of scattered villages rather than compact towns. As R. I. Mason writes:

In the Weald towns are small whilst villages are large, so that the distinction is often difficult to draw and local pride may be readily offended by an incautious classification. Even in undoubted villages, place-names like 'New Town' and 'Old Town' are fairly common. These may of course arise from the Wealden bent for cynicism which, among the farmsteads, finds expression in names like 'Little London', 'Mockbeggar', 'Starvecrow' and 'Rats Castle'.[6]

Bayleaf House, c. 1400, is a restored Wealden house which may be seen at the Weald and Downland Open Air Museum at Singleton in Sussex. It was transferred from Chiddingstone in Kent to make way for a reservoir.

The characteristic of the Wealden house is the jettied or projecting upper storey of the end bays, leaving the hall to occupy the two bays in the middle. The hall thus appears to be recessed under the eaves, which run continuously from end to end, and are supported in the central section by curved braces. The recession is not, of course, reflected in the plan.

The jetties can be found continuing round the side and sometimes the back, particularly in town houses. Fine examples from c. 1480 are Pattenden, Goudhurst, and the Priest's House, Headcorn. In such houses there is likely to be a strong corner-post with carved ornament, and a diagonal or dragon beam into which the joists of the upper floor are jointed at 45°. This feature can also be seen at the Guildhall, Lavenham, Suffolk.

The house was entered, as always, at the lower end of the hall, with a through passage divided from the hall with screens. In some cases, there would be a spere-truss in this position, as already mentioned. In Bayleaf House, the central hall truss is enhanced and strengthened by two massive arched braces. They had to be replaced in the reconstruction, and were cut from a single curved tree. Each piece is nearly 13 ft (4 m) long and weighs four hundredweight.

On the tie-beam of this truss sits the crown-post, the final and most enduring solution to the architectural problem of glorifying the upper space of the hall. It was usually moulded to appear like a stone column, with base and capital, above which four arched braces sprang to connect with the collar and collar-

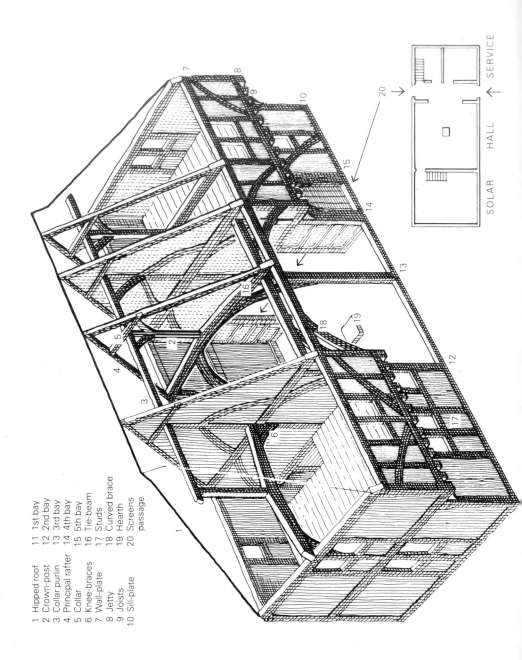

1 Hipped roof
2 Crown-post
3 Collar purlin
4 Principal rafter
5 Collar
6 Knee-braces
7 Wall-plate
8 Jetty
9 Joists
10 Sill-plate
11 1st bay
12 2nd bay
13 3rd bay
14 4th bay
15 5th bay
16 Tie-beam
17 Studs
18 Curved brace
19 Hearth
20 Screens passage

SOLAR   HALL   SERVICE

purlin. The collar-purlin was not a direct part of the support of the roof, like an ordinary purlin. Instead, it ran parallel to the roof ridge but below it, linking the collars of the various trusses, and the collars of the rafter couples. It took the place of the ridge piece, which was discovered to be structurally redundant, although earlier periods had invested it with considerable superstitious significance. A rare example of a late-fifteenth-century crown-post in the form of four colonettes can be seen at Stoneacre, Kent. It was realized by the early sixteenth century that the crown-post, too, was more decorative than functional, and the last stage of the open hall featured windbracing flat against the slope of the roof between the principal rafters, as at Lytes Carey, Somerset (c. 1460).

Unlike the king-post of the north and west, the crown-post did not extend right up to the roof ridge, and thus marks a further stage in the understanding of the mechanics of a roof structure, for the ridge bears nothing but its own weight, while the greatest compressive force comes at the point, about a third of the way down the roof slope, where the collar is usually placed. This understanding led to the adoption of the 'side-purlin' roof which, with the demise of the crown-post around 1500, was usually braced with curved struts rising from the tie-beam. The purlins thus took the main weight of the roof.

The change in living habits in the early Tudor period can be seen in the alterations which were made to Wealden houses, including Bayleaf. The great hall had ceased to be a vital centre of daily life in the houses of the aristocracy a hundred years before, since they had retreated into the solar and great chamber to eat, away from the servants and retainers of the household. As at Bayleaf, a fireplace and first floor were often introduced into the hall of a smaller house to make a more intimate principal living room in emulation of the aristocratic example. It may seem odd that chimneys, which were built in stone houses by the Normans, took so long to become a common feature. One can imagine that the symbolic importance of the open hearth kept it in favour. It is also the best way of providing heat for more than a few people at a time and, if skilfully managed, the smoke need not be disagreeable. Knowing the hygienic standards of the time, it must have been a positive asset to have permanent fumigation.

Fig. 6. Bayleaf, a Wealden house at the Weald and Downland Museum probably built in two phases, 1400–1405 (hall and service bay) and 1500–1515 (solar bay, probably replacing an earlier structure). The upper floor is jettied on the front and one end. The design is orderly, but far from symmetrical.

The effect can be tested at the two open-air museums already mentioned. At the Avoncroft Museum, the Merchant's House from Bromsgrove (late fifteenth century) has a rare survival of a smoke-hood over the fire which is made in a corner behind the hall door. Such hoods were a common feature in the north and west long before chimneys became widespread in the south-east.

The survival of the open hearth was characteristic of medieval conservatism, in common with many other vernacular features. As A. R. Myers writes, 'it was still presumed that innovation and experiment were bad, and were to be tested, not by empirical methods, but by their degree of correspondence with traditional beliefs and authorities'.[7] The same was equally true of Scottish vernacular, where features such as wheel, or spiral, stairs persisted into the eighteenth century, and a castle-like appearance was favoured in the seventeenth century for houses from the slightly fantastic Craigievar Castle (1600–1626) to the tenement 'Lands' of Edinburgh Old Town.

The widespread use of chimneys was hardly a generation old even in 'advanced' Essex in 1577, when William Harrison wrote his *Description of England*:

There are old men yet dwelling in the village where I remain which have noted three things marvellously altered within their sound remembrance: one is the multitude of chimneys lately erected, whereas in their young days there were not above two or three, if so many, in most uplandish towns (the religious houses and manor places of their lords always excepted, and peradventure some great personages), but each one made his fire against a reredos in the hall, where he dined and dressed his meat.[8]

Harrison goes on to complain that wainscoting and fireplaces have brought ailments which fresh air and smoke kept at bay.

When chimneys were inserted into Wealden and other houses, they were usually of brick, and built across the lower end of the hall, backing on to the cross-passage which took the place of the screens passage. Alternatively, the stack could take two flues, from the hall and the ground-floor parlour. At the same time the hall was floored over at tie-beam level, and some of its structure might be cut away to make a more usable space above. In humbler farmhouses

11. (*top*) Stoneacre, Otham, Kent. A screens passage in the early-sixteenth-century hall.

12. (*bottom left*) Lytes Carey, Somerset. The hall, *c.* 1453, has an elegant roof with cusped windbraces, reflected in the arch (*c.* 1530) which leads to a stair.

13. (*bottom right*) The Merchant's House (originally from Bromsgrove) a late-fifteenth-century post and truss house now at the Avoncroft Museum; the house still has an original timber-framed smoke-hood filled with wattle and daub in the hall.

there remained a prejudice against using the upper rooms except as workshops or for storage.

Regional Variations

While the structural systems employed in timber building in all parts of the country were roughly similar by 1500, the main difference still observable today when travelling in the different regions is in the way the frame of the building is composed and filled. Typical of the midland and western region is the box-frame, in which the vertical and horizontal members have equal prominence, forming square intervals on the surface. When constructional ingenuity was no longer a challenge, the impetus of building went into ornamentation, the universal characteristic of the late Gothic style. The square spaces in the frame were braced diagonally, making chevron patterns and quatrefoils with dazzling effect. This can be seen at Little Moreton Hall, Cheshire, a simple hall-house enlarged and elaborated through the sixteenth century, with the final crowning addition of a long gallery at third-floor level. Other well-known examples in the same region are Speke Hall and Hall i'th' Wood, Bolton, both saved from destruction in the Edwardian period by that architectural philanthropist, the first Lord Leverhulme. The profusion of gables and cresting ornaments in these houses demonstrates the change from the grand simplicity of the Middle Ages to the conscious display of the Tudor period.

The alternative to the box-frame, found in many places but most typically in the south-east, was the close-studded wall, with many studs or vertical timbers placed close together in parallel lines. To use a lot of timber in such a way was a mark of wealth, and William Harrison was well aware of this geographical class distinction:

The greater part of our building in the cities and good towns of England consisteth onlie of timber . . . In old time the houses of the Britons were set up with a few posts and many radels, with stables and all offices under one roof, the like whereof is to be seen in the fennie countries, and the northern parts unto this daie, where for lack of wood they are enforced to continue this ancient manner of building. It is not in vaine therefore in speaking of building to make a distinction between the plaine and woodie soiles: for as in these, our houses are commonly strong and well-timbered, so that in many places, there are not above foure, six or nine inches between stud and stud; so in

14. Little Moreton Hall, Cheshire, late fifteenth and mid sixteenth century.
The most extreme example of decorative filling of a box-frame.

15. A Wealden house at Bignor, West Sussex, sixteenth century. The hall window
in the centre has been filled in with brick nogging and a smaller window substituted,
probably when the chimney was inserted and the hall roofed over.

the open and champaigne countries they are inforced for want of stuffe to use no studs
at all, but onlie franke posts, raisins, beames, prickeposts, groundsels, summers (or
dormant) transoms, and such principals with here and there a griding, wherewith they
fasten their splints or radels, and then cast it all over with a thick claie to keep out the
wind which otherwise would annoy them.[8]

16. Paycocke's, Coggeshall, Essex, c. 1500. A spectacular display
of close-studding with brick infill for a wealthy clothier. The facade is the result of
radical restoration by Lord Noel Buxton in 1910.

In an example like the Clergy House at Alfriston, an early Wealden house,
the front wall of the hall is decoratively composed of curved timbers, while
the service end (where the priest's housekeeper lived in a 'self-contained'
apartment, decently entered by a separate door at the back) is made of regular
vertical studs. Smallhythe Place, near Tenterden in Kent, is a later Wealden
house with much closer studding, while the late-sixteenth-century Wealden
house at Bignor in Sussex – a favourite subject for romantic views – betrays its
humble status in the wide spaces in the frame.

In Suffolk, Eric Sandon comments on the 'lean and vigorous austerity'[9] of
the timberwork, although the individual members were increasingly carved
and ornamented, as can be seen in houses at Lavenham, and at Paycocke's,
Coggeshall, just across the border in Essex. In this clothier's house of 1500 the
continuous plate over the jetty is treated with running foliage, terminating
with a dragon of the kind often found on the rood beam of a church. In

between there are charming fantastical figures which emerge from flowers or dive back into them head first. Inside, the exposed joists of the ceilings are elaborately carved with personal emblems and foliage. There is no double-height hall, and the fireplaces are built into the back wall rather than the cross-walls, innovations which did not penetrate into the upland regions for at least another hundred years.

STONE HOUSES

As Harrison tells us, in 1577 Tudor England was still chiefly housed in wooden buildings but a few manor-houses had been built in stone in the two previous centuries. Sometimes they can be explained by special local circumstances, like the Priest's House at Muchelney in Somerset, built around 1400 of blue lias

17. Clevedon Court, Avon, c. 1320. The stone hall
with porch and unique oriel window, lighting a chapel.

with dressings of Ham Hill stone, evidently worked by the masons of the adjoining Abbey.

Clevedon Court, near Bristol, is a house almost too large and exceptional to be strictly called vernacular. It was built in the early fourteenth century as an addition to a stone tower of a defensive character – the porch has a portcullis groove. The exceptional feature, however, is the chapel at the dais end on an upper floor. As Sir Nikolaus Pevsner wrote, 'Its windows must at first be considered a wild Victorian invention',[10] but the bold reticulated ogee tracery, an allusion to St Peter's fishing net, is of the same date as the hall.

At Lytes Carey in Somerset, a manor-house of the mid fifteenth century, a previously existing chapel of a century earlier was built into the structure. The hall roof is a good example of the last phase of the evolution of the carpenter's art, when the transverse members were made less significant and attention was directed to the patterns on the sloping sides, with curved windbraces cut decoratively with cusps making three tiers of arches. Within a generation a fashionable bay window at the dais end of the hall had been added, making a small space which could be screened off for private dining. It has its own fireplace and a loophole for watching people coming and going at the adjacent chapel.

Oriels and bays – the term oriel is normally used for a bay projecting from an upper storey – were to become prominent features for architectural display in the last phase of Gothic architecture. Treasurer Ralph Cromwell's magnificently ruined palace at South Wingfield Manor, Derbyshire, built in 1440, has a fine example, and the fashion spread down the social scale. Grevel House in Chipping Campden, Gloucestershire, of the late fourteenth century, product of the fortunes in wool that were amassed after the Black Death, has a two-storey projecting bay with the mullions (the solid vertical divisions) continued in typical Perpendicular style through a blank panel between, making a crisp linear arrangement.

It is surprising that the wealth of stone in England was not exploited earlier on. It can only be attributed to the persistence of folk custom in using timber, and the foreignness of stone building. As William Harrison noted, the Normans preferred to import Caen stone and the indigenous stones were still being neglected in the Tudor period:

Our elders have from time to time, following our natural vice in misliking of our own commodities at home, and desiring those of countries abroad, most esteemed the Caen stone that is brought hither out of Normandy: and many even in these our days following the same vein, do covet in their works almost to use none other. Howbeit experience on the one side, and our skilful masons on the other (whose judgement is

18. Grevel House, Chipping Campden, late fourteenth century. A house built on a wool fortune with Cotswold limestone. The bay window rivals the finest church work of the time.

nothing inferior to those of other countries), do affirm that in the north (and south) parts of England, and certain other places, there are some quarries which for hardness and beauty are equal to the outlandish great.[11]

The most versatile English stones are found in the limestone belt running from Portland Bill to the Wash. They can be used for walling, roofing and fine carving, and buildings gain a unique unity of colour and texture from their use. There is also a consistency of style between, for example, the Cotswolds and the Lincolnshire wolds. The predominant grey yields a wide variety of colour under different lights, from yellow to blue and green. There has also been a remarkable historical consistency in the way these stones are used, so that changes in style are only superficially assimilated.

There are softer stones, like chalk (or clunch as it is called in building), and many harder ones: sandstones, slates, blue lias, flint and granite. By the Tudor period all were beginning to play a part in the further development of the vernacular.

No account of stone-built manor-houses can omit Ightham Mote, near Sevenoaks, Kent. As usual, the hall is the earliest part of the house, from the early fourteenth century, with a remarkable stone arch in the centre bay spanning the whole width, and echoed in wood in the end trusses. In contradiction to the normal pattern, there never seems to have been a screens passage here, although the two doors to the buttery and pantry at the service end are clearly apparent. The ensemble of courtyard, gate-tower and jettied half-timbering grew up through the next two centuries, and was restored in 1872 by Norman Shaw, who tried to capture the rambling picturesque effect in his new work.

GATEHOUSES AND MOATS

At Ightham Mote, two other important elements of late medieval domestic architecture are present: the gatehouse and the moat. Both were features of military building which were frequently adopted for houses in the troubled fifteenth century. Moats had many practical uses besides protection from attack, as they provided a reservoir of water and a source of fish. Thus a surprisingly large number of farmhouses in East Anglia were moated, or their sites can be identified by the traces of a moat. There is no need to doubt that the builders of moated houses enjoyed as much as we do the surprising effect of walls rising sheer out of water, as at Leeds Castle, Kent, a residence of the English queens from 1272 onwards or, on a humbler scale, at Parham Moat Hall in Suffolk (c. 1500) with its twin surviving bays of diapered brick.

The square artificial island at Parham is entered by an arched brick gateway, with small figures of 'wodwose', or wild men, in niches. Whether as a habitable building, or as token barrier, the gatehouse was the outcome of building a forecourt round the hall. John Aubrey, writing in the seventeenth century about Bradfield Manor in Wiltshire, says:

> The architecture of an old English gentleman's house was a good high strong wall, a gatehouse, and a great Hall and Parlour; and within, a little green court where you came in, stood, on one side the Barn. They then thought not the noise of the threshold ill music.[12]

Bradfield Manor has lost its wall and gatehouse, but Aubrey's description works for many late medieval houses, such as Cotehele in Cornwall, built in its present form by Sir Richard Edgcumbe soon after 1485. The granite gatehouse hides the hall from view as one approaches, and leads into just such a green court as Aubrey mentions. In this case the magnificent barn stands

19. Cotehele, Cornwall. The barn and hall court, with gatehouse
to the right, c. 1485; hall, c. 1530; tower to the left, 1627. Informal planning with
consistent local materials over 150 years.

outside, and the main court, together with another court to the side, was given over to retainers' lodgings. These were a necessary accompaniment to the houses of great men of the time, although royal power under Henry VII tried to limit the size of such private armies. A set of retainers' lodgings in almost unaltered condition can be found at Dartington Hall in Devon, begun in the

late fourteenth century by John Holland, Duke of Exeter and half-brother to
Richard II. Dartington seems ideally adapted to its twentieth-century use as a
college; the traditional college plan of Oxford and Cambridge hardly differs
from that of a late medieval great house.

Timber-framed gatehouses are found at Stokesay Castle and at Lower

20. Lower Brockhampton House, Herefordshire. A late-fourteenth-century house
with a fine base-cruck hall and cross-wing. The picturesque gatehouse
was built a hundred years later and there is a ruined chapel in the farmyard beyond.

Brockhampton, both post-dating the houses they protect by long periods.
Apart from serving as a porter's lodge, a gatehouse was seen, in the late Gothic
period, as an opportunity for architectural display. The generation before the
Reformation saw a new wave of monastic building, one of the glories of which
is the flushwork gatehouse at St Osyth's Priory, Essex, of the late fifteenth

21. Oxburgh Hall, Norfolk, 1482. The late Gothic gatehouse becomes
a formal architectural statement.

century. The flat papery patterning of fictive arcades is carried over the whole
surface, although the inner face of the building is comparatively plain. A tall
gatehouse was a practical advantage in flat country, and at Oxburgh Hall in
Norfolk, built in the 1480s, the seven-storeyed towers necessarily eclipse the
two-storeyed ranges of the house itself.

At Layer Marney in Essex the gatehouse of the 1520s rises through nine
storeys to gain a view of the sea, and Lord Marney so overreached himself that
the gatehouse alone was built, topped off with some of the earliest Renaissance
ornament in England, in the form of terracotta shells and dolphins. Smaller
structures of the same period, like the gatehouses at East Barsham Manor,
Norfolk, and West Stow Hall, Suffolk, were also made the opportunity for the
most impressive architectural display in the whole house, benefiting from the
ease with which ornament can be created in brick and terracotta.

22. East Barsham Manor, Norfolk, *c.* 1520–30. The porch seen through the gatehouse, both exploiting the decorative possibilities of brick in late Gothic style.

BRICK HOUSES

Although bricks were used at Little Wenham Hall, built in the thirteenth century, they are rarely found until the fifteenth. One of the largest brick buildings of the late Middle Ages, Tattershall Castle in Lincolnshire, built for the Treasurer, Ralph Cromwell, in 1456, is also one of the earliest. Historians used to assume that the bricks were imported, but it has been proved that in this, as in nearly all other cases, the bricks were locally made, perhaps with the help of foreign workmen. For the two succeeding centuries, the history of the English house can be adequately described using brick buildings alone as examples.

As with timber-framed buildings, there is a temptation to look for a chronological sequence in the way bricks were used. The size of the brick and the method of laying or bonding are the determinants, but although early bricks are generally longer and narrower than post-Tudor ones, the buildings elude such easy classification. Early bricks tended to be uneven in shape, and were laid in thick mortar. It is surprising to learn that the rich red colour, which is now admired, was originally covered with a coat of limewash or lime plaster, as were timber and stone buildings of the Middle Ages.

As well as the brick chimneys introduced into earlier timber-framed houses, the timber frame began to be filled with brick during the sixteenth century. Called brick nogging, it can be laid in a straight or herringbone pattern. This was more enduring and weatherproof than the earlier wattle and daub, and could be easily substituted in an existing building. On the other hand, the structural use of timber remained a deep-seated instinct in the English builder, and up to the nineteenth century many wooden tie-beams were built at random into brickwork to bind a house together. Wood remained the only material for carrying loads over openings, as well as for flooring and for studwork partition walls. In the London terrace houses built in large numbers during and after the Napoleonic wars the construction within the enclosing brick walls is entirely of timber and, with its studs, braces and ingenious trusses, looks remarkably like a country cottage when stripped down – 'The Colonel's lady and Judy O'Grady are sisters under the skin.'

OTHER BUILDING MATERIALS

The use of unbaked earth for building pre-dates the use of brick, but the earliest surviving examples are of similar date. It was the main building

material in areas, like Cumberland, which are now associated with stone. There
are two techniques: *pisé de terre* or rammed earth, which is mostly found in
the chalky soils of the midlands, and cob, built up from wet earth and straw,
which is found particularly in the south-west. Hayes Barton Manor in Devon,
the birthplace of Sir Walter Raleigh, is an E-plan house of the sixteenth century

23. Hayes Barton Manor, Devon. A sixteenth-century example of the local cob.

built of cob, with the usual accompaniment of a thatched roof. By the end of
the sixteenth century, cob had become a poor man's way of building, and
Richard Carew noted that 'The poor cottager contenteth himself with cob for
his walls and thatch for his covering.'[13]

Up to the end of the fifteenth century, the use of stone, even in areas where
it was readily available, was still an indication of exceptional wealth. While

Chipping Campden was built with fine stone houses from 1400, neighbouring Burford lagged behind. As Mary Sturge Gretton writes,

> Until the mid-1400s the houses were almost entirely of wood, built throughout of timber uprights joined by laths filled in with plaster ('wattle and daub'), the whole set on a very low plinth of stone. No quarry appears in our manorial documents until 1435. And it was not till considerably later that stone was at all freely used in Burford. Moreover, when it was employed, it was at first seldom used higher than the ground-floor storey – upper storeys still being of timber with wattle and daub.[14]

In Cumberland and the Lake District, mud and earth building (employing a technique quite unlike that of Devon) was almost universal before the seventeenth century and persisted thereafter in combination with loose stone building. This regional influence spread up the west coast of Scotland – Burns wrote of 'the auld clay biggin' in *The Cottar's Saturday Night*. Otherwise, the Scots seem always to have used the rough stones and boulders which are their most abundant building material. Roof coverings were of heather thatch or turf. The attractive red pantiles of the east coast were an innovation of the seventeenth century.

The scarcity of building timber is often seen as one of the major causes in the evolution of the medieval house. In the fifteenth century the firing of bricks actually used up much timber which might otherwise have been used for building. Oaks of large growth were needed for ships as well as houses. A great deal of faster-growing hardwood was made into charcoal for use in the iron industry, probably the greatest cause of deforestation up to the eighteenth century. The demand for oak meant that pieces were often re-used, a feature commonly found in sixteenth-century houses.

THE GREAT REBUILDING

Allied to the changing availability of building materials was the growth in wealth and expectations of comfort. The luxuries of chimneys, wainscoting, glazed windows and boarded floors all spread down from the highest level, to which they had been confined in the fifteenth century, to become commonplace. These gradual changes accelerated in the last quarter of the sixteenth century to become what is known as 'the great rebuilding' or 'the

FIG. 7. Pendean farmhouse, late sixteenth century, at the Weald and Downland Museum, retains many medieval features like unglazed windows and unplastered interior walls. On the other hand, the complete flooring over the upper level and the brick chimney-stack serving three fireplaces show the changes made in the Tudor period.

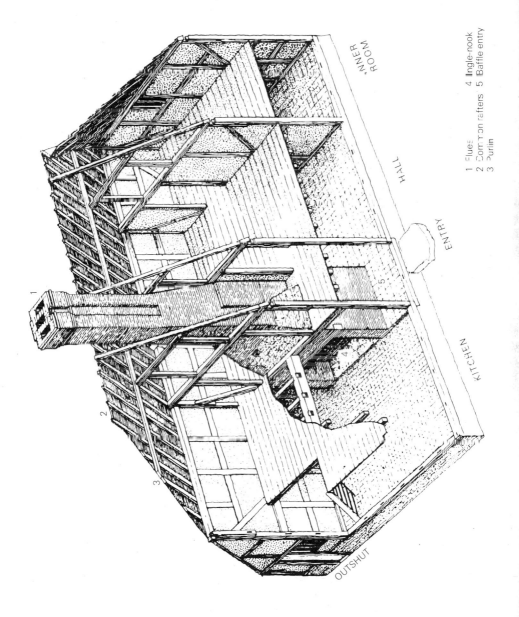

INNER ROOM

HALL

ENTRY

KITCHEN

OUTSHUT

1 Flues   4 Ingle-nook
2 Common rafters   5 Baffle entry
3 Purlin

housing revolution', which lasted until the Civil War. The majority of surviving vernacular houses can be dated from this period, and there were few earlier ones which did not undergo substantial changes to bring them up to date. While the court and aristocracy adopted ideas of planning and ornament from the continental Renaissance, building on the manor-house and farmhouse level was often only superficially affected by these aspirations.

The nature of the changes can be studied in the Pendean farmhouse moved from Midhurst to the Weald and Downland Museum nearby. The three-room configuration of the plan follows through from the Middle Ages, but the hall was floored over from the first. The functions of hall and kitchen are more distinctly separated, and both have wide fireplaces backing on to a single chimney-stack. A simple ladder stair leads out of the kitchen to the three rooms separately partitioned on the upper floor. Because of the placing of the chimney-stack directly in front of the entrance door, no space is lost in passages, although some relief from draughts and 'the noise of the threshold' is afforded. In spite of these advances, the windows are still unglazed and the walls unplastered. In the same museum, the house from Walderton shows the adaptation of an earlier building to a seventeenth-century standard of comfort with glazing and plaster, and simple furniture. In the chronological succession, it is probably the first house in which people of the twentieth century could imagine themselves living rather than camping. This is another 'baffle-entry' house, where the chimney-stack is in line with the front door.

On certain sites a through-passage of the medieval type persisted. In a normal three-celled house, it could run at the opposite end of the hall to the chimney, or alternatively across the back of the stack. The thickness of the stack might also house a small, domed bread oven, built-in spice cupboards and seats in the ingle-nook. There might also be a hot-air vent for drying clothes on the floor above. With the gradual enclosure of common land, which increased greatly in the eighteenth century, wood for burning was hard to find and was made to perform several functions at once.

Plaster assumed a more important role in the list of building materials. The first plaster ceilings occur in England in the 1520s, moulded in imitation of stone, but soon to become a showcase for the Elizabethan imagination, like tapestries and painted walls. As William Harrison describes it:

In plastering likewise of our fairest houses over our heads, we use to lay first a line or two of white mortar, tempered with hair, upon laths, which are nailed one by another . . . and finally cover all with the aforesaid plaster, which, beside the delectable whiteness of the stuff itself, is laid on so even and smoothly as nothing in my judgement can be done with more exactness. The walls of our houses on the inner sides in like sort be either hanged with tapestry, arras work, or painted cloths, wherein either divers

24–27. Pargetting (upper left and right), tile-hanging (lower left) and
weatherboarding (lower right). Three methods of weatherproofing and
decorating a timber-framed house which were popular in the seventeenth and
eighteenth centuries, and often disguise the presence of an earlier house beneath,
thus being at risk from improper antiquarian curiosity.

histories, or herbs, beasts, knots, and such like are stained, or else they are ceiled with oak of our own, or wainscot brought hither out of the east countries, whereby the rooms are not a little commended, made warm, and much more close than otherwise they would be.[15]

At the vernacular level, plaster was generally used as a complete covering for timber-framed houses after 1600, and frequently ornamented with incised patterns or 'pargetting' in relief. It is therefore quite wrong to strip houses of this date back to their timber frame, and such 'restorations' should only be made on any building with the greatest caution. The plaster would be protected with limewash, either in white or using a natural earth colour which modern paints strive unsuccessfully to imitate.

Other methods of covering the timber frame arose, especially in the fashion-conscious south-east. Tile-hanging is found particularly in Kent and Sussex, where protection against the weather is welcome. It is usually applied only to the upper storey down to the jetty. The tiles were shaped into a variety of patterns to create a 'fish-scale' effect. Weatherboarding is also found in Kent, but is chiefly associated with Essex and Middlesex. The lapped boards create a horizontal pattern which accords well with the spirit of the vernacular, and is often found on water-mills and windmills which need a light covering. It was one of the chief architectural exports to the well-wooded American colonies.

In Cornwall, slates are often hung on the walls, not on a timber frame but as extra protection against the weather for rough stone walls. A purely cosmetic covering, favoured in Sussex and elsewhere in the eighteenth century, was the 'mathematical' tile, specially made to be nailed on to a wooden-framed house to imitate the effect of brickwork. In a few freakish examples, blocks of wood are even used to imitate the effect of rusticated masonry.

In spite of these sophistications, certain elements persisted which link later vernacular houses to those of the Middle Ages. In plan they were seldom more than one room deep under the main roof, and seldom more than two storeys high. When additional rooms were made, they were accommodated under the slope of the main roof extended down towards the ground, or in cross-wings built at right angles. Two cross-wings and a central block continued the three-celled medieval division.

With the growth of classical ideas, the desire for a symmetrical show front was incorporated gradually into the vernacular level of building particularly when, as frequently happened, houses were re-fronted and altered internally. When this occurred, the order of hierarchy between service and privacy which ran from end to end of a medieval house was changed into a hierarchy between back and front which is still a feature of most houses.

28. Little Grange, Blyford, Suffolk. A three-celled lobby-entrance house of the mid seventeenth century. Much information about the plan and date can be inferred from the placing of doors, windows and chimneys.

29. Lumb Beck Farm, Addingham, North Yorkshire, 1670. A house of coursed rubble, with the door at the extreme right-hand end. Inside, the fireplace is protected from the door by a short wall called a heck, which has a window in it. The left-hand end of the house is a later rebuilding.

Classicism with a high level of expertise cannot be called vernacular, but the style of the Restoration, plain except for a carved doorcase and dominated by an emphatic hipped roof, was taken up in many regional variations. The character of the details changed, but, as John Harvey writes

> Plan, construction, and the handling of materials; these were the legacy of Gothic art to what came after. Like many a great line, the House of Gothic Architecture left no male heir; yet in the warmth and cheerful proportions of brick houses of Anne and the Georges we may recognize the lineaments of Tudor Gothic's bastard son.[16]

It is in the smaller houses of the seventeenth and eighteenth centuries that the continuation of the vernacular must be sought. With travelling conditions hardly improved since the Middle Ages, there was still a considerable time-lag between the south-east and the north and west. Cruck construction continued in Yorkshire and Cumberland well into the eighteenth century, in combination with stone or clay walls. In stone houses, mullioned windows continued to be used when other parts of England had adopted the sash window. Internally, the broad hearth on which peat and turf could be burnt was almost a room in itself, with a special 'fire-window' to light it and a built-in settle and spice cupboard.

As Beatrix Potter wrote of her own seventeenth-century house, Hill Top, Near Sawrey, Cumbria, in *The Tale of Samuel Whiskers*, 'The chimney itself was wide enough inside for a man to stand up in.'

COTTAGES

The vernacular thread continues into cottage building. The houses of men with no direct stake in the land were never sufficiently well built before Elizabethan times to have survived. In the early seventeenth century, a group of stone-built cottages at Bibury, Gloucestershire, Arlington Row, was specially built for weavers to supply the adjoining fulling mill, but such early stone-built cottages are the exception. At this time, cottages of a single storey or a single room were common, and the most primitive materials were still in use. Celia Fiennes, travelling between Penrith and Carlisle in 1698, noticed 'the little hutts and hovels the poor live in like barnes some have them daubed with mud-wall others drye walls'.[17]

Surviving cottages of the eighteenth century generally look much older, but lack the large timbers and solid walls of earlier vernacular buildings. The spread of enclosure aggravated the problem of rural housing, and there was resort to the 'squatter's right' to build a house on waste land and to light a fire in it between dusk and dawn. Richard Jefferies, writing in the 1870s, described the process, which had hardly changed since the earliest recorded times:

The ground plan is extremely simple. It consists of two rooms, oblong, and generally of the same size – one to live in, the other to sleep in – for the great majority of the squatters' hovels have no upstairs room. At one end there is a small shed for odds and ends. This shed used to be built with an oven, but now scarcely any labourers bake their own bread, but buy of the baker. The walls of the cottage have been carried up some six feet or six feet six – just a little higher than a man's head – the next process is to construct the roof, which is a very simple process. The roof is then thatched, sometimes with flags cut from the stream but more usually with straw and practically the cottage is now built, for there are no indoor fittings to speak of. The chimney is placed at the end of the room set apart for day use. There is no ceiling, nothing between the floor and the thatch and the rafters, except perhaps at one end where there is a kind of loft. The floor consists simply of the earth itself rammed down hard, or sometimes of rough pitching stones, with large interstices between them. The furniture of this room is of the simplest description. A few chairs, a deal table, three or four shelves, and a cupboard with a box or two in the corners constitute the whole.[18]

Humanitarian and aesthetic motives caused eighteenth-century landowners to build estate cottages to a higher standard, although vernacular plans and materials were usually adopted. Rows of cottages and semidetached 'double-dwellers' indicate greater financial resources. In the later years of the century, leading architects might be called on to provide cottage designs in combination with their work on the 'big house', as did Sir William Chambers for the *pisé de terre* and thatch cottages at Milton Abbas, Dorset, in the 1770s. Thus in cottage building the true vernacular finished, and its artificial revival began, stimulated by the new aesthetic doctrine of the picturesque.

VERNACULAR REVIVAL

The Picturesque movement, whose origins are described in Chapter 3, brought a new, but initially superficial, appreciation of vernacular building.

By the end of the nineteenth century, however, we come full circle to the Clergy House at Alfriston and the work of the Society for the Protection of Ancient Buildings. So thoroughly had their architects willed themselves into the vernacular mentality that they attempted to build new cottages on vernacular lines.

Alfred Powell built the remarkable Long Copse at Ewhurst, Surrey, in 1897, at the same period as his restoration of the Clergy House. The original cottage, later enlarged, consisted of two rooms on the ground floor, set at a slight angle

30. Long Copse, Ewhurst, Surrey, 1897. An attempt to revive vernacular methods
by Alfred Powell, who restored the Clergy House, Alfriston, in the same year.

to each other, a plan hardly ever found in real vernacular. Much of the work was done by university men on vacation, but there is an excellent standard of stone-laying. Powell bought the materials and supervised the work on site.

In the same year, his colleague Detmar Blow was building a more rugged cottage, Stoneywell, in Charnwood Forest, Leicestershire, in collaboration with the architect Ernest Gimson. Gimson himself built a substantial cob house at Budleigh Salterton. The skills which these idealistic young men had learnt from restoring old buildings were transferred into new work, but the result cannot be wholly convincing. It is like the folk-song arrangements of composers of the time, such as Percy Grainger's 'Country Gardens', slightly too good to be true.

Nonetheless, Blow went on to restore many larger houses, like Lake House, Wilsford, Wiltshire, and Broome Park, Kent. Powell settled in the Cotswolds and continued to do much valuable work with cottages.

It is not surprising that this new interest in the vernacular coincided with the earliest scholarly studies of the subject. In 1898 a Sheffield solicitor, S. O. Addy, published *The Evolution of the English House*. In the preface he complained that

English writers on domestic architecture have been content for the most part with describing the remains of great villas, or the picturesque timber houses which adorn our old cities. Such buildings are more attractive to the casual eye than wattled huts or combinations of dwelling house and cattle stall.[19]

Another Sheffield man, C. F. Innocent, added a technical counterpart to Addy's work of social and philological history in *The Development of English Building Construction* (1916). Both authors were aware of the need to record buildings which were continually being demolished. At a time of housing improvements, many vernacular dwellings were thoughtlessly condemned, and in 1927 Stanley Baldwin issued an appeal, *The Preservation of Ancient Cottages*, to which was added a note by Thomas Hardy. The cottage at Higher Bockhampton, Dorset, where Hardy was born is preserved by the National Trust, and he claimed to have seen one of the last mud wall and thatch cottages being built when he was a child. His novels and poems speak even more eloquently, if indirectly, of the old rural order which had produced the vernacular buildings and by its passing had left them irreplaceable. The present could only feel nostalgic for the lost innocence which that world represented.

⊡ TWO ⊡

THE CLASSICAL INFLUENCE

'God damn my blood, my Lord, is this your Grecian architecture?
What villainy! What absurdity!'

Lord de la Warr, 1758

From the time of the Roman Empire to the sixteenth century, nothing which was built in England can be described as Classical. From the sixteenth century to the early nineteenth, and indeed onwards, nearly all houses were Classical which did not conform to the definition of vernacular.

What does Classicism imply in architecture? It is the consciousness of an architectural link, however remote, with the Mediterranean, and more specifically Classical Greece and Rome. It is not that Englishmen did not visit Italy throughout the Middle Ages, or that English poets and scholars were unaware of the literary remains of Greece and Rome. Chaucer borrowed the story of *Troilus and Criseyde* from the Greek, but he set it in an English vernacular house, and his readers must have been unaware of any incongruity in this. It was only when England became infected with the Italian Renaissance fervour for a physical re-creation of the ancient world that Classicism may be said to have arrived as a complete architectural package. Classicism can, however, be divided into a number of separate elements, some of which arrived in England ahead of the rest.

The most fundamental, perhaps, were the orders: three Greek – Doric, Ionic and Corinthian – and two Roman – Tuscan and Composite. These descriptions apply to columns, and are immediately recognizable by the decorative form of the head or capital. Around them was built a complicated system of proportions and moulding profiles for the base and the beam supported by the column. (See fig. 8.)

The orders may be used in their primary function of providing support, or they may be used decoratively. They may appear in spirit but not in physical form, like the key signature governing a piece of music, controlling all the relationships of proportion and the character of the mouldings without actually appearing on any column. In this way, the whole facade of a building – base, shaft and entablature – may be treated in terms of an implied order. The same

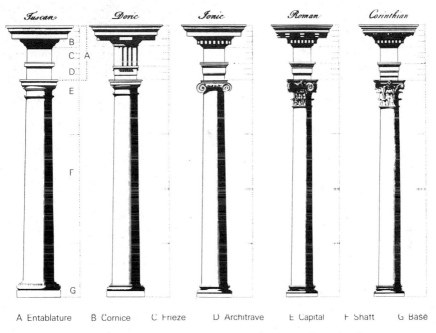

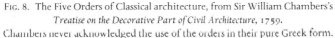

A Entablature   B Cornice   C Frieze   D Architrave   E Capital   F Shaft   G Base

FIG. 8. The Five Orders of Classical architecture, from Sir William Chambers's
Treatise on the Decorative Part of Civil Architecture, 1759.
Chambers never acknowledged the use of the orders in their pure Greek form.

process can apply to the dado, wall and cornice making three ascending divisions inside a room.

Following from the order in its simplest form are combinations of columns in twos, fours and increasing even numbers. They may be surmounted by a pediment, the triangular formalization of a gable end peculiar to the temple architecture of the ancient world. The entablature may support a further row of columns in the style given antique authority in the external wall of the Colosseum. A column must always rise above another for reasons as much practical as visual, since Classicism is based on the structural laws of stone building. Columns may also support arches of semicircular form, either individually, or treated as arcades.

This and much more information was rediscovered and valued by the architects of the Italian Renaissance who, by an imaginative leap, started designing new buildings based on those of the ancient world to express their humanist culture. There was ample evidence of ancient remains from which to reconstruct an ideal world of antiquity. In addition there was a single ancient text on architecture, the Ten Books of Vitruvius written in the first century AD. The book is illuminating and mystifying by turns, but was sufficiently suggestive to fuel the imaginations of architects and patrons.

In interpreting the past, the Renaissance architects added their own qualities of space, decoration and visual rhythm, quickening the dead marmoreal forms with lively improvisation in decoration. The great architecture of temples and baths was adapted to churches and palaces, castles and houses. Architecture was removed from the exclusive control of the masons and made a subject of more general intellectual speculation, together with the other fine arts which were, of course, so frequently practised in combination.

In Italy, the urban palace had become a fruitful field of experiment in the composition of facades and courtyards by the sixteenth century. In association with the School of Raphael, interior decoration became a sumptuous and surprisingly accurate re-creation of antiquity. Great houses in the country were now beginning to abandon the castle style and aim at the antique openness of the *villa*, the nobleman's place of repose and scene of the simple enjoyment of country pleasures as described by Horace or Pliny the Younger.

It is the villa which provides the principal thread in the history of the Classical English house. It is important to realize that little direct evidence of the villas of antiquity survived. Imaginative skill was needed in suggesting the spirit of the ancient Roman world, drawing on the available forms from other types of buildings. The architect who made the villa form particularly his own was Andrea Palladio (1508–80), working from 1540 onwards in the country round Venice.

THE ENGLISH RENAISSANCE

Classical architecture was introduced to northern Europe in the years following 1500. Italian skill was admired and emulated in all the arts. Italian artists and workmen were summoned to the court of François I of France, after which French architecture developed uninterruptedly on Classical lines. In England, François's contemporary and rival, the young Henry VIII, employed a handful of Italian sculptors and carvers in the mid 1520s, but their remarkable work had little relevance to the history of the smaller English house. Terracotta ornament like that of Hampton Court was raised aloft on the gate-tower at Layer Marney, Essex, and domesticated at Sutton Place, Surrey, by Sir Richard Weston, who had accompanied Henry VIII to France to the Field of the Cloth of Gold in 1520. Sutton Place dates from the years following this, and was

finished in 1533. As well as the tiny cherubs above the door, the symmetry
and regularity of the court (originally enclosed by a fourth range) are striking
evidence of a new attitude to building.

After Henry's death in 1548, the protectorate in Edward VI's minority
provided a second phase of the English Renaissance which may be represented,
on a small and a large scale, by two houses in Wiltshire, Lacock Abbey and
Longleat, testifying to the individual tastes and the originality of Sir William
Sharington and Sir John Thynne for whom they were built. If it still survived,
we could also include the Strand mansion of the Protector Earl of Somerset.

Lacock is a house of many periods. What concerns us here are incidental
details, chimneys, fireplaces and stone tables which formed part of Sharington's
adaptation of the former monastic buildings.

31. The Satyr Table, Sharington's Tower, Lacock Abbey, Wiltshire, c. 1650.
An example of the precocious Classicism of the mid-Tudor court circle.

Following the dissolution of the monasteries (1536–8), many new country house sites with readily available building materials passed into the hands of those with sufficient cash or royal favour. Medieval crypts were often incorporated into new houses, as at Lacock and Anglesey Abbey, Cambridgeshire. Exceptionally, a new dwelling could be made within the walls of a great abbey church, as at Buckland Abbey, Devon. In other cases the name abbey or priory survives without any original building fabric visible, as at Woburn Abbey, the fictitious Northanger.

A further consequence of Henry's break with Rome was that Italy was placed at a diplomatic distance much harder to overcome than the physical obstacles of France and the Alps. Like present-day visitors to the West from behind the Iron Curtain, the few Englishmen who went to Italy were closely watched by their own country's spies. Excessive interest in Italian culture, with its inevitable Catholic overtones, would have incurred its penalty at home.

Longleat is an exceptional house in many respects. The Italianate spark of Lacock was fanned into a steady blaze of Classicism in the course of the many changes undergone by Sir John Thynne's house between 1546 and 1580. Numerous masons and workmen whose names are recorded were involved, but Thynne himself emerges as the effective architect in the letters which he sent almost weekly, even when imprisoned in the Tower of London.

In 1553, when Longleat was under construction, John Shute, the first Englishman to call himself an architect, published *The First and Chief Groundes of Architecture*, the earliest English book to describe the five orders, but no buildings can be securely attributed to him. In the later stages of Longleat, the first effective English architect does, however, emerge. Robert Smythson went to work at Longleat after the great fire of 1567 and remained for twelve years. He would have learnt from Alan Maynard, William Spicer and John Chapman, the leading Classical carvers and designers of the time. He went on to design two of the greatest Elizabethan houses, Wollaton, Nottinghamshire (1580–88) and Hardwick Hall, Derbyshire (1590–97). He can also be associated with a number of smaller buildings, Barlborough Hall, Derbyshire (1583–4) and Doddington, Lincolnshire (c. 1593–1600), which develop a similar vocabulary – regular windows as great in area as the adjoining wall, and projecting towers which stand forward from the face of the wall and rise above the main roof-line.

These smaller houses stand apart from the elaborate Elizabethan architecture which developed on the lines of Wollaton, and owed as much to Gothic inspiration from the English past as to ancient Rome. Admittedly, a house like Chastleton, Oxfordshire (c. 1602), does not look very Italian with its

32. Chastleton, Oxfordshire, *c.* 1602. Traditional forms in a regular pattern, under the influence of Robert Smythson.

battlemented towers and sharp-pointed gables. When we look at the plan, however, it is clear how far the English house had moved from the late Middle Ages. External symmetry has become an imperative to which traditional features are subordinated. The hall, with its screens passage, survives, but has to be entered by a curious side-step through a rather overlit vestibule. The

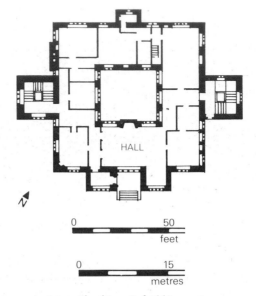

FIG. 9. Chastleton, Oxfordshire, c. 1602.
The plan shows the difficulty of fitting a traditional hall
into a symmetrical facade. With its open central court,
the house is still effectively one room deep,
although impressively massive outside.

open court in the centre serves only to give light, not as the focus of arrival and departure. For the sake of symmetry there are two staircases in the side-towers, which seem to have been directly inspired by Hardwick. At the upper level, a long gallery celebrates the Elizabethan delight in height and prospect, as well as being a new domestic amenity.

The use of Classical details is irrelevant to considerations such as these, which give a distinctive character to the houses of Elizabethan England, isolated and embattled as it was against most of the rest of Europe. Many houses represent a half-way stage in the emergence from the vernacular. Higher and more

33. Thorpe Hall, Horham, Suffolk, c. 1560. A brick hunting-lodge
displaying the Tudor love of height.

conspicuous sites were chosen, and the houses themselves grew upwards to
survey the surrounding landscape. Thorpe Hall, Horham, Suffolk, is a red-
brick hunting-lodge of c. 1560 in which the chimney-stacks and four-storey
porch achieve a remarkable impression of height. The addition of such a
feature to a simple single-ridge roof is a regular occurrence.

The double-pile house, with one set of rooms directly behind another,
remained relatively rare, and a commoner way of gaining accommodation was
to emphasize the ends of a house with clustered towers, leaving a single width
in the centre to contain the hall. At Montacute, Somerset (c. 1600), the central

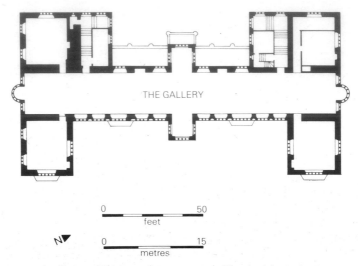

THE GALLERY

0 ————— 50
feet

N▼   0 ————— 15
metres

FIG. 10. Montacute, Somerset, c.1600. The plan is massed
at the two ends of a thin central spine, internally uninterrupted
in the spectacular Long Gallery on the second floor.

piece of the 'H' plan is thin enough for the third-floor Long Gallery to enjoy
views on both sides. The curved gables at Montacute are sober descendants of
the five which decorate the roof-line at Trerice, Cornwall (1572). Here, in an
old-fashioned part of England, the great hall still proclaims its importance
with a huge mullioned window, upsetting the otherwise regular facade.
Richard Carew, who married an Arundell of Trerice, called it a 'costly and
commodious building' in his Survey of Cornwall of 1602.

A common alternative form was to project the ends of the house forward as
wings, resulting in what is known as the 'E' plan. It is apparent as early as 1520
at Barrington Court, Somerset. Two differing treatments of it may be seen at
Long Melford, Suffolk, in Melford Hall (1550s) and Kentwell Hall (1564). The
turrets with onion-shaped caps which occur in both these houses are a common
feature of Tudor building from Henry VIII's Nonsuch Palace (1538). They are
associated with the revival of chivalry and tournaments whose architectural
implications are discussed in the next chapter. From a more practical point of
view, they accommodated staircases giving access to the different suites of
apartments. Elizabethan planning was still an *ad hoc* process, and the
architectural treatment of the staircase was to become one of the major points
of development in the following two hundred years.

34. Trerice, Cornwall, 1572. Decorative Classicism is expressed in the gables of
the Arundells' house, but the traditional hall window breaks the symmetry.

That Elizabethan architects were interested in the theory of planning can be
deduced from the collection of drawings by John Thorpe (c. 1565–1655)
showing many of the great houses of his time. He includes a typical Elizabethan
'conceit', a plan in the shape of the letters IT, his own initials, and such strange
diagrammatic plans as the triangular Longford Castle (1591). Architecturally,
the effect has nothing to do with Classicism, which is essentially rectilinear and
subordinates such literary 'devices' to visual coherence – a quality which they
frequently lack.

One place where Classicism and the conceit are not in conflict is the house
in the form of a Greek cross built by the recusant Sir Thomas Tresham at

35. Lyveden New Bield, Northamptonshire, 1605. Sir Thomas Tresham's emblematic Greek cross house was never completed.

Lyveden in Northamptonshire (1605). The house, which was never completed, was to be a prospect or banqueting house associated with the older Tresham mansion at Lyveden. The Elizabethan period is notable for the growing diversity of such domestic building types, which undoubtedly stimulated architectural innovation. Hunting-lodges, belvederes and banqueting houses all needed height and compactness of plan. They could be used for a kind of retreat known as 'secret house' – it seems that while an audit and spring-clean were being carried out in the main house, the lord lived in semi-state with a reduced household in his retreat.

A more direct form of literary 'conceit' is found at Felbrigg, Norfolk, a rather *retardataire* house of 1620 whose parapet carries the inscription 'GLORIA DEO IN EXCELSIS'.

With the Renaissance came architectural books – books of theory and speculation and picture books of designs. The Elizabethans displayed a particular fondness for pattern books of ornament from the Netherlands and Germany. Links of religion, politics and trade reinforced this affinity. Perhaps the first traceable instance is the influence of Hans Blum's *A Description of the Five Orders* (with the books of Shute and Serlio) on Kirby Hall, Northampton-shire (1570–75). Here the grand order of pilasters (as pioneered in Michelangelo's Capitoline palaces in Rome in 1547) makes a unique Elizabethan appearance.

Amongst the most widely known pattern books were those of Vriedman de Vries and Wendel Dietterlin, noted by James Lees-Milne in *Tudor Renaissance* for their 'strong streak of sadism' and 'hideous and displeasing patterns'. Their excesses were, however, modified in adaptations such as the screen at Audley End, Essex. The principal area of Flemish influence was in the design of church monuments.

In spite of the provincialism of Elizabethan architecture and its often wilful misunderstanding of Classical intentions, the first century of Renaissance influence in England had left its mark. The attitudes of 'polite' as opposed to vernacular building had spread down to the manor-house level, accompanied by ornaments such as pediments over windows, strapwork plaster ceilings and stone chimney-pieces. The appearance of the house was considered in relation to its facades and their formal arrangement, and these in turn displayed the governance of a symmetrical plan. The 'Great Rebuilding', noted as a feature of vernacular houses in the 1570s, also played its part in creating a new pattern for small manor-houses, which displayed evidence of the new current of ideas. An example is Quebec House, Westerham, Kent (early seventeenth century), which has old-fashioned hood-moulds, but an insistent regularity in its three gables.

THE IMPACT OF INIGO JONES

A new reign and a new century may both produce architectural change, but the first years of James I saw no new beginnings. In houses like Hatfield (1607–11) and Blickling, Norfolk (1619–28), both designed by Robert Lyminge for great men of the court, there is only an expansion of Elizabethan themes. At Hatfield, the south front has the expected Classical centrepiece, dated 1610, but perhaps a little more tightly organized than usual. This may be because in 1608 the builder of Hatfield, Robert Cecil, first Earl of Salisbury, had commissioned a design for a New Exchange in the Strand from a rising man at court, Inigo Jones. His reputation was for designing elaborate scenery for the masques on which the Queen, Anne of Denmark, loved to spend her time and her husband's money, and the Exchange was probably Jones's first design for a real building, although it was not carried out to his scheme.

Inigo Jones (1573–1652) was the first Classical architect to work in England. The changes he introduced were so radical that the Tudor prelude to Classicism taught him nothing. For the first time since the 1520s, the direct route to Italy was reopened and the Classicism which had hitherto arrived as an incomplete set of parts lacking a proper instruction manual was now remedied in both these defects.

The effect of Jones's revolution can be seen in his one surviving, incontestably documented, domestic building, the Queen's House at Greenwich. Here, in effect, is the Classical villa as developed by Palladio in the Veneto only fifty years or so previously.

36. The Queen's House, Greenwich, by Inigo Jones, 1616 and 1630.
A mature adaptation of Palladio, the first completely Classical house in England.

Between the Exchange design and the Queen's House, Jones had visited Italy a second time, setting out in 1613 with the Earl of Arundel. With him on the journey, Jones seems to have had a copy – which survives, with his annotations – of Palladio's *Quattro libri dell' architettura* of 1570. It is, as Sir John Summerson says, 'a document fraught with great significance for English architecture'. It was the textbook which had been missing from English architecture, although there is a justifiable claim that the designer of Hardwick Hall knew the plans in it. Jones was able to put the book to use, however, because he visited Palladio's buildings and the ancient architecture from which they had been

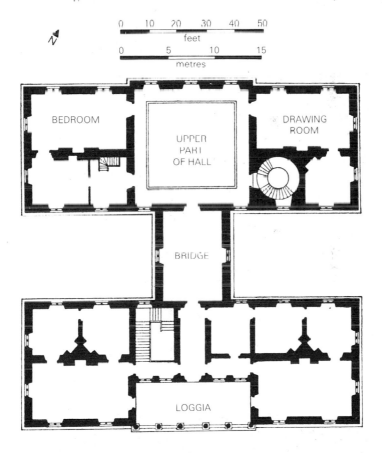

FIG. 11. The Queen's House, Greenwich, by Inigo Jones, 1616 and 1630.
The plan shows the original form of the house in two blocks with a bridge across the public road.

adapted. In addition, he acquired from Palladio's pupil, Scamozzi, a large number of original drawings.

The Queen's House was begun in 1616. It is almost a 'conceit', bridging the public road that ran through the royal park at Greenwich, but it did its best not to look like one and has been altered externally to conceal its origins. There are two ranges, clearly planned in three square divisions. Building was suspended in 1619 when Anne of Denmark died, and only resumed in 1630–35 for Queen Henrietta Maria, but there is no reason to doubt that this extraordinarily mature synthesis of Palladio and Scamozzi was clearly in Jones's head from the outset. Out of the world of Mannerism and incipient Baroque which he had encountered in Italy, Jones had gone unerringly for an architect of unimpassioned reserve, that quality so often attributed to the English but so lacking from Elizabethan houses. We have Jones's own words for how he liked architecture: 'sollid, proporsionable according to the rulles, masculine and unaffected'.

The rules were those outlined in Palladio's book and at the beginning of this chapter. It is often said that Classical architecture is a game, and the benefit of the rules is to make the players concentrate on excellence. Originality does not greatly matter, it is the creative use of precedent which is the standard of judgement.

What made Jones's work so significant for the following century was that he was not only the first proper player in England, but a very fine one. Before the outbreak of Civil War concluded his career, Jones had built surprisingly little, but had established the foundations on which a genuinely Classical style could be built.

One of Palladio's signal innovations was the adaptation of the temple portico to the villa. Jones adapted one to a church at Covent Garden, but never to a dwelling. The credit for this goes to his pupil and successor John Webb (1611–72) at The Vyne, Basingstoke, Hampshire, 1645–6. A quite different house, also to his design but with more of a *palazzo* feeling, is Lamport Hall, Northamptonshire, 1655–7. Although Webb never went to Italy, the Vyne portico has more of a genuine feeling of Palladio than any of its eighteenth-century successors. It is a feature ideally suited to the hot Italian sun, but in the north it can still evoke Mediterranean light and warmth.

The important question of the staircase was solved at the Queen's House with an elegant 'geometrical' stair with cantilevered treads in a circular well. At Ashburnham House, Westminster (pre-1662), there is an even more ingenious use of a square well. This may be by John Webb or possibly by William Samwell, architect of the original house at The Grange, Hampshire.

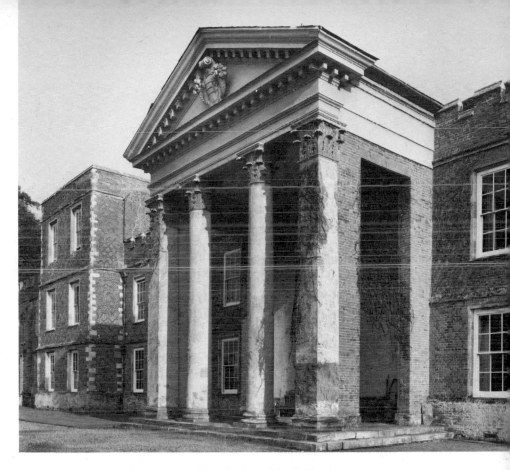

37. The Vyne, Hampshire. Portico by John Webb, 1645.
The first use of this grandest of Classical features in an English house.
The Corinthian columns are surmounted by a bold pediment.

Unlike Jones, Webb was a professional architect rather than a *uomo universale* of the visual arts. One of his contemporaries, Sir Roger Pratt (1620–85), was typical of the tradition of the gentleman amateur. In the succeeding hundred years, Pratt's adaptation of Jones's Palladianism was most influential. In his own words, should you be unable to design your own house, you should get 'some ingenious gentleman who has seen much of that kind abroad and been somewhat versed in the best authors of Architecture; viz. Palladio, Scamozzi, Serlio etc. to do it for you'.

In fact, Pratt did far more than just the original design of the buildings in which he was involved. English workmen were still getting to know the

38. Coleshill, Oxfordshire, by Sir Roger Pratt, 1649–62. One of the finest
mid-seventeenth-century houses, with a double-pile plan. Burnt out and demolished in 1953.

Classical language, and needed constant supervision. Perhaps the most beautiful
house with which Pratt was involved was Coleshill, Oxfordshire, 1649–62,
built for his cousin, Sir George Pratt. The work began soon after Roger Pratt
had returned from six years abroad, but Coleshill was quite unlike an Italian
or French house. To James Lees-Milne, the house was like 'a sonnet by Milton
wherein are compressed infinite subtleties of meaning'.[20]

Here Pratt made one of the first English uses of the 'double-pile' plan which
he advocated in his manuscript writings on architecture. A central corridor
runs the length of the house on each level, with substantial rooms on each side.
This was justified as being snugger and more convenient, but one suspects that
it was chiefly recommended by the effect of solid exterior mass that could be
obtained with it. Coleshill was an outstanding example of an astylar, or
columnless house, with its horizontal breadth emphasized by a simple cornice
and string course. The windows were disposed with great skill in the plain
facade. Inside, the palatial staircase and the quality of carving and plasterwork
were the beginning of a new epoch. But Coleshill was destroyed by fire in 1953
and is only a memory.

39. Belton House, Lincolnshire, 1684–8. One of many derivatives of
Pratt's short-lived Clarendon House, shown here in a painting attributed to Henry Bug,
the porter standing by the gate.

Pratt's house at Kingston Lacy, Dorset, 1663–5, survives, but only under a
Victorian skin by Barry. Perhaps his most influential design was the most
short-lived, Clarendon House in Piccadilly, 1664–6, which set the tone for the
domestic architecture of the Restoration. To John Evelyn, it was 'without
hyperbolies, the best contrived, the most useful, graceful and magnificent
house in England'. It was a more relaxed and traditional design than Coleshill,
on an H-plan, the centre emphasized with a pediment and roof lantern. A
slightly reduced version of it, built at Belton, Lincolnshire, 1684–8, shows
what a simple and effective design it was.

THE RESTORATION

The Restoration was the age of Wren, yet no surviving domestic work can be
firmly attributed to him. Winslow Hall, Buckinghamshire, 1699–1702, is,
however, so distinguished a design that the evidence linking it to Wren is
usually willingly accepted. Here Pratt's restful horizontality is pulled up to
attention.

40. Fenton House, Hampstead, 1693. The easy-going Classicism of the smaller
Queen Anne house which was much admired and imitated by the Edwardians.

Wren's colleague, as scientist and architect, Robert Hooke (1635–1703) was
more responsible for the continuity of the Pratt type of house. Ramsbury
Manor, Wiltshire, 1680–83, is almost certainly by him, and Uppark, Sussex,
1685–90, closely follows the same manner. Another figure from Wren's circle
was Hugh May, whose design for Eltham Lodge, Kent, 1664, introduced in
actuality the pilasters which Pratt's pediments implied. The parallels with a
contemporary Dutch building, the Mauritshuis, The Hague, are inescapable.
Holland was also involved, with France and England, in the development of
the sash window during Charles II's reign. By abolishing mullions and
transoms, sash windows emphasized the void of the window against the solid
mass of the wall. The glazing bars also played their part in making the facade
a grid of modular proportions.

Pratt's hipped-roof design could be adapted to a smaller scale with or without
the projecting wings. It was frequently built in brick with stone dressings, like
the three houses just mentioned. Examples may be seen in the London

41. Mompesson House, Salisbury, 1701. A fine stone facade taking its place in a varied but homogeneous group of buildings in Salisbury Cathedral Close.

suburbs, then several miles into the country, at Fenton House, Hampstead, 1693, and Eagle House, Mitcham, 1705. It was adapted with some subtlety of elevation for Mompesson House, in Salisbury Cathedral Close, 1701, with a stone facade, and it was raised an extra storey in height for Lord Craven's hunting-lodge at Ashdown, Oxfordshire, c. 1660. Kip's engraving shows how the cupola and viewing platform dominated the straight rides through woods.

The formal setting of Restoration houses was often swept away in the late eighteenth century, but survives in the charming arcaded brick forecourt of Antony House, Cornwall, 1710–21, and in the gate piers and fine ironwork at Nether Lypiatt, Gloucestershire, 1700–1705.

The Clarendon House model was not the only one for houses in the aftermath of Inigo Jones, and we must go back in time to account for different ways of building. The Tudor and Jacobean affection for an elaborate skyline was not easily suppressed. Sir John Summerson has noted that one of the sources of the 'artisan mannerist' style of Charles I's reign lies in the London

42. Ashdown House, Oxfordshire, 1660. A hunting-lodge built
by the first Lord Craven and intended for use by Elizabeth, the Winter Queen of Bohemia.
The chalk downland is still remote and unpopulated.

houses of around 1619. These were distinguished by curved gables surmounted by pediments, and a profusion of mouldings and ornaments, in marked contrast to the restraint of Jones. Examples of the style, in ascending order of gabled fantasy, are the Dutch (or Queen's) House, Kew, 1631, Swakeleys, Middlesex, 1630, and Broome Park, Kent, 1635–8.

The direct links with Holland are surprisingly difficult to find, but 'Dutch' gables continued to be an important feature of vernacular building in the eastern counties through the eighteenth century. Features of the Flemish version of the style, without the gables, appear at Cromwell House, Highgate, 1637–8, linked to the architectural taste of Rubens, possibly through the intervention of Sir Balthasar Gerbier, an occasional architect and opponent of Jones.

At the same time, the town house was coming under the Jones influence. Covent Garden was surrounded in 1630 with his regular, uniform 'piazzas', arcaded on the ground floor, with simple pilasters linking two floors above. Seven years later and a short distance away, William Newton developed a row of houses in Great Queen Street. Instead of their individuality being stressed, as in the 'artisan Mannerist' style, a continuous cornice runs through the block, and the pilasters assume a stronger architectural character. A more directly Palladian version of the design can still be seen in Lindsay House (from 1640) in Lincoln's Inn Fields. In general outline, it resembles Palladio's palaces at Vicenza, and if the design was not by Jones, as was supposed through the eighteenth and nineteenth centuries, he would probably have sanctioned it. Remove the pilasters and cornice, and what is left is the London terrace house in its essential anatomy up to the 1840s.

The proportions of the windows were carefully calculated so that a series of diagonal lines will 'place' the important heights and widths within a consistent geometrical system. The earliest surviving examples of the pilastered house-front built as a terrace are Nos. 52–55 Newington Green, London, built in 1658, but only recently recognized by historians.

Two other points arise from Lindsay House. It was built by Newton as a speculation, not for his own use, and thus sets the pattern of finance and organization by which English towns were generally to develop. After the Civil War, London was enlarged by the house building of a colourful entrepreneur, Dr Nicholas Barbon, operating on the southern parts of Bloomsbury. Lindsay House also enjoys the amenity of open land in front of it, the prototype of the London square, which in turn became the model of squares all over England.

THE BAROQUE

The calm and comfortable style of Sir Roger Pratt was not the only aspect of Restoration architecture. The age of Wren was also the age of the Baroque style. Baroque is a form of Classicism in which emotion and sensation are allowed to control the rules of composition. There are many precedents for Baroque effects in the architecture of antiquity, and the style, which was of Roman origin, enabled architects in northern Europe to get closer to the spirit of Rome.

In the restricted terms of the English house, one general effect was to conceal the roof by flattening it or raising a parapet as the Elizabethans had done. The house then appeared as an impressive single mass. Buckingham House (the core of the present Buckingham Palace), designed by William Winde in 1702, was important in establishing this pattern.

The turn of the seventeenth century was the beginning of the brief but intense period of Baroque house building in England. The leading figures were

Nicholas Hawksmoor and Sir John Vanbrugh, both associated with Wren in the Office of Works. Their work was mostly with great houses – Castle Howard, Blenheim, Easton Neston – but they influenced local architects, builders and craftsmen who then worked for similar effects on a smaller scale. Thus William Wakefield, a Yorkshire gentleman, continued the style of Vanbrugh in examples like Duncombe Park; William Townesend, a mason on Vanbrugh's houses at Blenheim and King's Weston, built his own house in Oxford with a giant columnar frontispiece. Woodperry, Oxfordshire, was built by Townesend in 1728 for the bachelor banker, John Morse, with many Vanbrugh features. Out of a family of masons like the Townesends, it was not unusual for one member to become eminent as a designer of buildings.

In the same connection we may mention the prolific brothers Francis and William Smith of Warwick. Their houses lack Vanbrugh's originality, but they are full of superb craftsmanship in wood panelling and carving and in plasterwork. A facade of Francis Smith's at Sutton Scarsdale, Derbyshire, 1724, is full of poetry in its ruined state. When Smith introduces such authentic Baroque motifs as the illusory projecting front (achieved with curved parapet and cornice), and the Borromini-like doorcase at Chicheley Hall, Buckinghamshire, 1719, one assumes that another mind is at work as well. These features can be linked to Thomas Archer (c. 1668–1743), one of the most original 'gentlemen amateurs' in architecture.

In Italy, Archer was among the few Englishmen of his generation to see and appreciate the new work of Bernini and Borromini, and to give it an idiosyncratic English form in well-known churches like St John, Smith Square and St Philip, Birmingham. His name is associated with several houses of the smaller size, notably Chettle House, Dorset, c. 1710, and Marlow Place, Buckinghamshire, c. 1712–20. These have in common the red brick of which they are built, a grand order of pilasters and a vigorous modelling of the mass of the house. By placing the service offices in a basement, it was possible to make every side of the house a 'show front', each one being different.

An even more compact design on the same theme is Iver Grove, Buckinghamshire, 1722–4. With its full Doric entablature and pediment, the west front has a Palladian air not unexpected for its date, but the treatment of the south front with a giant arched centrepiece is distinctly Baroque. Hawksmoor's associate John James has been suggested as the designer of this 'small, trim, pretentious, suburban retreat'.[21]

Archer's influence is found in the use of an Ionic capital with inturned volutes, based on Borromini, in the town houses of the Bastard brothers at Blandford Forum, Dorset, which they rebuilt with considerable personal style

43. Iver Grove, Buckinghamshire, 1722. A small house showing the
rhetorical Classicism of the Baroque.

after a devastating fire in 1731. By this time, Baroque was well out of fashion
in the capital. It did, nonetheless, become an important style for small country
builders, encouraging improvisation in decoration and materials. The side wall
at Bradbourne, Kent, 1713–15, is a *tour de force* of different coloured brick,
used in receding planes.

Colour contrast and the modelling of planes is the essence of the extraordinary
multum in parvo facade of Sherman's, Dedham, Essex, *c.*1730. The use of
pilasters at the extremities of the facade is a recurrent feature of 'builders'

44. Sherman's, Dedham, Essex, *c. 1730*. A Baroque front to a vernacular building in the main street of a small country town.

45. Tintinhull House, Somerset. A Classical facade added in 1700 to an earlier farmhouse, and retaining its original mullioned windows.

Baroque'. It occurs in the attractive if muddle-headed facade of Finchcocks, Goudhurst, Kent, c. 1725, where each pilaster has a section of Doric entablature, although it does not reach the line of the first-floor window heads. The whole idea of a pilaster representing (if only symbolically) an element of constructional support is missing.

Isolated pilasters can occur more predictably beneath a pediment in the centre of the facade. At Tintinhull, Somerset, a facade of Ham Hill stone was added in 1700 to a house of Charles I period, mixing the hipped-roof style with a touch of Baroque through the use of pilasters. The house was known as Pitt Farm in the eighteenth century, and was held by a junior branch of the Napper family. It still has a farmhouse air from the rear, although the eighteenth-century facade is now seen framed by the fine twentieth-century garden.

Even further from architectural orthodoxy is the facade of Reddish House, Broad Chalke, Wiltshire, of the early eighteenth century. The pediment is

46. Reddish House, Broad Chalke, Wiltshire, early eighteenth century.
An attractive distortion of Classical rules.

47. The Manor House, Hale, Lancashire, 1700. A facade of extreme grandeur
on a relatively small village house.

nearly squeezed into an equilateral triangle, and the finely carved Corinthian
pilaster capitals look as if they might have been waylaid on the road to a
grander house. It is still 'a house of great character, noble yet rustic'.[22] Sir Cecil
Beaton lived here for many years. This, like Tintinhull, is a village house.

Not far away, at Netherhampton, is a house of c. 1710–20 in which the
facade is far grander than the cottage dwelling at the rear could justify. This
amiable pretence, which sometimes included making building materials seem
other than they actually were, was a feature of the dissemination of Baroque
ideas among country builders. A similar display of cheap grandeur can be seen
at the Manor House, Hale, Lancashire, which was given a fine facade of red
sandstone in 1700 by the vicar, the Reverend William Langford. This is a
much more sophisticated design than Reddish House, reflecting the French
manner of Petworth and Boughton, with a military trophy in the pediment
and œil-de-bœuf windows which turn out on inspection to be done in paint –
the house behind does not rise to this height.

THE PALLADIAN DISCIPLINE

While the Baroque was going native in remote parts of the country in the 1720s, London had become the centre of a new wave of Classicism. Dissatisfaction with Baroque was partly the result of the cycle of taste revolving, but it also reflected antagonism to France and to Catholicism in general, the political stance of the Whig party.

One might have expected the architecture of Whiggery to abjure any foreign style, especially a foreign style connected with the Stuart dynasty, but by a strange set of correspondences, the architecture of English nationalism in the early eighteenth century modelled itself on that of ancient Rome, as interpreted by Palladio and Inigo Jones.

The narrowness of this artistic aim undoubtedly helped its achievement. The rules inherent in the works of Palladio and Jones (which they themselves often transgressed) were boiled down as a standard by which all building work could be undertaken. It was believed that an absolute standard of good taste could thereby be attained.

The Palladian movement began in 1715 with the publication of a translation of Palladio's *I quattro libri dell'architettura* with new copperplate engravings by Giacomo Leoni, which greatly improved on Palladio's originals. In the same year was published the first part of *Vitruvius Britannicus*, a luxurious architectural picture-book with an emphasis on new country houses. The publication of country-house views had in fact begun in 1707 with the charming bird's-eye perspectives by the Dutchman, Leonard Knyff, engraved by Johannes Kip, in *Britannia Illustrata*. Part of their charm is that they recorded old and new houses, standing in fields and orchards, as the illustrator happened to see them. *Vitruvius Britannicus*, although it included some Baroque houses, was a book with a mission. Colen Campbell, its editor, an ambitious Scot, was concerned with the serious professional treatment of architecture. The buildings are shown almost entirely in plan and elevation, rather than in perspective. The book was also concerned to present Campbell's own designs, begun in the year of publication, for a massive mansion at Wanstead, Essex, in the most favourable light. His two alternative designs for Wanstead show that the new Palladianism was more severe in character even than its models, with minimal ornamentation of the skyline, and a great Corinthian portico in the centre.

No English house had ever looked like this before, but in the course of the next fifty years, the central portico, the rusticated basement storey, and the square-shouldered silhouette were to become distinguishing marks of even the most provincial country house.

Campbell's other country-house designs, Stourhead, 1721, Houghton, 1722, and Mereworth, 1723, also established important precedents. Houghton revived the towers which terminate the facade at Wilton, then believed to be a pure work of Inigo Jones, although now attributed mainly to Isaac de Caus. Stourhead and Mereworth are of greater significance for the history of the smaller house, as they are based on the prototype of the Palladian villa rather than the palace. Stourhead is based on Palladio's Villa Emo at Fanzolo, one of

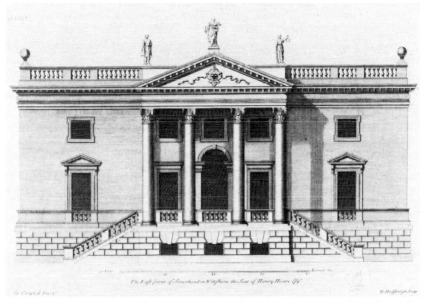

48. Stourhead, Wiltshire, by Colen Campbell, 1721. The essential Palladian features, seen in an engraving from Campbell's *Vitruvius Britannicus*.

the purest statements of Palladio's villa type, although Stourhead differs in having a projecting portico, roof parapet, and two small flights of steps up to the portico rather than one central ramp. The plan compromises with English precedent by avoiding the double-height central hall of Palladio's originals, and putting the main staircase in the core of the house. In other respects, particularly the carefully proportioned rooms based on intersecting tripartite divisions, the model was closely followed.

Mereworth is a more directly derivative version of Palladio's famous 'conceit', the Villa Capra (or Rotonda) at Vicenza of 1566–70. The original was a belvedere or banqueting house rather than a genuine country retreat with a

49. Villa Emo, Fanzolo, Italy, by Andrea Palladio, 1559. Of all Palladio's villas,
this was the inspiration for English architects.

working farm, and the extreme formality of having four identical facades with
porticos linked to a central circular space imposes a strain on its adaptation for
the more varied life of the English country house, making it a difficult model
to repeat very often.

It is often thought that the young Lord Burlington looked to the Villa Capra
when building an addition to his house at Chiswick in 1725. His general desire
to improve English taste in the arts was channelled into architecture by
Campbell's example, but he soon became his own designer, educating his
protégé William Kent. In 1719 he made a second journey to Italy with the
specific intention of studying Palladio's work, and acquired the master's
drawings of Roman antiquity, uniting them with the portion of the Jones–
Webb collection which had descended to the architects John and William
Talman.

Chiswick is no simple derivative, however. It borrows from many sources – Palladio, Scamozzi and (especially inside) Jones. Each of the three main facades is different, making important use of the 'Palladian' or 'Venetian' window, which is hardly a theme in Palladio's own designs at all. This arrangement of a three-light window, the centre one wider and raising its arched head from a springing which makes the architrave of the other two, was to become a useful leavening in popular English Palladianism.

Chiswick was an old family estate of Burlington's, close to London by road or water, and enjoying the amenities of the river and country air. It was a place to visit to play at being in Italy and to play at being in an ideal ancient Roman landscape. The gardens at Chiswick were, and mostly still are, as remarkable as the house. The severe interpretation of artistic law and human dignity of the house was tempered by a more forgiving attitude to nature, so from its earliest times the English Palladian villa acquired an air of pleasing make-believe.

Without going far up river from Chiswick, we come to Twickenham, where the poet Alexander Pope, an admirer of Burlington, lived in a small Palladian house, to which was attached a garden seething with poetic symbolism. Also at Twickenham, we may enjoy the Countess of Suffolk's villa, Marble Hill, 1724–9. She had suffered an unfortunate marriage, but was still an influential court figure in her own right, and such distinction was nicely served with an attractive villa à la mode. The designer was Roger Morris, possibly with the advice of Lord Herbert who had built an interesting villa in Whitehall to Campbell's design a few years before. Marble Hill has more of Campbell's authentic Palladian tranquillity than Burlington's intellectual electricity. The two main facades are ordered in the manner of the Villa Emo and Stourhead, although the steps are missing and the columns are only pilasters. The 'envelope' of the building is made as simple as possible. Inside, the influence of Wilton is especially apparent in the double-height Great Room on the first floor, which is in fact a single-cube room decorated in the rich and restrained style of the Double-cube Room at Wilton. This room was flanked by Lady Suffolk's bedroom and the dressing room.

Across the green from Marble Hill, we can still see the Octagon at Orleans House, designed in 1720 by James Gibbs. Gibbs had travelled to Rome to train for the Catholic priesthood, but returned as an architect instead. Had the Palladian revolution and the installation of the Hanoverian dynasty not occurred so soon after his return, it is likely that he would have given new life to English Baroque from his first-hand knowledge of modern Rome. As it was, Gibbs's Tory patrons supplied him with plenty of work, and he modified his style towards Palladianism. The Octagon is Baroque, but not treasonably so.

50. Marble Hill, Twickenham, by Roger Morris, 1724–9. One of the
most influential early Palladian villas in England.

There is another aspect to Gibbs's work of more widespread importance.
The eighteenth century became a great age for architectural books; there were
large and expensive ones, like *Vitruvius Britannicus* and Leoni's edition of
Palladio, and there were many smaller and cheaper pocket-books for builders.
If we are looking at smaller houses outside London, these handbooks are
usually the clue to the evolution of the design; a columned doorcase or a
rusticated window surround may prove to have been lifted directly from one
of them.

In this popular subculture of architecture, James Gibbs supplied many of
the forms which responded to the country builder's desire to make a brave

show of a house front. His *Book of Architecture* (1728) was the starting-point, and was backed up by *Rules for Drawing the Several Parts of Architecture* (1732). The Palladians had surrounded the orders of architecture with daunting geometrical mystery, but Gibbs simplified the rules to a formula which could be readily understood and applied. Palladio's name was still a passport to success, however, and as Rudolf Wittkower remarks, 'there are books which carry Palladio's name in the title like a trademark. In the eighteenth century, Palladio was a saleable proposition. So one adopted the name without much or even any of the substance.'[23]

The chief authors of pattern books which mingled Palladio and Gibbs for popular consumption were William Halfpenny and Batty Langley. They also mixed in a diet of Gothick and Chinese, which does not concern us here. The fruits of their labours can be seen particularly well at Stamford, Lincolnshire, one of the most beautiful English towns on the limestone belt. The main streets assemble a catalogue of popular builders' forms of the 1720s onwards: shouldered architraves and the 'Gibbs' surround with blocky quoins. In the small Cotswold town of Painswick, Loveday House by the churchyard is another example of the same phenomenon. Pattern books such as publications by William Kent and Isaac Ware showing designs by Inigo Jones for chimney-pieces, alcoves and other interior details were also valuable.

The first half of the eighteenth century saw a considerable growth in small country towns. Country gentlemen built town houses to enjoy assemblies and assizes. Such houses, some designed by John Carr, can be seen in Micklegate, Castlegate and Bootham in York. In Bury St Edmunds one can still see the pattern of Georgian social life in the Athenaeum, the elegant Town Hall, the Angel Hotel and the Theatre Royal. Merchants, people living on annuities, retired officers and the professional middle classes were also building town houses. Wherever trade and industry were thriving, we find the surplus profit going into architecture. At all levels of society more was spent on building than at any time before or since. On the North Brink at Wisbech, Cambridgeshire, we find a fine succession of houses from the mid century, each keeping level with its neighbours until we come to Peckover House, 1722, which is detached and slightly set back, with a reticent Quakerish facade.

Further into the fens, at Spalding, Lincolnshire, there still survives the Gentlemen's Society, founded in 1710 for antiquarian and scientific discussion. It seems that provincial obscurity actually encouraged intellectual life – the further from the metropolis, the greater the need for local pride and self-reliance. At Kirkwall in the Orkneys the major families built themselves houses in town for the winter, and a writer of 1775 remarked that there was 'perhaps as brilliant an appearance of Ladies as any of an equal number in Britain, without exception, both as to figure, education, virtue and every other amiable qualification'.

THE RISE OF THE VILLA

'I had before discovered that there was nowhere but in England the distinction of *middling* people,' wrote Horace Walpole on returning from the Continent in 1741. 'I perceive now, that there is peculiar to us *middling houses*: how snug they are!' The second half of the eighteenth century shows how the first truly middle-class house-type, the suburban villa, became an established part of the architectural repertory, copied by the aristocracy and by foreign countries.

To rise in society before the reforms of the nineteenth century (and for a long time after) it was necessary to have a landed estate. It was the qualification for voting, for serving as a magistrate, and, effectively, for entering Parliament. Land was difficult to acquire, making the prize seem more estimable. Extravagance in building or misfortune at the gaming tables were frequent reasons why estates changed hands. A new owner might improve his property by enclosing common land, in contradiction of the old style of paternalism. R. J. Mingay comments, 'declining owners found themselves supplanted by a medley of merchants, lawyers, bankers and tradesmen whose intrusion in the countryside aroused deep hostility and not a little envy'.[24]

For such people in search of a compact but fashionable house, the villa form was the answer. By 1793, when Charles Middleton wrote *Picturesque Views for Cottages, Farm Houses and Country Villas*, the name and the definition had become well established:

> Villas may be considered under three different descriptions – first, as the occasional and temporary retreats of the nobility and persons of fortune from what may be called their town residence; secondly as the country houses of wealthy citizens and persons in official stations, which cannot be far removed from the capital; and thirdly, the smaller kind of provincial edifices, considered either as hunting seats, or the habitations of country gentlemen of moderate fortune. Elegance, compactness and convenience are the characteristics of such buildings . . . in contradistinction to the magnificence and extensive range of the country seats of nobility and opulent gentry.

Chiswick and Marble Hill were examples of the first category. It was in the second category that the architectural development of the villa in the mid eighteenth century took place. The key figure seems to have been the architect Robert Taylor, who built a sequence of villas near London in the 1750s and

51. Asgill House, Richmond, Surrey, by Robert Taylor, 1761–4. A striking addition to the many Thames-side villas and source of many innovations.

1760s which turned the form away from purely Palladian models to a new and more versatile architectural idiom. Taylor's villas, Harleyford, Buckinghamshire, 1755, Coptfold, Essex, 1755, Danson Hill, Kent, 1762, and Asgill House, Richmond, Surrey, 1761–4, are astylar (that is, without columns), and instead of the square block of Marble Hill, the exterior masses are varied, with pieces projecting and receding. Taylor's particular innovation was the canted bay, sometimes, as at Danson Hill, applied to three sides of the house. This gave more space and variety to the rooms within and an outlook on three sides. All these villas, like their Palladian prototypes, were raised on a rusticated basement, which enabled the main rooms of the first floor to command better views, and the house itself to be more conspicuous from the surrounding country. In the case of Danson Hill, a grand entrance was contrived with curving walls to the sides of the house, linking it to stable and office buildings. For the rest, the domestic services were situated on the ground level of the 'rustic'. The first floor was reached by outside steps, and consisted, in all cases, of a series of rooms intercommunicating with each other round a top-lit stair. Such an arrangement offered both convenience and the opportunity for display in the staircase.

Marcus Binney, who has drawn attention to the importance of Taylor's villas and masterminded the rescue of a probable Taylor villa, Barlaston Hall, Staffordshire, c. 1753, writes of the domestic novelty of these houses:

> Most of Taylor's villas have only four rooms on the principal floor – hall, saloon, dining-room and library. The anterooms and cabinets that formed sets of apartments for husband, wife and guests in early-eighteenth-century houses disappear. The bedrooms are almost always all above the main floor, anticipating modern modes of living.[25]

The new ways of living in Taylor's villas reflected the 'new money' and 'new land'. Sir Charles Asgill, whose Thames-side villa has recently been restored – it can be glimpsed from Richmond Bridge – rose to fortune through hard work and a good marriage. Sir John Boyd, of Danson Hill, which still survives although in need of much work, was a merchant with West and East Indian connections.

Taylor's villa-building career came to a triumphant conclusion with Sharpham, Devon (c. 1770), for Captain Philemon Pownall.

Compared to Taylor's villas, an example like Clifton Hill House, designed by Isaac Ware for the merchant Paul Fisher in 1746, in a growing suburb of Bristol, looks conventional and old-fashioned, in spite of its delightful Rococo plasterwork.

In Middleton's second category of 'country houses of wealthy citizens and persons in official stations which cannot be far removed from the capital', we may think also of Lord Mansfield's villa at Kenwood, on Hampstead Heath. Mansfield was a notable judge, whose town house in Bloomsbury Square was burnt by the Gordon Rioters in 1780 because of his humane leniency towards Catholics. Luckily, according to legend, the rioters were waylaid at the Spaniards Inn on their way to Kenwood and so Robert Adam's recasting of an earlier house, carried out between 1767 and 1769, was saved. Such remodellings are continual in the history of English houses.

Without the wings of 1795 in the forecourt, Kenwood would seem more compact, although Adam extended the south front to make the library into the one really grand room in the house, with a balancing orangery. The use of the library as a general sitting-room was a fashion which was to spread through the rest of the century.

Adam was one of a new generation of English architects who were aware of developments on the Continent. French theorists had objected that a portico raised up on a basement storey is absurd. The function of the portico is to offer shelter, and the beauty of columns is best seen when they rise directly from the ground. The effect of this new doctrine can be seen at Kenwood, where the main rooms are indeed on the ground floor, and the handsome Ionic portico can act as a *porte-cochère*.

The credit for making this change should, however, be given to Adam's rival, Sir William Chambers, at Duddingstone, outside Edinburgh, 1762, a villa for the eighth Earl of Abercorn. This is a scholarly refinement of the

52. Duddingstone, Edinburgh, by Sir William Chambers, 1762.
The traditional Palladian formula updated by omitting the basement storey.

53. Berrington Hall, Herefordshire, by Henry Holland, 1778.
A reinterpretation of the villa with aspects of French Neo-classicism.

Stourhead type, and although the principal suite of rooms is on the ground floor, there is still a magnificent cube-shaped staircase hall.

As Middleton indicated in his third category, the villa could effectively be a small country house, with all its complement of a household of servants. The smaller establishment of villa size might suit a younger son improving part of the family property as his own 'seat'. An example is found at Berrington Hall, Herefordshire, built for the Hon. Thomas Harley, who, although a younger son of the third Earl of Oxford, had in fact made a fortune on his own account.

Berrington was begun in 1778 to the design of the fashionable Whig architect Henry Holland, son-in-law of Capability Brown, the landscape gardener. The enormous span of the portico at Berrington seems to be an attempt to make the house seem smaller than it is. At the rear, the stable court is made a formal part of the composition, but allows the villa to be seen on its own as part of the scenery. Brown's influence on the development of landscape from the 1740s onwards was to simplify the arrangements of grass, trees and water, leaving the house serenely floating in an uninterrupted sea of green, composed in the approved manner of landscape painters.

54. Basildon Park, Berkshire, by John Carr, 1776.
Palladian features persist, but ingeniously modified.

The rusticated basement gradually went out of fashion. In 1824 the architect C. R. Cockerell wrote, of James Wyatt's conventional Bryanston House, Dorset (demolished in the 1890s):

This is a house built for a city – all the architecture be raised, the lower part looking like a prison, the windows inaccessible, uninviting & no communication whatever with the garden or lawn. There is none of that confidence, that palatial and garden look so delightful to encounter with the residence of a country gent.[26]

Another country house of villa character is Basildon Park, near Pangbourne, Berkshire. It was designed in 1776 by John Carr of York, who had adapted the Robert Taylor villa pattern to a more conservative Palladianism. The originality comes in the placing of steps to the first-floor level *inside* the basement wall of the portico *in antis*, a neat and surprisingly theatrical device. The house is placed on the edge of a bluff, so there are fine views from the canted bay on the east front. The client, Sir Francis Sykes, was another Yorkshireman who had made his fortune in India. So many of his fellow 'nabobs' had gathered in the locality that it was known as 'the English Hindoostan'. Following the decline and collapse of the Sykes family, the house was sold in 1838 to a London merchant prince, James Morrison. Thanks to Brunel's Great Western Railway, the situation had suddenly become almost suburban, and Morrison welcomed the novelty and convenience:

We shall soon not want a Town House. In three years all the best physicians will recommend a ride in a steam carriage an hour before dinner as much better than a ride in the Park, and my cards will run thus; Train off at 6; dinner on table 7 precisely; return steam up at ½ past 10; carriages to Paddington at ¼ past 11; Brunel and 50 miles an hour.

After the 1770s, the canted bay rarely occurs. It evolved instead into the curved bay; this had in fact been used at Harleyford and Barlaston by Taylor, and also by Chambers and Adam, but it became something of an obsession in the villa designs of a younger generation. French architects had been interested in the pure circular form since the 1750s, and the half-round projection in the middle of a facade, finished off with a dome revealing a fully circular room inside, became the high fashion in Paris following examples like the Château of Bagatelle in the Bois de Boulogne, Paris, 1777, and Ledoux's Hotel Thelusson of the same period.

In England, the curved bay became a favourite device of Samuel Wyatt (1737–1807), who started his architectural career by using one at Doddington Hall, Cheshire, in 1776, although the dome is missing. It became so much part of his architectural repertory that he even suggested adding a rounded bow to Marble Hill in 1783 'in preference to the angular one as it will be more gracefull in appearance & give more space in the Room'. The bow is found again in the terminal pavilions of his design for Shugborough, Staffordshire, 1790–95. His younger brother, the erratic genius James Wyatt, had already used the bow with columns at Heaton Hall, Manchester, in 1772, and was to make a villa-sized version of it at Bowden Park, Wiltshire, in 1796.

To see the usefulness and potential of this device for the smaller sort of villa, we must look at the early work of John Soane (1753–1837). In the 1780s Soane was busily laying the foundation of a practice in East Anglia, designing modest houses of villa character whose external austerity (in finely coursed brick) was not only in the fashion but was good value for money. At Letton Hall, Norfolk, 1783–4, a semicircular bow came and went on the garden front as the drawings were prepared; as built, the entrance had a semicircle of Doric columns to the height of the first floor.

Saxlingham Rectory, Norfolk, 1784–7, does without such embellishment, but has a stronger form in shallow curved bays which rise above the roof line on both of the main fronts, making a solidly knit mass reminiscent, in a

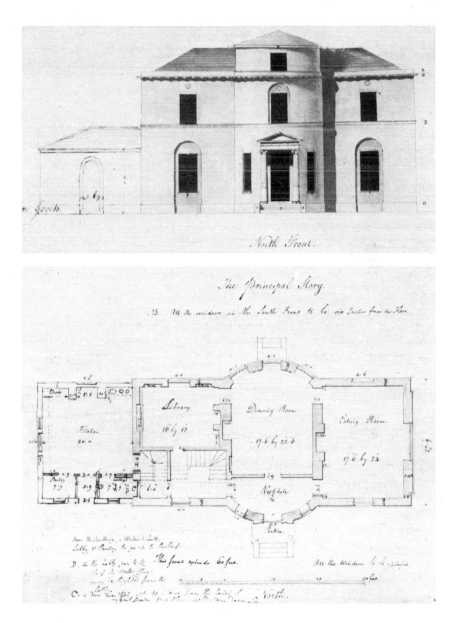

55. Saxlingham Rectory, Norfolk, by John Soane, 1784. Classicism reduced to its essential forms in a small house, but a gentleman still needed two staircases.

different style, of the original Palladio villas. Palladio would also have approved of the achievement of architectural effect in a cheap building. As Du Prey writes, 'what had started with ambitious and fashionable villas for the rich, had ended up with an inexpensive parsonage for a cleric who could not pay his bills on time'.[27]

Soane's reductive treatment of Classicism could even be effective on a farmhouse scale, as the remarkable Butterton Farm House, Staffordshire, 1816, shows. Given greater resources, Soane could mould this style to produce a masterpiece like the now demolished Tendring Hall, Suffolk, 1784–6. At Tyringham Hall, Northamptonshire, 1793, the bow appears complete with Corinthian columns to betoken his arrival in the architectural establishment. There was no dome here until an Edwardian francophile added one in imitation of the Bagatelle.

THE CHALLENGE OF THE PICTURESQUE

In contrast to Soane's rather prickly rectitude is the easy-going career of John Nash (1752–1835). Following his early bankruptcy and divorce in London, he spent some time in Wales and met several of the important theorists of the new Picturesque movement, who were to stimulate many changes in the architecture of the 1790s onwards. His design for Southgate Grove, 1797, has an almost Baroque swagger. Soane's Pitzhanger Manor, in a similar suburban situation, is a greater work of learning, but arguably not of architecture.

Soane worked hard for his originality; Nash's seemed to come by happy accident. Cronkhill, Salop, 1802, is a small agent's house attached to Attingham Park. Sir John Summerson observes:

> Here is a new departure altogether. The round tower is not a Gothic castle tower but the tower, perhaps, of an old Italian *castello* which has been made into a villa or farm; and the arcade along the front of the house is so simple that 'loggia' and 'verandah' seem descriptions altogether too exotic. The combination of these elementary forms is the essence of the 'picturesqueness'. Cronkhill is apprehended at once as a comment on the landscape in which it stands, landscape of sweeping fall and rise from the dawdling meadow above which the house stands to the far distant Wrekin.[28]

Cronkhill is an English architect's version of the kind of Italian vernacular building which is seen in the much-esteemed landscapes of Claude and Poussin – a vital source for Picturesque theory. It is the origin of the asymmetrical Italianate architecture which was for some years restrained by the Classical discipline, but eventually overcame it. We can trace its descent through Nash's

56. Cronkhill, Atcham, Shropshire, by John Nash, 1802.
The prototype of the Italian rustic style.

remarkable 'Park Villages', which were applied as an afterthought to his Regent's Park scheme in 1823. They are charming irregular compositions in Italianate style, with some Castle Gothic thrown in. The broad eaves of Cronkhill (which we could also trace back to Asgill House) make frequent appearance. The houses in Park Village were an immediate inspiration to the discerning middle classes.

Much of Nash's success in the promotion of the villa as part of the Picturesque movement is due to the landscape gardener Humphry Repton and his son John Adey Repton, who acted as a draughtsman in Nash's office. The Reptons designed and laid out a modest country house of particular charm on the north Norfolk coast, Sheringham Hall, in 1812. Although it is more a country house than a villa, the effect of mass is diminished by the low facade without central emphasis. The clients, Thomas and Charlotte Upcher, were typical of the sensitive, earnest side of the Regency which produced the Romantic poets. As Christopher Hussey wrote, they were 'romantic, emotional, virtuous and

57. Park Village West, London, by John Nash and James Pennethorne, 1823.
The Italianate style of Cronkhill is one of many in a suburban setting.

58. Sheringham Hall, Norfolk, by Humphry and John Adey Repton, 1812.
The original design presented in its landscape context, from one of Repton's famous Red Books.

deeply religious'.[29] They treated the creation of their home with the seriousness which one associates more with the Victorians, and indeed they offer a foretaste of the changed attitude to the home which was soon to prevail.

GREEK REVIVAL

The Classical repertory of architecture was enlarged after the 1760s by the adoption of genuine Greek forms, the fruit of archaeological researches undertaken in Greece and Asia Minor. Their effect on English houses was widespread but generally superficial. Greek orders replaced Roman, and mouldings became more refined, but the essentially Palladian patterns of composition continued. This continuity can be seen in rather crude form in the Doric Villa, Regent's Park, designed by Nash in 1828, with a Doric portico of four columns attached to the front of what is actually two houses. By this date, the Greek Revival style could become subtle to the point of ennui, as at Arlington Court, Devon, 1822, by Soane's pupil Thomas Lee, which James Lees-Milne thought 'plain to ugliness'.[30] Only small relief is given by the half-round Doric porch on the entrance side. Inside, however, the austerity is compensated for by such typically Regency treatments as *scagliola* (artificial marble), elaborate low-relief plasterwork, gilding, upholstery and fake maple graining.

59. Arlington Court, Devon, by Thomas Lee, 1822. A plain villa of the late Greek revival.
The service wing is a mid-Victorian addition in which all sense of
Classical refinement has been lost.

The Greek Revival was a strong influence on architects working outside London, like the Norfolk architect W. J. Donthorn, designer of several villa-type houses with 'great hardness and decision in the edges', or John Dobson of Newcastle, whose masterpiece in the domestic field is probably Longhirst Hall, Northumberland, 1828, with its spectacular staircase and double-height hall; that is, if one excludes Belsay Castle, 1807–17, perhaps the greatest Greek Revival house of all, in which Dobson carried out the designs of the owner, Sir Charles Monck.

THE VILLA AND THE SUBURB

The Classical style could not go further in the direction of austerity. Donthorn, Dobson and most of their contemporaries did Gothic designs as well. For a more decorative attitude to Classicism we must look back to Regent's Park. In Nash's original scheme for the Park, a large number of villas were to be built, but terraces were eventually preferred for the majority of buildings. Some villas were nonetheless built, one of the earliest by James Burton, a builder who had often worked with Nash. His son Decimus, aged eighteen, designed The Holme in 1819 in a rather conventional manner with a bow of Ionic columns. St John's Lodge which adjoins it was built at the same time to a more

60. The Holme, Regent's Park, London, by Decimus Burton, 1819. A conventional youthful essay
by an architect who developed important villa suburbs in spas and resorts.

ambitious design by John Raffield. It combined Doric columns at the entrance
(and Coade stone lions by John Flaxman) with Corinthian pilasters in the upper
storey and some incised lines in the stucco in the manner of Soane to ornament

61. St John's Lodge, Regent's Park, London, by John Raffield.
The villas of Regent's Park helped to spread the popularity of the villa form.

the wings. By 1846 this was out of date, and the financier Isaac Lyon Goldsmid had the villa remodelled in Charles Barry's Italianate palazzo style, which represented the last phase of English domestic Classicism. The other six principal villas represented the variety of Classical styles to which an architect could turn.

Variety was also apparent in the social position of the original occupants. James Elmes commented in *Metropolitan Improvements* (1826):

> Trim gardens, lawns and shrubs; towering spires, ample domes, banks clothed with flowers, all the elegancies of the town, and all the beauties of the country are co-mingled with happy art and blissful union. They surely must all be the abodes of nobles and princes! No, the majority are the retreats of the happy, free-born sons of commerce, of the wealthy commonalty of Britain, who thus enrich and bedeck the heart of their great empire.

It is to the middle-class adoption of the villa, however, that we must turn. The mercantile origins of Robert Taylor's clients have been noted, and contemporaries were quick to see the villa as the symbol of pitiful or ridiculous pretensions:

> Suburban villas, highway-side retreats,
> That dread the encroachment of our growing streets,
> Tight boxes, neatly sashed, and in a blaze
> With all the July sun's collected rays,
> Delight the citizen, who, gasping there,
> Breathes clouds of dust and calls it country air . . .
> There, pinion'd in a parlour snug and small,
> Like bottled wasps upon a southern wall,
> The man of business and his friends compress'd,
> Forget their labours, and yet find no rest.[31]

Villas of this kind, probably of little architectural distinction, have largely vanished from the suburbs of London of which they were once a dominating feature. Only a few examples remain, like Keats's house in Hampstead – in a district of Regency suburbia.

The growth of middle-class patronage can be seen in the multitude of books of architectural design published in the early nineteenth century. Instead of the old style of elevations and plans in line, like *Vitruvius Britannicus*, the new books had perspective views in aquatint which the most untrained eye could appreciate. With small houses and cottages, the books were aimed at the suburban market, although every building stands apparently in open country.

62. Belle Isle, Windermere, Cumbria, by John Plaw, 1774.
A severe Classical house in a romantic lake-island setting.

Indeed, the most remarkable design in John Plaw's *Rural Architecture* (1785 and later editions), the circular porticoed house on Belle Isle, Windermere, could not have had a more secluded situation.

Perhaps the leader in such publications was J. B. Papworth, whose designs appeared amidst fashion plates and fabric samples in *Ackermann's Repository of the Arts* between 1809 and 1828. His *Rural Residences* (1818) mixes 'cottages, decorated cottages' and 'small villas', including such useful suggestions as 'a villa designed as a residence for a small family', 'a villa adapted to park scenery (to afford accommodation to a small family of moderate fortune)' and 'a villa designed as the residence of an artist (also suited to the man of literary study, or to the amateur of taste)'. E. Gyfford's *Designs for Elegant Cottages and Small Villas* (1806) includes an executed design for a villa at Walthamstow for Mr Cooke, a bookseller. In the following year, Gyfford published *Designs for Small Picturesque Cottages and Hunting Boxes*, showing how the new popularity of hunting among the middle classes provided yet another opportunity for architects.

Papworth specialized in improvements to properties on the rural fringe of London: Crouch End, Chigwell, Balham and Clapham. His clients were drawn from city merchants and bankers, for whom he also advised on warehouses and other buildings. Papworth was involved, too, in the layout and planning of new developments in Dulwich, Cheltenham, Dover and the never-begun city of Hygeia on the Ohio River.

It was through such speculative developments that the villa burgeoned into the standard Victorian middle-class dwelling. The Eyre Estate in St John's Wood, London, is crucial to the history of this change. As early as 1794 a plan for the estate, which was to benefit from the Crown's development of Marylebone Park (now Regent's Park), was drawn up. Sir John Summerson has observed:

the remarkable thing about it is that the whole development consists of *pairs of semi-detached houses*. So far as I know, this is the first recorded scheme of the kind – a kind which was to become almost universal for suburban development in the later nineteenth century and which remains almost universal today.[32]

When the Eyre Estate finally came to be developed in the 1820s, it did indeed consist of detached and semidetached houses with space between them.

FIG. 12. Nos. 107 and 109 Clifton Hall, St John's Wood. Typical villas of the period after Waterloo.

In the same period, developers who could not afford this use of land still endeavoured to give a villa character to their terraces, as in the charming paired pedimented houses in the Lloyd Baker Estate in Finsbury. This formula has lately been successfully revived for houses in Lanark Road, Maida Vale by Jeremy Dixon, although here the pairs are not joined.

63. Lloyd Baker Street, Finsbury, possibly by W. J. Booth, 1820–40. The villa pediment
disguises the monotony of the terrace and suggests a non-existent detachment.

As with Nash's Park Villages, the informality of the villa suburb was an invitation to architectural variety. St John's Wood has examples of Classical and Gothic styles, as does Decimus Burton's development at Hove (see Chapter 4). When Burton was developing Calverly Park in Tunbridge Wells in the 1830s, there was a fine balance between the need for individual architectural expression and the tradition of uniformity. John Britton wrote in *Descriptive Sketches of Tunbridge Wells* (1832), 'In designing and placing these houses, the architect has evidently studied variety but restrained his fancy to such simple forms and sizes as seemed best adapted to economical expenditure.' This was evidently a response to the idea that the villas would attract 'the generality of persons who can only occasionally exchange their abodes from the metropolitan close streets to the broad expanses of rural scenery'. Such people would be well served by the short-term letting of furnished houses which was a common feature in resorts until the last war.

Writing in 1936, G. M. Young asked, 'Who are these Victorians?... What creed, what doctrine, what institution was there among them which was not at some time or other debated or assailed? I can think of two only: Representative Institutions and the Family.'[33] Belief in the family was the reason for suburbia's success in the nineteenth century. To uphold the values of the family, it was necessary to have privacy from neighbours and privacy for the individuals in the house, for servants from those they served and for each member of the family from the others. A villa, even semi-detached, went far to achieve this, and mid-Victorian terraced houses swelled in size to make it possible without physical separation.

Among the institutions which the Victorians successfully challenged was the 'rule of taste', the Classical standard in the arts. From the 1840s onwards there is a transformation in the architectural appearance of the villa. Only in Glasgow and a few other bastions of old values did the purity of the Greek Revival persist past the mid-century. Elsewhere, eclectic decoration of no certain architectural description became the rule. The desirable quality was 'character'. It may be seen in developments of the 1850s like the Tufnell Park Estate (surveyor George Truefitt), Maitland Park (Wehnert and Ashdown) and Highbury New Park (Charles Hambridge). These designs, combining elements of several styles, seem to have arisen from an architectural 'underground', in which no figures of distinct talent can be perceived. Their social ambiance was accurately described by Sir John Betjeman in *St Saviour's, Aberdeen Park*:

> Geranium beds for the lawn, Venetian blinds for the sun,
> A separate tradesman's entrance, straw in the mews behind,
> Just in the four-mile radius where hackney-carriages run,
> Solid Italianate houses for the solid commercial mind.

'High Art' architecture only came back into speculative suburbia with the development of Bedford Park in the 1870s.

By that time, the mid-Victorian eclectic style was following the developing railway system and producing the 'workman's villa' in outer suburbs linked to city centres by workmen's trains.

Thus, as Sir John Summerson wrote,

these villas ... bring the ancient word 'Villa' down to a level inconceivable when Lord Burlington built the first and loveliest of English villas at Chiswick a century and a half before. At last, this ancient romantic word, Roman in ancestry, lordly in association, was brought down to the mud of Walham Green and trodden into the marshes of Leytonstone.[34]

THE VICTORIAN TERRACED HOUSE

At the same time, the onward march of bricks and mortar was continued in the traditional form of terraced houses. In London, the development of the 1840s and 1850s was mainly westward. Thomas Cubitt's bold and successful venture of Belgravia on the land of the Grosvenor Estate set the style for stuccoed houses with individual porches, arranged in long grandiose streets. A stranger led blindfold would have difficulty in distinguishing between North Kensington, Paddington, Bayswater or Pimlico, all developed in the 1850s.

Speculative builders tended to aim for the higher class of tenant, but each area rapidly found its social level. As a newspaper correspondent wrote of 'Stuccoville' – Pimlico – in 1877:

Here are squares and churches. South Belgravia is genteel, sacred to professional men of various grades, not rich enough to luxuriate in Belgravia, but rich enough to live in private houses – for this is a retired suburb. Here people are more lively than in Kensington, though not so grand, of course as Albertopolis [the Queen's Gate area], and yet a cut above Chelsea, which is only commercial, and ever so much more respectable than Westminster, dreadfully behind the age, vegetating on the other side of Vauxhall Bridge Road.

Often houses were built ahead of demand, and successful development, undertaken by families like Galsworthy's fictional Forsytes or real-life tycoons like Sir Charles James Freake, depended on judging the right moment to build. Behind the actual contracting builder lay a shadowy realm of lawyers, financiers, mortgagors and surveyors who contributed to getting houses built. The names of architects are usually hard to find. The enormous cliffs of stucco which Freake and his contemporaries erected in 'Albertopolis' in the 1860s are varied with surface ornament, but follow a standard pattern within.

Today it is hard to imagine these houses as single family dwellings, but the subdivision of services and the need for privacy described in Chapter 4 so inflated the Victorian terraced house that the standard plot 22–5 feet wide was filled back to a depth of 80 or 90 feet with the service quarters at the back, and raised up to five storeys with basements and attics. Private gardens were unpopular and hard to accommodate, but communal gardens were created in front of the houses across the road, or sometimes to the rear with private access from each group of houses. The builder would contribute to the layout of the garden, and the residents would pay for its upkeep.

Planning control was still exercised by ground landlords, whose surveyors laid out street patterns and placed shops, churches and mews in appropriate parts of each estate. Long straight streets were varied with rectangular 'squares' and the occasional crescent or circus, perpetuating the forms canonized by John Wood's Bath developments of the mid eighteenth century.

Thus Victorian London developed as a series of self-contained pockets linked to the main highways, but often cut off from neighbouring estates. By continental standards it was never fully 'urban' and, as Stefan Muthesius has pointed out in *The English Terraced House* (1982), the terraced house retained 'suburban' features like the private garden and individual plot which are quite unlike the courtyard forms of the Continent.

The grand Classical terrace had a final flowering in the work of Alexander 'Greek' Thomson in Glasgow. His Great Western Terrace of 1869 has a dignity and reserve which had hardly ever existed in the south. Its privacy is emphasized by a massive earthen embankment. Elsewhere, a terrace might assume the guise of a country house protected by lodges and gates. Front gardens were rare, but a delightful exception is Bede's Terrace of the 1860s in Sunderland.

By the 1880s the idea of Classical unity, on which the aesthetic aspect of the terraced house depends, was at its lowest point. One result was the attempt to build terraces in the picturesque Queen Anne style, which can be seen in Courtfield Road, South Kensington, in a block designed by Walter Graves for the builder John Robinson Roberts in 1881. These houses could hardly compete, however, with the individual town houses of George and Peto in Harrington Gardens which were rising in the next street at the same period.

The tendency, described in Chapter 5, towards suburban and rural living hastened the decline of the upper-middle-class terrace. In 1883 a book on estate development made the simple distinction, terraces for the lower orders, villas for the better classes.

PALLADIAN EPILOGUE

This is not quite the end of the genuinely Classical villa, however. In Chapter 5 we trace the rise of the romantic neo-Georgian house, whose plan was based on quite un-Georgian informality. By the 1930s, a younger generation of architects was looking with renewed enthusiasm at the architecture of English Palladianism, which the older generation had despised as cold and foreign. It was exactly these qualities of formal splendour and intellectual challenge which now seemed specially attractive.

In 1938, John Seely (1900–1963) and Paul Paget (b. 1901) built the remarkable hunting-box at Templewood, Norfolk, using fragments from demolished Georgian buildings. The plan consists of a large central room, of Palladian proportion and grandeur, to which small suites of apartments are attached at each corner – a perfect answer to the twentieth-century demand for the feeling of generous scale without an excessive bulk of building.

At the same time, Raymond Erith (1904–73) was pursuing an individual line of Classicism which led him to design after the war several villas of more direct Palladian inspiration than even the English Palladian villas of the eighteenth century. Among these, Wivenhoe New Park, Essex, 1962–4, and Kings Walden Bury, 1969–71 (with his partner and successor, Quinlan Terry), are especially notable. The Palladian influence is also uppermost in the work of Claud Phillimore, as in the new house in Arundel Park for the Duke of Norfolk, 1960. In all these houses, the simplicity and economy of Palladio's original villas has been a valuable guide for adapting to twentieth-century requirements. The Classical influence is even returning to public housing projects, with a fondness for 'pavilion' forms with pyramidal roofs. It seems unlikely that a general understanding of the principles of Classical architecture, such as existed in the eighteenth century, will return, but it is encouraging to think that a growing number of specialized architects and craftsmen are capable of carrying the style into the twenty-first century, five hundred years after Inigo Jones roused English architecture from backwardness and barbarity.

◧ THREE ◩

THE ROMANCE OF
THE PAST

In one of those beautiful vallies, on a bold round-surfaced lawn, spotted with juniper, that opened itself in the bosom of an old wood, which rose with a steep but not precipitous ascent, from the river to the summit of the hill, stood the castellated villa of a retired citizen.

Thomas Love Peacock, *Crotchet Castle*, 1831

When the Italian style came to England in the sixteenth century, it had as its premiss an idealization of ancient Rome. Yet, paradoxically, this harking back to the Classical world represented everything that seemed most up to date in architecture at the time. The subsequent development of Classicism down to the Edwardian period was largely the story of one fashion following another, each seeming more chic and advanced than the one before. Only in our own day – since the Second World War – has Classicism in turn come to appear romantic and backward-looking; the vanished age to which some recent country houses appeal is located as much in the eighteenth century, or even the 1930s, as in the first century AD. They look back to periods of apparent stability and order that, to some people, seem preferable to the chaos of the present.

But choosing to be old-fashioned, or to set your face against the prevailing trend, is nothing new. Even when Classical architecture was at its height, there were men and women who rejected it – not because they knew no better, but because for special, often personal reasons, perhaps to do with family or religion, they favoured the associations of other styles. Usually this meant an idealization of the Middle Ages, with its codes of chivalry and courtly love, rather than of ancient Rome or Greece. Many arguments could be advanced for it: some saw the Middle Ages in Christian terms, with large swathes of Britain ruled over by the Church; others conceived it as a period of social cooperation symbolized by the guild system; others again rather unhistorically envisaged Gothic as first and foremost a British style. By the middle of the nineteenth century, the Gothic Revival had swept the board almost as completely as Classicism had done previously. But signs of a romantic yearning for the past can be perceived much earlier than that – almost before the Middle Ages were over. As likely as not, they can be associated with individualists, or dreamers, with highly developed tastes, idiosyncrasies or obsessions – or a special pride in family history, and perhaps the sense that the present was just not as good as the past. One may at times be tempted to think that individualism has always been a highly regarded quality of the English house, but not so; quite the reverse in the Georgian period, for instance. Perhaps these early individualists in house architecture were the precursors of a typically modern taste. Those whose names have come down to us built great houses or castles, but their work probably would have found a parallel in the more modest houses for which documentation in this early period is scarce.

Identifying early examples of revivalism can be something of a problem. Revival is easily confused with survival. The Middle Ages in England did not, of course, conveniently come to an end all of a sudden at the Battle of Bosworth Field. Similarly, because communications were bad and ideas travelled slowly, Gothic forms did not die out everywhere at the same time; in some parts of the country, remote from centres of fashion, they lingered on in the repertoire of traditionalist masons and carpenters, who handed on their skills and mannerisms from father to son. And more up-to-date craftsmen also remembered the old ways, even if they did not generally practise them. When attempts were made to resuscitate Gothic in the seventeenth century, particularly by the High Church party that put a special value on tradition, it was possible to draw on the folk memories of such craftsmen. They knew how it was done. This was no longer the case in the nineteenth century, when architects found that, if they wanted a piece of neo-Gothic work doing properly, they had to give very detailed instructions and possibly train their own craftsmen, or even do the thing themselves. Gothic survival, as opposed to Revival, was unselfconscious. Traces of it have been found as late as the first half of the eighteenth century.

Unless builders of houses helpfully put their thoughts down on paper, and that paper has survived, it is by no means easy to say when old forms were used as a deliberate gesture and when not. It is difficult to classify Tattershall Castle in Lincolnshire, for instance. Although the point of possessing a castle as a centre of power decreased considerably as cannons became more powerful and more reliable, some people still wished to give the impression that their new houses were castles, or had elements of castles about them.

From 1430 to 1460, Henry VI's treasurer, Lord Cromwell, replaced the old early-thirteenth-century castle at Tattershall, which had been a genuinely

64. Tattershall Castle in Lincolnshire, built in the second quarter of the fifteenth century. It was designed to look like a castle, although the big window openings show that it could not in practice have stood out to a significant force for long.

defensive structure, with a tall brick keep – which both looked spectacular in the flat landscape and provided a vantage point from which the owner could survey the coast. This building only looked like a castle. There were battlements along the roof-line, but the ground floor has doorways and large windows that could easily have been penetrated by an enemy. So much for the 'great tower called le Dongeon', as the keep is referred to in the accounts. Cromwell was extremely conscious of his rank, and wanted a house that would create a sense of seigneurial grandeur appropriate to it.

Equally, the crenellated parapet of a house like Athelhampton in Dorset, built for Sir William Martyn, a wealthy skinner and Mayor of London, in 1495, is too small to be of military use. Ten years after Bosworth, it did not seem necessary to build anything more than a comfortable country house, and the licence to crenellate which Martyn obtained was not more than a kind of planning permission. Castle forms passed into the decorative language of a wholly domestic way of building and survived well into the sixteenth century.

It was the sophisticated, outward-looking court of Henry VIII that first adopted the Italianate ornament of Pietro Torrigiani and the other foreign sculptors and craftsmen who were brought to England (a taste that never became general). Yet the same court also saw a revival of chivalry. Jousts were held in the royal lists, with the king himself taking part. They were accompanied by an elaborate and colourful pageantry, and highly complex heraldic symbolism. In *Tudor Renaissance*, James Lees-Milne describes the joust held by Henry VIII at Christmas 1524. A herald called 'Chasteau Blanche' rode into the queen's chamber wearing a 'coat of arms of red silk, beaten with a goodly castle, of four turrets silver, and in every turret a fair lady, standing gorgeously apparelled', who declared 'to all kings and princes, and other gentlemen of noble courage' that a certain 'Captain will near to his Castle of Loyaltie raise a Mount, on which shall stand an Unicorn, supporting four fair shields.' Such imagery reached a high point of elaboration at the Field of the Cloth of Gold, that grand contest of royal egos between France and England, for which Henry employed three thousand workmen to erect a mock palace. Although the fountains in front of the gatehouse were 'ingrailed with anticke work' (that is to say, Renaissance motifs), the one-day-wonder palace was in the form of a square castle with a round tower at each corner and statues of armed men standing at the loopholes and battlements. A similar combination of the Italianate and the medieval can be seen in Henry's real, but long-since-demolished palace of Nonsuch in Surrey – the most ostentatious building of the age. The quaint octagonal corner towers and the fantastic skyline looked back, whether consciously or unconsciously, to a heroic past.

Chivalry was even more in the minds of Gloriana's courtiers, who might have read Spenser's *Faerie Queen* and observed the extravagant behaviour of Sidney, Essex and Raleigh. Tournaments were held several times a year, notably on Accession Day to celebrate Elizabeth's mounting the throne. Mock castles of wood and canvas were frequently erected to accompany these and other ceremonies that bolstered the prestige of the monarch and helped satisfy the popular love of spectacle.

Again, it had its parallel in architecture which, as John Aubrey commented in the next century: 'Under Elizabeth . . . made no progress but rather went backwards.' A self-conscious revival of Gothic forms is evident in the work of the Smythsons – Robert and John – who dominated the second half of the sixteenth century. Historians have emphasized Robert Smythson's Classicism and sophistication – his eager interest in Italian sources, his translation of them into symmetry and window walls of glass; and houses such as Longleat and Hardwick were indeed staggering, spectacular and something very new when they were built. But what of Wollaton? The immense central tower, rising up improbably behind the four balanced facades of the outer walls, derives from the castle tradition rather than from an Italian palace.

Even more obviously castle-looking houses were built at Lulworth in Dorset, Ruperra in Glamorgan and Bolsover in Derbyshire. The first two had towers at each corner of a four-square plan, while Bolsover was the most extravagant with a Little Castle in the form of a Norman keep standing before an arc of medieval curtain wall, and a long terrace range running off on a spur. The Little Castle was built by Sir Henry Cavendish, a son of Bess of Hardwick, in the 1610s; the terrace was added about 1630 by his son.

Following the execution of the 4th Duke of Norfolk for treason in 1572, this great Catholic family had some cause to 'look back with nostalgia and reverence to a lost world of Catholic piety and aristocratic Privilege', as the historian of the Dukes of Norfolk has pointed out. 'The urge to revive, relive or commemorate adequately that lost past became a powerful force determining the behaviour to a greater or lesser degree of all subsequent heads of the family."[35] This urge expressed itself in a taste for antiquarianism, a preoccupation with genealogy and an enthusiasm for Gothic architecture that lasted from the sixteenth to the twentieth centuries. A similar devotion to the past is seen in the castle restorations of Lady Anne Clifford (1590–1676), a formidable lady who married twice and could style herself Countess of Dorset, Pembroke and Montgomery. Although severe in her personal tastes (her first husband, the Earl of Dorset, urged her to spend more money on clothes), she was a devoted Royalist, unlike her second husband, the Earl of Pembroke and

Montgomery. After the Civil War, she left London for the family estates she had inherited in Cumberland, and with daunting energy set about restoring or rebuilding the castles of Skipton, Appleby, Brougham, Brough and Pendragon, and Barden Tower. (She also built one almshouse, restored another, and erected a pillar to mark the spot where she last parted from her beloved mother.)

For the rest of the seventeenth century the spirit of revivalism shows itself less in domestic architecture than in churches and chapels attached to houses or colleges. To the High Church followers of Archbishop Laud, the old Gothic style seemed consciously anti-Puritan and was used for the library of St John's College and the chapel of Peterhouse, both Cambridge. Wren was not blind to the merits of some Gothic architecture and, on occasion, even designed in Gothic where circumstances demanded it. But again he did so only in churches. By the time we re-emerge with Gothic as a style fit for the house – and especially the park – in the 1720s, a good deal of researching and recording of the medieval period had gone on. Topographical books published by scholars such as Sir William Dugdale and William Stukeley described and, more importantly, illustrated medieval remains, perhaps more out of a fascination with the past than because they were interested in architecture, while a little later Browne Willis visited every English and Welsh cathedral except Carlisle. Willis took a leading role in the Society of Antiquaries, which was founded in 1707 and reconstituted in 1717. With the spread of awareness about real Gothic, the element of survival in building gradually faded away; in its place there developed a style that self-consciously imitated features from the Middle Ages. At first these details were more likely to be taken from churches and abbeys than from domestic buildings.

THE PICTURESQUE

Antiquarianism as a learned hobby became almost a craze for some educated gentlemen, probing into the past from the comfort of their country-house libraries. But one doubts that Gothic or ruin architecture would have really caught on if it had not become part of a much broader vision, which took in landscape as well as architecture, and encouraged sophisticated people to see buildings in the context of other ideas. This vision has, since the mid eighteenth century, been called the Picturesque, because of the influence of the idealized representation of landscape in the seventeenth-century paintings of Salvator Rosa and Claude Lorrain on the organization of landscape parks and the buildings, including houses, within them. Rich young gentlemen had seen such paintings while making their Grand Tours in Italy, and they had also, indeed, seen the real landscapes of the Roman Campagna on which they were based. It was extremely piquant to try to turn your own estate at home into one of these half-real, half-imaginary landscapes; you might even choose to look at the result in a mirrored Claude glass, which had the effect of instantly varnishing Nature with a golden glow – the rays of the long afternoon sun that produced that hue in the originals being all too often absent in Britain. By the third quarter of the eighteenth century, Horace Walpole could exclaim that 'every journey is made through a succession of pictures'.

Some of the 'pictures' had been created by the hand of man, in moving hills, damming up streams to form lakes and planting clumps of trees, which were also good for the foxes. But Nature herself, especially in what was thought of as the wild and romantic scenery of Wales and the Lake District, could also be regarded as a series of painterly views. It was less of a question, for some writers, of paintings being judged according to their fidelity to the natural world, as of Nature corresponding to an artistic ideal: a curious inversion of values.

But an eye for pictorial effects, however important, was only one element of the Picturesque. Intellectual and poetic notions also played their part in a broadening of sensibility, so that buildings came to be appreciated not merely as architecture, but for the pleasurable, or even fearful, thoughts or feelings they inspired.

Many of the strands that came together in the Picturesque can be perceived, in embryo, in Vanbrugh's Memorandum of 11 June 1709, on the preservation of Woodstock Manor near Blenheim Palace. Vanbrugh, the great Baroque architect of Blenheim and Castle Howard, may seem a strange starting-point for the Picturesque. But architecture was only one of his talents; he was also a playwright, and a suggestion of theatricality is present in most of his houses, which were designed more for effect than for comfortable living. Typically, his own house – Vanbrugh Castle on Maze Hill at Greenwich – was one of his most eccentric, having been designed as a castle, albeit one constructed of unattractive yellow London stock bricks. At Castle Howard, Vanbrugh also built a series of mock fortifications in the park, which partly look neo-medieval, although he probably thought of them as Roman. But designing new works in dramatic styles was one thing, seeking to preserve the ruin of an old manor house, such as that at Woodstock, was another. Vanbrugh had become interested in the building while working on Blenheim; he had then, without authority from the Duke of Marlborough, or, more particularly, his

The Remains of Woodstock, as they appeared in 1714.

65. Woodstock Manor at Blenheim. Vanbrugh urged that it should be restored
because of its associations and because of its role in the landscape.
His Memorandum on the subject is seminal to the theory of the Picturesque.

forceful Duchess, Sarah, set about rehabilitating it as a residence for himself.
Caught in the act, he found it necessary to promulgate a theory for the
preservation of old buildings. In the Memorandum, he advanced a number of
arguments, such as that '. . . they move more lively and pleasing Reflections
(than History without their aid can do) on the Persons who have inhabited
them; on the remarkable things which have been transacted in them, or the
extraordinary occasions of erecting them'. As Dr David Watkin observes, 'Here
the case is formulated for the first time for buildings that are evocative,
associational, and which recall periods more remote and perhaps more colourful
than our own.'[36]

66. Vanbrugh's fortifications at Castle Howard.
They were designed to evoke associations of a heroic past.

And Vanbrugh continued:

There is still more to be said on other considerations. That part of the Park which is seen from the North Front of the new building has little variety of objects. Nor does the country beyond it afford any of value. It therefore stands in need of all the helps that can be given . . . Buildings and Plantations. These rightly dispos'd will indeed supply all the wants of Nature in that place. And the most agreeable disposition is to mix them: in which this old Manour gives so happy an occasion for: that were the enclosure filled with Trees (principally fine Yews and Hollys) promiscuously set to grow up in a wild thicket, so that all the buildings left might appear in two risings amongst 'em, it would make one of the most agreeable objects that the best of Landskip painters can invent.

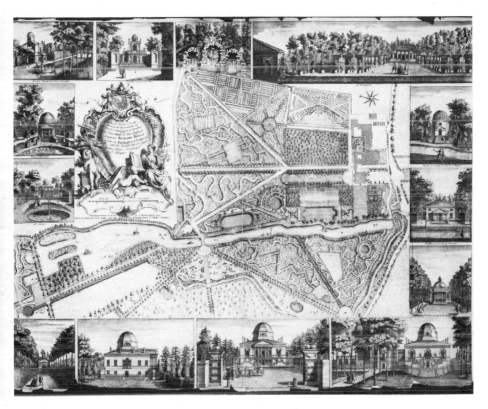

67. Plan of Lord Burlington's gardens at Chiswick villa, engraved by Rocque, 1736.
The curling walks in the Chinese-influenced landscape were terminated with buildings,
shown around the edge of the print.

House and landscape are seen as parts of the same unity: so much so that the
house does not stand four square in the centre of vision, but seems to be a
romantic incident in the landscape, glimpsed between thickets. This was a
distinctly new way of looking at buildings, and it was to have profound
implications for how they were to be designed. Vanbrugh also anticipated the
informal style of landscape gardening later associated with Capability Brown,
who abolished the old formal garden, with its parterres and avenues and
brought the greensward of the park up to the foot of the house.

The first eighteenth-century gardeners to show a taste for informality did so on the authority of the Chinese. Very few people had actually seen the gardens of China, but travellers' engravings indicated grottoes, wildernesses, serpentine paths and an absence of topiary. Chinese influence can be seen in the wriggling paths of the garden Lord Burlington laid out around his Palladian villa at Chiswick. The garden was probably laid out with the help of Charles Bridgeman, who was later to work at Rousham and Stowe and Wimpole Hall. But at least to begin with Lord Burlington himself took a strong hand. 'The whole contrivance of [the gardens] is the Effect of his Lordship's own Genius, and singular fine Taste,' wrote Macky in 1724; 'Every Walk terminates with some little Building, one with a Heathen Temple, for instance the *Pantheon*; another a little Villa, where my Lord often dines instead of his House, and . . . another Walk terminates with a Portico, in imitation of *Covent-Garden* Church.'

An important technical innovation of about 1710 was the ha-ha – a fence sunk in a ditch or just a deep ditch with one sheer side. It was thrown round the grounds immediately surrounding the house, and prevented cattle or sheep from trampling over what, later in the century, was to be beautifully tended turf. The name derived from the exclamation of surprise uninitiated visitors made when, unawares, they came upon the trick. For the ha-ha was invisible except close to. Looking out from the house, there appeared to be no division between the parkland beyond it and the grounds within. Horace Walpole called the ha-ha 'the leading step' on the road to informality. 'No sooner was this simple enchantment made, than levelling, mowing, rolling, followed.'

Follies – the Pleasure of Ruins

Just as Vanbrugh had imagined that Woodstock Manor would be a pleasing object to be glimpsed from the other end of the park at Blenheim, so an increasing number of gentlemen were coming to feel that a landscape was not complete unless dotted with suitable buildings – and most such buildings, unlike Woodstock, had to be specially erected. Often they were no more than 'follies': small structures erected for little other purpose than to catch the eye, and not infrequently made in a gimcrack way. Throughout the course of the century an immense number of follies were built. They appear to fulfil every kind of whim, although on closer inspection most belong to one of four main groups: temples, ruins, castles and follies in medieval style. While these engaging structures should not be allowed to detain us too long in a study of the English house, it is important to remember that they are more than mere jokes, because – being relatively cheap and inconsequential – they offered an ideal opportunity for experiment (as did stables, lodges and other estate buildings). Both the earliest Greek Revival and the earliest Gothic Revival buildings in Britain were follies.

The landscapes of Claude are adorned with Classical temples, and such buildings in British parks had a special appeal for gentlemen steeped by education in the classical authors. Many a budding statesman must have imagined himself a second Cicero as he looked out from behind the columns of a portico.

A ruin – specially constructed, of course – was likely to arouse other sensations. Certain poets had been using ruins as the stock stage properties of a genre that was in some respects the equivalent of the video nasty of today. They revelled in graveyard scenes that were intended to make your flesh creep. None but the most susceptible would have lost sleepless nights from the Gothic horrors of this poetry; the *frisson* of being shown ghastly sights was evidently in some way pleasurable or the verse would not have been read. The sensation was akin to that which Edmund Burke would later analyse as 'sublime'. More drily, antiquaries such as Thomas Whately responded to the pleasure of ruins by recording and describing them. Scholarship sometimes spilled over into architecture, and vice versa. Whately concluded his description of Tintern Abbey with the recommendation: 'Upon such models fictitious ruins should be formed; and if any parts are entirely lost, they should be such as the imagination can easily supply from those which are remaining.'

Ruin follies represent the beginnings of a vogue for the ruinous which was to be stimulated by the thrilling visions of decay of the great Italian engraver, Piranesi. In the second half of the eighteenth century, some architects, including Sir William Chambers and Robert Adam, had draughtsmen picture their buildings in a state of poetic collapse even before they were built. This made the buildings seem as powerfully romantic as the enormously admired ruins of ancient Rome.

A number of people, including the poet William Shenstone of the Leasowes, Worcestershire, contrived ruined monasteries by moving genuine medieval ruins to their grounds. But monastic ruin follies were not common: the work of the antiquaries exercised greater influence on real architecture, as we shall see.

On the other hand, there were plenty of battlemented follies, whether ruinous or no. One of the first was Alfred's Hall, built by Pope's friend the 1st Earl Bathurst in the grounds of Cirencester Park in 1732. Sanderson Miller erected a castle at Edgehill, in Warwickshire, in 1745–7. Miller was a gentleman architect, and his estate at Radway included the Civil War battlefield of Edgehill, which he planted with different species of trees to represent the

68. Mow Cop in Cheshire, built by the local squire, Randle Wilbraham.
It was intended as a dramatic hill-top silhouette to be glimpsed from the grounds
of Wilbraham's house, Rode Hall.

regiments that took part. The castle supposedly stands on the spot where
Charles I raised his standard and its form was derived (without connection
with the Civil War) from Guy's Tower at Warwick Castle. The building soon
became a local landmark – the kind of place that neighbouring gentry made
the object of an afternoon drive. Previously, Radway itself, which is a Tudor
house, had been partly remodelled, with pointed arches and pinnacles.
Although Miller also designed in a Palladian style – he is thought to have been
the architect of nearby Farnborough Hall, home of his friend and neighbour,
William Holbech – he acquired a reputation for ruins. The year after the

Edgehill castle he built another at Hagley (the same park as would see the erection of Athenian Stuart's temple, the first Greek Doric building in England); and it was not long before he was in demand all over the country. The Gothic tower he designed for Wimpole Hall in Cambridgeshire was not built until 1772, by James Essex or Capability Brown. However, it is not known who designed the National Trust's dramatically ruinous castle at Mow Cop, Cheshire, which — like Miller's at Edgehill — is strikingly perched on top of a steep and rocky escarpment, to provide a romantic silhouette that would be visible from the lawn of the comfortable Georgian house, Rode Hall.

A form of Gothic style was tried by James Gibbs – the Baroque architect of St Mary-le-Strand, in London – in the Gothic Temple at Stowe. It was built in 1741–2, of red sandstone, on a triangular plan. First known as the Temple of Liberty and dedicated to the Liberty of our Ancestors, it symbolized, however unhistorically, the origins of British political liberty before the Norman conquest, since Gothic was believed to have been the architecture of the Saxons. King Alfred was enjoying something of a vogue: reference has already been made to Lord Bathurst's Alfred's Hall, while at Stourhead a tower was built between 1769 and 1772 to mark the spot where Alfred rallied his troops before defeating the Danes in 878. The Stourhead tower, which is on a hill, contrasts with the Convent in the Woods – an ecclesiastical folly built some time before 1770 which originally contained painted panels of nuns; its low-lying position accorded with Shenstone's doctrine that wooded vales suited religious buildings.

The year that Gibbs built his Gothic Temple at Stowe, William Kent, the Palladian architect who had trained as a theatrical scene-painter, designed a Gothic choir-screen, with ogee arches, crockets and quatrefoils, for Gloucester Cathedral. In doing so, of course, he was under the influence of the surrounding architecture, as he had been when building Esher Place, Surrey, in 1730 (now rebuilt), where he incorporated existing Tudor work and made the original gatehouse more Tudor, adding a new ogee-arched porch and redesigning the windows. 'Esher I like the best of all Villas,' wrote Horace Walpole many years later, 'Kent is Kentissime there!' About this time Kent also designed the ruined Hermitage for Queen Caroline in Richmond Gardens, a Classical grotto with trees sprouting from the shattered roof. 'Every man, and every boy, is writing verses on the Royal Hermitage,' wrote Pope – although few of the verses were complimentary. Five years later, in 1735, he added another folly called Merlin's Cave, which was Gothic and thatched, and which contained figures of Merlin, Elizabeth (wife of Henry VII), Queen Elizabeth I and the rustic poet Stephen Duck.

Picturesque gardens with follies, albeit shorn of their portentous symbolic and Classical allusions, were not confined to grand houses; more modest examples, with overtones of rustic *fausse naïveté*, were Woburn Farm near Weybridge, in Surrey, and Shenstone's The Leasowes. (It seems to have been Shenstone who coined the term 'landskip, or picturesque-gardening'.)

Gothick

The frame of mind which made it possible for some people to use styles from history allowed others to employ styles from abroad. Within the decorative language of Rococo, the old-world accents of Gothic mingled with the eastern patois of Chinese. The Chinese style became as popular in decoration, plasterwork and furniture as it had already become in gardening. To us, with our keener awareness of history, geography and style, it may seem strange that in the 1740s Chinese and Gothic were treated as interchangeable, or that one was even confused with the other. But the aspect of Gothic that most appealed was the curving line of its arches – particularly the late-Gothic ogee arch – and the all-over pattern of tracery, and Chinese decoration shared this sinuous linear quality. Consequently, motifs from both styles were blended in the light and graceful Rococo hybrid known as Gothick.

Gothick was made popular by pattern books such as those published by Batty Langley. (Batty, incidentally, was his real name.) The son of a gardener, Langley himself did not have much luck as a practising architect. He is remembered for his attempt to explain Gothic architecture in terms of rules, and thereby to make it acceptable to a society brought up on rule-bound Classical architecture. This he did in *Ancient Architecture Restored and Improved by a Great Variety of Grand and Usefull Designs, Entirely New in the Gothick Mode for the Ornamenting of Buildings and Gardens*, which first appeared in 1741–2 and was republished under a different title in 1747. At one time it was fashionable for scholars to pour scorn on this work; now, the seriousness of Langley's purpose in trying to make sense of Gothic is understood. With the historical treatise Langley included his own designs for fireplaces and gazebos, to show that his learning could be synthesized for modern use. These designs are charmingly two-dimensional and quaint, the pungent flavour of the medieval originals scarcely discernible in a light and elegant eighteenth-century confection.

69. The Convent in the Woods at Stourhead, built before 1770.
It originally contained painted panels of nuns in different habits.

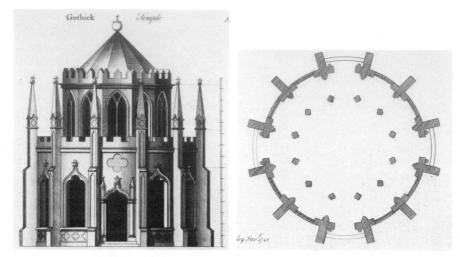

70. Design for a 'Gothic Temple' published by Batty Langley in 1742.
From *Ancient Architecture Restored and Improved* . . . Langley sought to classify Gothic,
and also to adapt it – in what now seems a delightfully fanciful way – to modern uses.

For houses, the key elements of Gothick were a battlemented parapet (the battlements usually diminutive) and pointed windows, with the option of crockets. Of necessity, pointed sashes were made to fit the windows, and these have a delightful form of pointed glazing bars. Often sash windows, whether pointed or plain, have hexagonal glazing bars, which are Chinese rather than medieval in derivation, and first cousin to the chair backs of Chinese Chippendale furniture.

Very much in the Batty Langley spirit were Hampden House, Buckinghamshire, where the papery decoration of the entrance front may well have been designed by Lord Hampden, the owner, and two buildings probably by William Halfpenny, Stout's Hill and the garden house at Frampton Court, both in Gloucestershire. In these, the design depends on a repetition of ogee-arched windows with octagonal glazing bars beneath a battlemented parapet. Halfpenny was really a carpenter – from the flimsiness of its ornament, Gothick is sometimes known as Carpenter's Gothic. He published numerous pattern books, the later ones, such as *Rural Architecture in the Gothic Taste* of 1752, popularizing Gothick.

About 1750 an increasing number of people of taste and influence were introduced to the style, when Horace Walpole began to display his villa at

71. Stout's Hill in Gloucestershire, probably by William Halfpenny. A diminutive parapet, ogee-arched windows and hexagonal glazing bars were among the ingredients of Gothick.

Twickenham, Strawberry Hill, which he had already begun to Gothicize. Walpole went on adding to Strawberry for many years – the office wing was not built until 1790; and as many as ten architects were employed at different times. Yet it was never a very big house, and if we are to believe Walpole, that was a prime reason for choosing Gothick. 'The Grecian is only proper for magnificent and public buildings ... The variety is little, and admits no charming irregularities. I am almost as fond of the *Sharawaggi*, or Chinese want of symmetry, in buildings, as in grounds or gardens.' The idea that a virtue of Gothic was irregularity was supremely Picturesque; in that irregularity implied adaptability and therefore fitness for purpose, it was transformed into a moral argument by Pugin and the Gothic revivalists in the next century.

72. Strawberry Hill, Twickenham, Horace Walpole's famous and much-visited Gothick villa.
The wing on the left is a later addition.

The evolution of Strawberry Hill was directed by a famous committee of taste, which comprised Richard Bentley (the son of the celebrated scholar of the same name) and the architect John Chute ('my oracle in taste, the standard to whom I submitted my trifles, and the genius that presided over poor Strawberry!' as Walpole described him on his death in 1776). Nevertheless, it was not ahead of the general fashion for Gothick. As early as 1754 a contribution to the *World* observed the prevalence of a debased Gothic style, mixed with Chinese: 'From Hyde Park to Shoreditch scarce a chandler's shop or an oyster stall but has embellishments of this kind.' Strawberry Hill, however, had better credentials than an oyster stall. By travelling, talking, going to parties and writing volumes of letters, Walpole made sure that everyone interested in architecture knew about Gothick, whether they approved or not. To some, the house will seem delightful but gimcrack. But Walpole also had antiquarian tastes and held such hybrids as those described in the *World* in contempt. He

73 and 74. Classical and Gothic at Castle Ward in County Down, built in 1770.
The house has a split personality, with a Palladian entrance front and a Gothic facade
to the garden. The choice of one style did not necessarily exclude another,
as it would have done in the mid nineteenth century.

sent Adam antiquarian engravings from which to take details. In fact, he had
his architects copy whole Gothic structures, such as tombs and chapels. Odd
though it may seem, this was a genuine tribute to true Gothic, and helped
make architects take Gothic more seriously.

For all its influence, Strawberry was something of a freak. Few people were
single-minded about 'charming venerable Gothic'. When Walpole met Chute
in 1740, he described him as 'an able Geometrician, and . . . an Exquisite
Architect, & of the purest taste both in the Grecian and Gothic styles'. At this
date Gothic and Classical architecture were not seen as incompatible. Architects
designed in both styles, and in one memorable house – Castle Ward, in County
Down, of 1770 – they were combined in a single building. In what seems to
have been an exemplary marital compromise, this mansion was given a

conservative Palladian front to suit the tastes of the owner, the recently created Lord Bangor, while the garden elevation was Gothic, with battlements, crockets and pointed windows – Lady Bangor's preferred style. The interior also exhibits this split personality. As yet, lack of consistency was not the crime it would appear to some Victorians. Even Walpole admitted that his Strawberry, in which the stone is usually plaster and the ornament papier mâché, was an imaginative evocation of Gothic, rather than a strictly accurate essay in the style. As he wrote himself, 'every true Goth must perceive that they (my rooms) are more the works of fancy than imagination'.

The Castle Mansion

A feature of Strawberry was a round tower with battlements evidently intended to suggest a castle. Walpole sometimes called Strawberry a castle, although it would hardly seem so. Most eighteenth-century castles are country houses with battlements and possibly a tower, with sometimes a wing thrown out to give a delusion of size.

We have already seen Sanderson Miller's castle folly at Edgehill. Exactly contemporary with that is Roger Morris's design for Inverary Castle, Argyllshire – a solid, centralized mass, with a projecting central keep and four corner towers. Morris knew about castles; he was appointed master carpenter to the Office of Ordnance in 1734. Inverary, which was executed after Morris's death by William, John and Robert Adam, looks forward to the castles built by Sir Robert Smirke, James Gillespie Graham and the Adam brothers, who designed the magnificent castle at Culzean, on the Ayrshire coast. These buildings, mostly for aristocrats, were generally very large and expensive, although Robert Adam designed a number of smaller (but still sizeable) castle-style mansions, such as Seton Castle in East Lothian, Dalquharran Castle in Ayrshire and Airthrey Castle in Stirlingshire – all within the seven years before his death in 1792. They are symmetrical, but with a lively contrast of round and square towers. Castles were thought to suit the landscape and traditions of Scotland, and it was in keeping that the ornament on Adam's castles was sparse. Less austere is Midford Castle in Somerset of 1775, built after designs by the antiquarian John Carter, who travelled widely drawing medieval antiquities and publishing the results.

There was an alternative to the centrally planned castle: the irregular castles inspired by Strawberry Hill and, in particular, Downton Castle, Herefordshire (1772–8), home of the theorist of the Picturesque, Richard Payne Knight. Such was the castle Nash built for himself at East Cowes on the Isle of Wight from

75. Robert Adam's Dalquharran Castle in Ayrshire, designed in 1782–5 and built in 1790 for Thomas Kennedy. A symmetrical, Classical composition with a minimum of castle decoration. Castles were thought particularly appropriate to Scotland.

76. Midford Castle in Somerset. Built about 1775 after designs by the antiquarian draughtsman, John Carter.

77. Downton Castle in Herefordshire, home of the Picturesque theorist, Richard Payne Knight.
Payne Knight decided on the castle style because he saw it in the architecture
in Claude and Poussin's paintings and wished the effect of his house in the landscape
to be similarly idyllic.

1798; it is massed in much the same way as his Italianate villa at Cronkhill.
East Cowes Castle was sufficiently grand for its owner to be able to entertain
his patron the Prince Regent, with whom he was on terms of rather doubtful
intimacy. (Another architect favoured by George IV, Thomas Hopper, built
Penrhyn Castle, an enormous neo-Norman pile, for the owner of a slate quarry,

in 1827–37.) The castle style's adaptability to rather smaller houses can be seen from Nash's Killymoon Castle, County Tyrone, of 1801–3; this charming building – designed to look larger than it is – contains only half a dozen modestly sized rooms on the ground floor. His Luscombe Castle in Devon of 1800–1804 is really quite a small house, its rooms arranged to take advantage of views on two sides.

The informal castle arrived in Scotland rather late. It was introduced by Robert Lugar at Tullichewan Castle in Dunbartonshire of 1808, which was shortly followed by the same architect's Balloch Castle nearby. Balloch Castle had only three principal rooms – drawing-room, dining-room and book-room – on the ground floor. The style was quickly picked up by the industrious Scot, Gillespie Graham, who built Culdees Castle in Perthshire in 1810 and several other picturesque castles over the next fifteen years. With Scotland's long tradition of fortified architecture and plentiful building stone, the castle seemed a particularly appropriate form for a house north of the Border. Gothick as a style for houses had never become popular in Scotland – it filtered up England as far as Northumberland but stopped mysteriously at the Border, as seeming presumably too soft for Scotland's rugged landscape and traditions. On the other hand, the castle style was less than ideal for all purposes, since it could only sensibly be applied to large houses. When therefore Abbotsford in Roxburghshire, home of the novelist Sir Walter Scott, was built in the more domestic style of the sixteenth century, the example was eagerly followed and what came to be known as Scots Baronial – characterized by crowstepped gables, mullion windows and pepperpot turrets – became the vernacular for middling-sized houses until the end of the century. The master of Scots Baronial was William Burn, who proved its adaptability by using it both for very large and luxurious country houses such as the House of Falkland in Fife (1839) and for much more modest ones like Auchmacoy in Aberdeenshire (1831) or Auchterarder in Perthshire (1832). In the second half of the nineteenth century, Robert Rowand Anderson adapted Scots Baronial to the middle-class suburban villa, such as the one he built for himself – Allermuir, at Colinton, in Edinburgh.

So deeply ingrained was the conviction of a castle being an Englishman's home that this form also percolated down the social scale. Dickens pursued the theme to an extreme in his affectionate description of Wemmick's castle at Walworth, garrisoned by the Aged Parent, in Great Expectations. Pip was surprised to discover a little wooden cottage with battlements, 'the queerest gothic windows (by far the greater part of them sham)', a 'real flag-staff', a bridge formed of a plank crossing a four-foot wide moat, and the famous gun

78. Luscombe Castle in Devon, by John Nash, 1804–8. The castle style was adapted to relatively small country houses, one advantage being that it permitted an irregular plan – which was useful for grouping rooms more informally and, in this case, for making the most of the views.

79. Abbotsford in Roxburghshire, home of the novelist, Sir Walter Scott. It was the progenitor of all revived Scottish Baronial – the dominant style of nineteenth-century house architecture in Scotland.

that fired every evening at nine o'clock, Greenwich time. Whether or not Wemmick's castle was based on a real example (it might well have been), Wemmick himself expressed an attitude shared by millions of commuters down to our own day: 'The office is one thing, and private life another,' he told Pip. 'When I go into the office, I leave the Castle behind me, and when I come into the Castle, I leave the office behind me.' Wemmick is not as far-fetched as he might seem – at least his castle stood on its own ground; perhaps the client who employed Ernest Trobridge to turn a small house in a perfectly conventional Edwardian terrace in west London into a castle before the First World War expressed an even odder taste (although echoed in the fashion for stone-cladding today).

The Cottage Orné

One consequence of the Picturesque was to stimulate a feeling for the countryside – particularly among people who were not landowners or practising farmers. Sentimental views of rural life were painted by George Morland and others, while poets like George Crabbe described the farm labourer as happy in his self-sufficiency:

> Behold the Cot! where thrives th'industrious swain,
> Source of his pride, his pleasure, and his gain;
> Screen'd from the winter's wind, the sun's last ray
> Smiles on the window and prolongs the day;
> Projecting thatch the woodbine's branches stop,
> And turn their blossoms to the casement's top:
> All need requires is in that cot contain'd
> And much that taste untaught and unrestrain'd
> Surveys delighted. . . .

Towards the end of the eighteenth century and particularly during the Regency, when urban life was becoming more and more artificial and complicated, such simple rustic cottages looked delightfully refreshing. For the first time in the history of the English house, it became the vogue to seem not grander, but poorer, simpler and less sophisticated than you really were. And in doing so, you showed yourself, perversely, to be at the height of fashion.

Elaborate cottage-like buildings or *cottages ornés* were built as holiday homes or rural retreats for the middle classes, or as playthings for the very rich.

Small rustic buildings in whatever style, Classical or Gothic, had been of concern to architects of the Picturesque, because they formed incidents in the landscape. The fact that you might be able to house a gamekeeper in your newly built temple was more an excuse than a reason for having it built. Sometimes whole villages were razed because they were too near the house and interfered with the Picturesque concept; but the new cottages that arose at the park gate were generally utilitarian, since they were no longer in view. A practical approach to improving the accommodation of farm labourers (still called 'peasants') was presented in the reports of the Board of Agriculture from 1797 to 1818. But in relation to these genuine cottages, the *cottage orné* was a kind of stage version – the dwelling of someone who liked, in the manner of Marie-Antoinette in her *hameau* at Versailles, to pretend that his tastes were simple and rustic when in fact they might be very sophisticated indeed.

When T. D. W. Dearn published 'A design for a cottage orné' in *Sketches in Architecture* in 1807, he explained their popularity in terms both of necessity and fashion:

In times like the present, when many sacrifices must be made and many privations endured; economy becomes a study, even to affluence. There are many who, without the most rigid attention, must stoop from that happy state of independence in which their lives have hitherto been passed, and depend for daily food on their daily exertions. That this species of building should from the peculiar circumstances of the times, become an object of general attention, may reasonably be expected and, under the sanction of fashion, we have seen royalty itself become the inmate and inhabitant of a cottage.

Queen Charlotte had an elaborately thatched cottage at Kew, which she is thought to have had a hand in designing herself. For her son, the Prince Regent, Nash built Adelaide Cottage or the 'Thatched Palace' in Windsor Great Park. Visitors to the Duke of Kent's Castle Hill Lodge at Ealing were greeted by six footmen at the door and perhaps, if they were very grand, the elderly French steward as well. It was full of musical novelties: cages of singing birds, organs with dancing horses, and musical clocks.

Through association with the Prince Regent and his circle, the *cottage orné* acquired a raffish reputation. One was owned by the decorator, Walsh Porter, who was a friend of the Prince and decorated the Throne Room at Buckingham Palace. Situated in Fulham, it was called Craven Cottage after the Margravine of Anspach, who built it when she was Countess of Craven. It contained only three rooms, but those were extremely elaborate. The 'principal saloon' was Egyptian 'supported by large palm-trees of considerable size, exceedingly well

Egyptian Hall in Craven Cottage Fulham built by Walsh Porter.

80. Sketch of Walsh Porter's Craven Cottage at Fulham. A pseudo-rustic *cottage orné*
might be intended to look modest outside, but in this case it was far from modest within.
Walsh Porter was a decorator and a friend of the Prince of Wales.

executed, with their drooping foliage at the top supporting the cornice and
architraves of the room . . . The furniture comprised a lion's skin for a hearth-
rug, for a sofa the back of a tiger, the supports of the tables in most instances
were four twisted serpents or hydras.'[37] This room gave into a large Gothic
dining-room, while the third room was a semicircular library.

Writers spoke of the *cottage orné* as a place of 'retirement', both permanent
and temporary. The businessman who ended his career 'without the attainment
of affluence yet not entirely destitute of success' was here 'free from the noise
and bustle to which he was hitherto been accustomed', as Hunt described a
design. Or if still working he could come to his *cottage orné* as a place of
tranquillity, far removed from daily cares. Both notions have a twentieth-
century ring. These houses were often built by the seaside – there was a colony
of *cottages ornés* at Lynmouth in Devon, which Southey described enthusiastically as the finest spot he ever saw, except for Cintra and the Arrabida. Another
favourite location was amid romantic wooded scenery which heightened the

81. Puckaster Cottage on the Isle of Wight, built for James Vine by Robert Lugar, before 1828.
It is a typical *cottage orné* – buildings of this kind were frequently located (as here)
by the seaside or by woods.

piquancy of the cottage image. Because the *cottage orné* was essentially a gentleman's residence in fancy dress, it was often filled with amusing novelties to save space, like mirrors that slide up to cover windows cunningly placed over fireplaces, transforming a small room into an elegant drawing-room.

Irregularity, both of plan and design, was made into a virtue: James Malton's *An Essay on British Cottage Architecture* of 1797, for instance, was subtitled 'being an attempt to perpetuate on Principle, that peculiar mode of building, which was originally the effect of Chance' (although in 1803 Richard Elsam, a minor and somewhat quarrelsome architect, published *An Essay on Rural Architecture* to defend the principles of symmetry and proportion, even in Gothick buildings).

The simplicity of these buildings all too often became quaintness. Coleridge, who had a real cottage at Nether Stowey in Somerset, was scornful of the fake modesty of the *cottage orné*, as this stanza, from *The Devil's Thoughts*, indicates:

> He saw a cottage with a double coach-house,
>   A cottage of gentility;
> And the Devil did grin, for his darling sin,
>   Is pride that apes humility.

82 View from the verandah of Endsleigh Cottage, past tree-trunk columns.
Endsleigh was built in 1810–11 by Wyatville for the 6th Duke of Bedford for his mother,
in a landscape by Repton.

Artifice was also ridiculed by Jane Austen; Mrs Dashwood in *Sense and Sensibility* found Barton Cottage 'small, comfortable and compact', but not sufficiently Picturesque: 'as a cottage it was defective, for the building was regular, the roof was tiled, the window shutters were not painted green, nor were the walls covered with honeysuckles'.

The style Mrs Dashwood would have preferred was that called the Rustic or the Picturesque. Even the most sober writers advocated porches flanked by young tree trunks with the bark left on, and an extreme was reached in T. J. Ricauti's *Rustic Architecture* of 1840, which showed cottages built only of materials 'procured by a judicious use of the woodman's axe'. A deep roof was of the essence. It was probably of thatch despite the admitted risk from fire. In *Hints for Picturesque Improvements in Ornamental Cottages and their Scenery,*

Edmund Bartell, junior, recommends a limited use of stained glass, although this would today seem most un-cottagelike; where this was not possible (and Bartell only suggested it for one room) you might encourage 'the tendrils of the ivy to mantle luxuriantly over the windows, opposing its transparent varnishing leaves as a screen to the too powerful rays of the sun . . .' These very rustic cottages were the successors to the hermitages built in some eighteenth-century parks.

The most enchanting *cottage orné* of all was built in 1795 by two much-travelled maiden ladies, the Misses Parminter, outside Exmouth in Devon. It was called A-la-Ronde, being circular – or more strictly, hexagonal – after the inspiration of San Vitale at Ravenna. The Parminters were the daughter and niece of a Devon glass manufacturer with business in Portugal. Their house was originally thatched, and has a lantern above and diamond-shaped windows alternating with the usual rectangular ones. Inside, it is planned around a central hall, 60 feet (18.3 m) high, the upper surfaces of which are encrusted

83. Home-made model of A-la-Ronde, outside Exmouth in Devon. The house was built for, and whimsically decorated by, two much-travelled maiden ladies, the Misses Parminter, the daughter and niece of a Devon glass manufacturer with business in Portugal.

with mosaics in shell and feathers, which like the rest of the decoration in the house was entirely home-made. Around the hall, the rooms are necessarily of curious shapes, and again filled with souvenirs and curios: a miniature bookcase of tiny books, pictures of sand and seawood. The cornice in the drawing-room is made out of coloured feathers.

Another master of the genre was Nash, popularly associated with white-fronted Classical terraces but just as much a genius of Picturesque town-planning, of which the terraces were but a part. In 1810–11 he built a group of nine cottages called Blaise Hamlet, near Bristol, for John Harford of Blaise

84. One of the Blaise Hamlet cottages designed by Nash. Blaise Hamlet is a group of nine elaborately Tudor cottages for retired estate workers, grouped as a village.

Castle, to house his retired servants. Some of the details – such as the tall twisted brick chimneys – are taken from Tudor architecture, but most are exaggerated versions of those seen in the traditional architecture of the country, put together with an elaboration of which no ordinary country labourer would have been capable.

Later in the nineteenth century genuine, rural cottages – as opposed to *cottages ornés* – were praised by Ruskin as embodying a natural harmony between landscape and architecture, especially in areas such as the Lake District where the mountains were on a smaller scale than the Alps and would therefore have suffered in juxtaposition to large, unbroken masses. In *The Poetry of Architecture*, an early work, Ruskin advocated the 'cottage-villa' as an appropriate building type for country mansions; and when he came to acquire a country home for himself in 1871, it was a white-painted, three-bay house that had originally been a cottage – Brantwood, on Coniston Water. It was bought unseen, although he knew the view across the lake to be one of the most beautiful in England. Over the next thirty years it grew to a house of some size – but in a series of sometimes haphazard additions, for Picturesque theory dictated that a building should grow as needs dictated. Brantwood prefigured the special reverence some Arts and Crafts architects had for cottages, described in Chapter 5.

'Old English'

After Blaise Hamlet, which Nash published in a lavish engraved edition, Tudor grew in popularity. Romantic, rambling buildings like Athelhampton in Dorset and Penshurst in Sussex were depicted as they might have been, peopled with figures in period costume, in Joseph Nash's evocative *Mansions of England in the Olden Time*. As a style for the present, Tudor was particularly championed in the 1820s and 1830s in a series of books by T. F. Hunt, who only produced his Italianate sketches on sufferance. In common with other authors, he thought the style especially appropriate for vicarages and parsonages, because of their proximity to the village church. He called the style 'old English', in anticipation of Richard Norman Shaw and William Eden Nesfield in the 1860s. His *Designs for Parsonage Houses, Alms Houses etc. etc.* of 1827 also conveys a keen sense of Church of England hierarchy. The ground floor of his parsonage house comprised entrance hall, study, drawing-room, dining-room, pantry or housekeeper's room, kitchen and water-closet. A little further down, the curate's house had front lobby, eating room, parlour, book-closet, kitchen, wash-house, store-room and lean-to or rustic verandah; while the lowly parish clerk made do with an office, parlour, kitchen and 'three Bed-rooms in the roof'. The success of Tudor was its being domestic and almost infinitely adaptable, particularly to low, spreading houses. Big Tudor bay windows offered architects a further note of variety in the planning of rooms, and in the Scots Baronial style of William Burn and David Bryce they were combined with pepperpot turrets and crowstepped gables in an evocation of Walter Scott's Waverley novels. Occasionally a 'genuine' castle was built in the Victorian period, the most spectacular being Salvin's Peckforton in Cheshire; but normally a ship-owner from Glasgow or a jute merchant from Dundee, while proud of his national architecture, did not want his drawing-room to be lit only by arrow slits.

The Swiss Chalet

In *Rural Architecture, or a Series of Designs for Ornamental Cottages* of 1823, P. F. Robinson published a design in the Swiss chalet style, which had been pioneered by Repton at Endsleigh. This was soon to be taken up in the famous Swiss chalet at Hampstead of 1829–32. Like Tudor, the Swiss style had a special appeal for the Victorians. The cult of the Highlands, itself a successor to Picturesque theories of the sublime, was matched – among those who could afford foreign travel – by an enthusiasm for the Alps. It was fostered by spirits as incompatible as Byron and Ruskin, the latter having discovered Switzerland on childhood journeys with his father, a sherry merchant who made annual business tours of the Continent. While most of Europe might be regarded with suspicion, Switzerland had the advantage that it was both Protestant and clean. The Swiss style was free from the contaminating associations of Roman Catholicism, tyranny and national degeneration which dogged other foreign styles – even if Ruskin found that the peasants who actually lived in the pretty, remote chalets, away from civilizing influences, lived coarsened lives, out of keeping with their majestic surroundings. Queen Victoria, who at Balmoral would shortly do much for Scots Baronial, had a Swiss chalet specially brought over to Osborne in the Isle of Wight, in 1853, as a playhouse for the royal children. Its appropriateness for the time was matched in the twentieth century by the miniature neo-Georgian villa built at Royal Lodge, Windsor, for the future Queen Elizabeth II and her sister, Princess Margaret. Dickens had a small Swiss chalet in the garden of his house at Gad's Hill in Kent. The popularity of Tunbridge Wells in the Victorian period can be explained by its being thought very like Switzerland.

The Many-splendoured Suburb

The Picturesque had opened a Pandora's box of styles and all the styles had flown out – out into the suburbs. The appearance of a substantial early Victorian suburb is shown by Decimus Burton's aerial view of his proposed development at Hove. It was never built, but would have been like many

85. Aerial view of development proposed by Decimus Burton at Hove. This shows the quest for stylistic individuality within a prosperous early Victorian suburb: from the tower of the castle you could have seen buildings that suggested Greek temples, rustic cottages and Italianate villas.

others. Each house is set in its own grounds, and partially shut off from its neighbours by trees and hedges. But not completely shut off, because the plots are quite small. So the owner of a fine Grecian portico would look out from his bedroom window over the towers of his neighbour's castle, while he who dwelt in simplicity beneath a rustic thatched roof could enjoy a fine prospect of an Italianate villa. The range of styles was widened further in Richard Brown's *Domestic Architecture* of 1842, in which was added Burmese, Egyptian, Venetian, Morisco-Spanish and Plantagenet Castle, Edward III. To this might have been added French Château, popular alike for suburban villas and immense Rothschild mansions in the 1850s and 1860s.

A RETURN TO PROPRIETY

Many architects believed that they should be masters of all the styles, with no special prejudice in favour of one more than others. This had the great benefit of giving clients what they wanted, or what they had been talked into wanting; but it was not conducive to purity of style. What Lugar, speaking of some rooms at his Tullichewan Castle, unblenchingly described as 'fancy decoration, unshackled by any particular style', was an eclectic mish-mash of different ingredients. This, along with the idea of the *cottage orné*, came to seem unacceptably frivolous, if not indecent, to a group of leading architects after 1830. The new note of seriousness emanated from university and church circles, particularly Cambridge, and was principally concerned with churches. The architect who embodied this seriousness – and who inspired a generation by his energy, zeal and downright rudeness towards opponents – was A. W. N. Pugin.

Pugin was the son of a French topographical draughtsman, who had come to England after the Revolution and worked for a time as an assistant to Nash. The family was Catholic. Ancestry, upbringing and religion help to explain Pugin's theories. They combine the rationalism of the French *philosophes* with a passionate, sometimes self righteous Christianity, and ideas derived from the Picturesque. Having acquired an unrivalled knowledge of Gothic architecture, he was able to help Charles Barry with the detail of the Houses of Parliament. He had a genius for two-dimensional ornament. But his interest in the Middle Ages was not confined to details or even to architecture: it was an all-embracing vision of society, the fundamental tenet of which was that Britain had been in decline since the dissolution of the monasteries in 1534. Before that date Britain had been a Catholic country, large swatches of which were ruled over by great religious houses, which dispensed charity, tended the sick and praised God. The values of Victorian Britain, as he saw them, were based on money-grubbing and were symbolized by Classicism.

Pugin formulated the vital elements of the Gothic or, as he preferred to call it, 'Christian' style in a series of principles: that buildings should contain nothing that was not strictly necessary for the sake of 'construction, convenience or propriety'; and that ornament should consist in the enrichment of construction. A question-mark hovered over the interpretation of 'convenience' and 'propriety' – Pugin believed, for instance, that extreme richness of materials and colour was indeed appropriate to the worship of God, so the principles are not as austere as they first sound. His object in emphasizing 'construction' was to attack the applied, 'sham' ornament of such buildings as James Wyatt's notorious Fonthill Abbey in Wiltshire, the tower of which collapsed in 1825. Anything as fanciful as a *cottage orné* was unquestionably taboo. He wrote:

> Let us look around, and see whether the Architecture of this country is not entirely ruled by whim and caprice. Does locality, destination, or character of a building, form the basis of a design? no; surely not. We have Swiss cottages in a flat country; Italian villas in the coldest situations; a Turkish kremlin for a royal residence; Greek temples in crowded lanes; Egyptian auction rooms, and all kinds of absurdities and incongruities, and not only are separate edifices erected in the inappropriate styles, but we have only to look into those nests of monstrosities, the Regent's Park and Regent's Street, where all kinds of styles are jumbled together to make up a mass.[38]

Pugin attacked the Picturesque, but his own point of view was not uninfluenced by it. He maintained, for instance, that the form of a plan should be expressed in the outside of a building. According to Pugin, the Georgian box involved artifice, and to an extent he was right; only the most skilful architects could ensure that, behind the symmetrical elevation, all the rooms were as grand and imposing as the size of their windows suggested. He argued that the hierarchy of functions – eating, sleeping, cooking, etc. – should be plainly visible: 'not *masked or concealed under one* monotonous front, but by their variety in form and outline increasing the effects of the building...' Variety in form and outline was exactly what the Picturesque theorists had been encouraging.

Despite an immensely busy practice, Pugin took no partners but drove himself to work harder and harder, until he died, burnt up and insane, at forty. (His son, Edward Welby, who took over the practice at the age of eighteen, inherited his father's work pattern and died at forty-one.) He built two large country houses – Scarisbrick Hall and Alton Towers – but most of his energy went into churches. His most interesting middling-sized houses were those he designed for himself, of which the first, St Marie's Grange, Alderbury, outside Salisbury, was built shortly after his first marriage, when Pugin was only twenty-three. Pugin said that St Marie's Grange would be 'the only modern building that is compleat in every part in the antient style'. The house bears the inscriptions '*Laus deo*' and '*Hanc domium cum capella edificavit Augustus de Pugin 1835*', but sadly he only lived there for two years. His second house was The Grange, next to a church he built at his own expense, at Ramsgate in Kent. Because Pugin had so good a knowledge of Gothic, he did not try to make it look like a church. It was constructed of yellow stock brick with stone dressings, and had a tower from which Pugin, a keen sailor, could watch for ships in trouble on rough seas. Its most striking characteristic is a rather solid simplicity – a shock after the richness one associates with his churches.

86. St Marie's Grange, Alderbury, outside Salisbury.
A. W. N. Pugin built the house in 1835, shortly after his first marriage,
when he was only twenty-three. Despite the romantic skyline,
it shows Pugin already using more sober, domestic detail
in preference to ecclesiastical motifs.
However, he only lived here two years and it was later sympathetically extended,
perhaps by Pugin himself.

The Parsonage Style

Equally, to Pugin's most talented contemporaries – G. E. Street, William Butterfield, J. L. Pearson and G. G. Scott – there was more excitement to be had from building churches than anything else, while town halls, railway stations and hotels offered the great challenge of suiting the Gothic style to distinctively nineteenth-century requirements. But building churches often also involved building houses, in the form of rectories, vicarages and parsonages. For this, Street and Butterfield evolved what has been called their 'parsonage style'. Although involved, almost Byzantine arguments surrounded the question of

87. Lympsham Rectory, a late-Georgian house designed to suit the church.

exactly which period of Gothic was appropriate to the church, the style of the parsonage was altogether more in the background. Like Pugin's The Grange, Butterfield's vicarages at Coalpit Heath, Gloucestershire, St Mawgan, Cornwall, and Sheen, Staffordshire, and Street's rectory at Wantage, Berkshire, are sober, straightforward buildings, which rely much more on the massing of gables, roofs, chimneys and porch than on ornament. Ornament, indeed, was necessarily kept to a minimum in most parsonages on grounds of expense (although sometimes zebra stripes of contrasting colours of brick were used as a cheap way of satisfying the Victorian zest for polychromy, as in the rectory of the 'rogue' architect, William White, at Little Baddow in Essex). Plain, soundly constructed parsonages were preferred by the *Ecclesiologist*, that all-important arbiter of High Church taste:

... Parsonage-houses in what may be called the villa-gothic style are not infrequent, but for the most part entirely deficient in the spirit of the originals. All these buildings are more or less characterized by a paltry pretence to ornament, while all solidity of construction is neglected. We have already insisted upon this point as of the first importance in the building of churches and it can scarcely be less important in a structure which is to be tenanted in constant succession by the pastors of the parish, and should therefore seem to partake of the stable and permanent character of the church itself ...

88. Vicarage and school by G. E. Street at Boyne Hill in Berkshire, begun in 1854.
In the parsonage style of Street, William Butterfield and William White,
Gothic detail is stripped down to its essence, but polychrome brickwork
and a variety of gables (expressing the internal lay-out) prevent monotony.

Butterfield even elevated the parsonage style to the status of a large country house in his only commission of that kind, Milton Ernest Hall in Bedfordshire.

Philip Webb

The parsonage style greatly influenced Philip Webb, Street's chief assistant. The son of a doctor, Webb was a naturally modest man who strove to keep his own personality from showing in his buildings. In Street's office, he met William Morris, and shared both Morris's socialist outlook and his passionate concern for old buildings. One of his first commissions was the now-famous Red House at Bexleyheath for Morris himself: not exactly a plain house (the roof ridges seem almost wilful in their complexity), but one largely without applied ornament. The interest for the eye lies in the massing, in the contrasting shapes of the windows (and how many there are!), and in the brickwork, with the different forms of relieving arch. At later houses such as Standen – a large house for a solicitor – austerity became something of a fetish, and the result, although beautiful, is always slightly awkward. From the discipline of his own life, in eschewing normal London practice and working on very few commissions at any one time, as well as his insistence on the very best workmanship and materials, he inspired a generation of idealistic young architects in the 1890s, some of whom he met through the Society for the Protection of Ancient Buildings.

Despite its importance for Webb, however, the parsonage style should not be overplayed. Seeming eminently rational and sober, it was perhaps given too much prominence by apologists of the Gothic revival in the 1960s, who were trying to persuade a public that still tended to regard the more extreme forms of Victorian architecture as the fruits of overtaxed brains. Not all that much was built, and it had little influence where it would have been most use, in the new suburbs.

Webb followed Pugin in rejecting what he regarded as sham architecture, which was epitomized by the stucco terraces of Nash, for stucco was originally jointed and painted to look like stone rather than plaster. He therefore clashed with Sir James Pennethorne, who had been trained by Nash, over the big town house he built for George Howard, a nephew of the Earl of Carlisle, at 1 Palace Green in 1867–9. As surveyor to the Crown Commissioners, Pennethorne objected to the use of plain brick as too humble for a house built on Crown land near Kensington Palace. Two further architects were called in to adjudicate on the design, and the ensuing correspondence illustrates Webb's attempt to achieve a 'styleless' form of building. 'That Messrs Salvin and Wyatt are "unable to discover what actual style or period of architecture" I have used, I take to be a sincere compliment,' he wrote. The idea of a styleless style was to have implications for Arts and Crafts architects at the end of the century, as will be described in Chapter 5. But no building can be without style altogether, and in the case of 1 Palace Green the basis was Gothic – as can be seen from Webb's strong objection to incorporating a stone cornice as Pennethorne desired.

89. Standen near East Grinstead, by Philip Webb. Even in quite large houses like this one,
built for a rich solicitor, Webb took his inspiration from cottages.

Shaw and Nesfield

Philip Webb was born in 1831, the same year as Richard Norman Shaw and four years earlier than Shaw's comrade in architecture, William Eden Nesfield. They were therefore about twenty years younger than the Pugin–Street generation and, to them, the most interesting challenge was not how to design churches but how to evolve an appropriately secular style for the house. They were not single-minded Goths. When they went out into the Home Counties on sketching expeditions in the 1850s and 1860s, they drew churches, certainly, but also the quaint old half-timbered pubs and cottages of the countryside, which belonged to no particular style in the accepted sense. This was the beginning of the self-conscious revival of interest in the vernacular described in Chapter 1. In the early 1860s, Shaw and Nesfield fused the vernacular elements of half-timbering, tile-hanging and hipped roofs into a new style for domestic architecture which they called Old English, echoing, perhaps unintentionally, Hunt's term for Tudor. A particular feature was pargetting – the traditional Essex technique of decorating the plasterwork of gable end with incised lines or embossed patterns. But Shaw and Nesfield did not restrict themselves to English sources. Moving in the sophisticated Bohemian high art circle of London, they were among the earliest collectors of Japanese blue and white porcelain, and from the decorative vocabulary of Japan they took the sunflower motif and the use of floating, asymmetrically placed discs which they irreverently liked to call 'pies'. These emblems were used to enliven gable ends, porches and fireplace surrounds.

Old English was a style for the country – although Nesfield did have the chance to bring it to town in a now-demolished lodge in Regent's Park (the kind of commission that would have been widely seen). Nesfield in particular began his career building numerous cottages and lodges on big country estates, since his father, William Andrews Nesfield, was a highly successful landscape gardener and his uncle, Anthony Salvin, a prominent country-house architect. Typical are those he built for Lord Crewe at Crewe Hall, where W. A. Nesfield laid out the gardens. In time, both Shaw and Nesfield (they were never strictly in partnership, although they shared offices) obtained commissions for country houses. One of Nesfield's first, Farnham Royal in Buckinghamshire, was remarkable for the introduction of a characteristic feature of country inns, the ingle-nook (a cosy arrangement of benches in the fireplace recess), which became hugely popular. Shaw had a special brilliance for planning which can be seen even in a – by Victorian standards – comparatively modest house such as Merrist Wood at Worplesdon in Surrey, of the mid-1870s. It has a double-

90. Chigwell Hall in Essex, by Richard Norman Shaw, 1875. One of Shaw's less exuberant houses, it succeeds by a combination of vernacular materials, overhangs, gables and tall chimneys, and so foreshadows much of the house-building of the last quarter of the century.

height great hall, but not one that could have been used for tenants' dinners or entertaining hunt meets as in the grandest Victorian country houses. Set at an angle to the entrance front, it is only thirty-two feet by twenty, and was in regular service as the dining-room. The evolution of the hall was the one decisive development that enabled a break away from the villa plan in the late nineteenth century.

Applied on a small scale, Old English created an aura of warmth and homeliness that struck a chord with the new emphasis on home values. However, the image of the home that it evoked was also shot through with romanticism. As a man Shaw was dreaming, home-loving, ebullient among friends but otherwise shy, and some would have said child-like in his enthusiasms. His personality is reflected in the little room or 'den', only ten feet by seven, from which he worked in his house, No. 6 Ellerdale Road in Hampstead. Tucked in over the drawing-room ingle-nook, it was reached by a special staircase and lit by a porthole window overlooking the road – 'a miniature parody of the Victorian artist's gigantic studio', as Shaw's biographer Andrew Saint has described it. In his Old English houses, the romanticism shows the sculptural massing achieved by low sweeping roofs, very tall Tudor chimneys, and a complex interlocking of roof ridges of gables. The texture is varied by rhapsodic bursts of half-timbering that are generally purely decorative rather than structural. While the elements are vernacular, the method of building on which they depended was thoroughly up-to-date, since Shaw made a liberal use of steel girders. The zenith of romance was reached at the armament millionaire William Armstrong's Cragside in Northumberland, a huge and meandering house that floats on a pinnacle above a forest; but within a smaller compass Shaw achieved scarcely less romantic effects working close to London – at for instance Pickards Rough and Pierrepont in Surrey and Grims Dyke (first the home of the painter Frederick Goodall, then of W. S. Gilbert of Gilbert and Sullivan, now a hotel) at Harrow Weald in London. Chigwell Hall in Essex is, however, less exuberant and so foreshadows much of the domestic architecture of the last decade of the century. In the work of Shaw's pupils and followers – such as J. M. Brydon, Gerald Horlsey and John Belcher – Old English survived as the most adaptable, most appropriate style for the middling-sized house into the 1910s and beyond.

Queen Anne Revival

Towards the end of the 1860s, Old English was joined by another eclectic style, which shared certain features (sunflowers, decorative plasterwork) but mixed them in with a different base. The style was the Queen Anne Revival. It had little to do with the reign of Queen Anne. The new type of building that architects such as Shaw, Nesfield, E. W. Godwin and J. J. Stevenson had rediscovered was what has since been dubbed 'Artisan Mannerist'. These Dutch-influenced houses of the mid seventeenth century were Classical, but built of brick, with curly gables, hipped roofs, tall chimneys and a curious interpretation in brick of Classical details such as pilasters. Queen Anne Revival architects not only had pilasters made of brick, but beautifully designed and delicately executed panels of sunflowers or Grinling Gibbons-style garlands, often placed over doorways. Later, terracotta – a harsher, if more adaptable, material – was greatly used, becoming a cliché in the streets around Sloane

Mathew Prior   1664-1721

A Letter
to Lady Margaret Cavendish Holles-
Harley, when a Child

My noble, lovely, little Peggy,
Let this my First Epistle beg ye,
At dawn of morn, and close of even,
To lift your heart and hands to
                    Heaven.
In double duty say your prayer:
Our Father first, then Notre Père.
And, dearest child, along the day,
In every thing you do and say,
Obey and please my lord and lady,
So God shall love and angels aid ye.

If to these precepts you attend,
No second letter need I send,
And so I rest your constant friend.

91. The new front added by W. E. Nesfield to Bodrhyddan Hall, in Clwyd.
With the Queen Anne Revival, architects such as Nesfield began looking with fresh eyes
at Classicism – especially the Dutch-influenced, red-brick houses of the
mid seventeenth century, whose influence can be seen here.

Square. While Old English implied casement windows and leaded lights, the
Queen Anne revival (here genuinely looking back to Queen Anne) nearly
always used sashes, which were really much more convenient. It by turns
saddened and outraged the older Gothic Revivalists, with their dream of a new
Gothic England – the younger generation had deserted the flag.

An interesting precursor of the Queen Anne Revival was the house built by
the novelist W. M. Thackeray for himself at 2 Palace Green, Kensington, in

1860–62 – next to the site that would be occupied by Webb's house for Howard. The Queen Anne Revival was more than simply an architectural movement: it encompassed gardening (with the revival of the 'old-fashioned' garden), furniture design (notably the black ebonized and Adam Revival furniture of firms such as Collinson and Lock) and even the children's picture books of Walter Crane and Kate Greenaway. Kate Greenaway was one of several artists to employ Shaw to build London studio houses, in her case 39 Frognal, in Hampstead. This little tile-hung house had a drawing-room and dining-room on the ground floor, a studio at the top of the house, and no back staircase, since Miss Greenaway was her own housekeeper. For the big names of the Royal Academy, the provision of staircases was a particular consideration, since they required a separate route to and from the studio for the models that posed for them: their wives did not wish to risk a chance encounter with girls who were not 'respectable'. Something of an artists' colony was established in Kensington, and Shaw built two houses – for Marcus Stone and Luke Fildes – in Melbury Road. Today, they can be identified from the blue plaques commemorating their former occupants; but even from a distance their purpose is declared by the very tall studio windows. Just round the corner from Melbury Road, in Holland Park Road, Lord Leighton was established in a house by Aitchison, to which a spectacular Arab Hall, lined with tiles that Leighton had brought back from travels in the Middle East, was added in 1877. Another group of Queen Anne Revival artists' houses was built in Tite Street, Chelsea, including one for Whistler by Godwin. For those who could not afford a detached studio house, studio terraces were built in Hampstead and Hammersmith, and there were also blocks of studio flats, including one in Tite Street. The difference between houses and flats with studios and other houses and flats is not always very great, however. They point to the growing fashionability of studios, not only for artists but for middle-class people with artistic leanings. For even more than Old English, the Queen Anne Revival was the in-house style of the Aesthetic Movement and the cult of Japan, parodied by Gilbert and Sullivan in their operetta *Patience*.

Other town houses by Shaw include 180 and 185 Queen's Gate in Kensington; Lowther Lodge (now the Royal Geographical Society) on Kensington Gore which typically – set back with a courtyard – looks more like a country house than the immense town mansion that it is; and the famous Swan House of 1875 on the newly made Chelsea Embankment. Swan House incorporates a set of three oriels derived from Sparrowe's House, a flamboyant

92. The architect William Burges's Tower House in Melbury Road, Kensington.

93. Marcus Stone's house, at 8 Melbury Road. Marcus Stone, principally a book illustrator,
was typical of the successful artists who built large studio houses
to display their position, and made Melbury Road something of a colony.

94. 14–17 Collingham Gardens, Kensington by George and Peto, 1880s.
While classical terraces disguised the individuality of each house, those by George and Peto
were as full of surprise and variety as the regulations permitted.
Verticality was emphasized and the stylistic details were taken from
the town houses of Flanders.

seventeenth-century town house in Ipswich. It is a sparkling building, helped perhaps by the fact that it faces the river and so there is nothing on the other side of the road. When the Cadogan Estate was redeveloped in the 1870s and 1880s, Queen Anne ran like a dark red rash through the streets around Sloane and Cadogan Squares. There are whole Queen Anne streets, in the way that there rarely were whole Gothic ones. Many of the new houses were designed by George and Peto, a firm better in their country work at sensitive detailing than thrilling composition, but extremely versatile in their handling of a London terrace street. This was about as thrilling as the terrace ever became. (There are also Queen Anne Revival terraces in new, more distant suburbs, like the Hever estate in Tooting, and by the seaside, in places like Aberystwyth.)

95. *The Rector's Garden, Queen of the Lilies* by Atkinson Grimshaw. The lily was the symbol of the Aesthetic Movement. The old rectory, with its 'old-fashioned' garden, shown here, was typical of the buildings the architects of the Queen Anne Revival admired.

Whereas the terraces of Nash and the great London developer Thomas Cubitt had been unified horizontally, those of the rebuilt Cadogan estate were organized vertically, to emphasize the individuality of each house. This was a legacy of the Gothic Revival, with its insistence that it should be possible to read a building's internal character from the exterior. As Cadogan Square and Harrington Gardens are even taller than Warwick Square, St George's Square and Eccleston Square – the tallest of the Pimlico terraces built forty years earlier – the verticality was highly pronounced. The obvious precedent for very tall, relatively narrow houses lay in Flemish architecture, and George and Peto's houses do incorporate gables and details of carved brickwork derived closely from Flemish sources. Sir Ernest George was remembered by Lutyens, who passed through his office for six months at the start of his meteoric career, as the supreme eclectic, who would spend his summer holidays in sketching tours of the Continent and quarry the results – finding a window here, a doorway there – for his designs for the rest of the year. It was a method of work that Lutyens and his contemporaries, with their reverence for the vernacular and sense of place, despised, but it had the merit of importing liveliness to streets that would otherwise have been cavernous and plain. And plainness was regarded almost with horror in High Victorian England.

A WALK DOWN MILLIONAIRE'S ROW

To savour sixty years of stylistic diversity at the top end of the market, let us take a walk through the private gates of Palace Green and down the road it turns into, Kensington Palace Gardens – aptly nicknamed Millionaires' Row. First comes Webb's house for Howard, rooted in Gothic; then Thackeray's house, with its Classical brick pilasters and doorcase. Next a row of Dutch- and Flemish-influenced Classical houses in brick with stone dressings of the Edwardian period (No. 5 Palace Green is by E. P. Warren, No. 10 by E. J. May). Kensington Palace Gardens itself was laid out in the 1840s and 1850s on the site of the old kitchen gardens of Kensington Palace, and the houses built on it, under Pennethorne's watchful eye, are mostly Italianate and stucco-fronted – Nos. 12 and 15 recall Barry's Italianate Travellers Club in Pall Mall. No. 13, on the other hand, is in an eccentric kind of Gothic by Decimus Burton with C. J. Richardson, strongly influenced by the owner, the Earl of Harrington. Despite the odd central belfry, it has conventional sash windows. Appearing over the parapet of No. 24 are the curvaceous turrets of 'the Moresque Style, which (though not usually adopted),' wrote Pennethorne to the Crown Commissioners, 'is admired by some persons and produces a picturesque effect'. The architect was Owen Jones, famous for his theories of polychromatic decoration derived from the study of Arabic architecture; his No. 8 was even more Moresque but has been demolished.

What does an Islamic house, for instance, have in common with its Italianate or Queen Anne neighbour? More than the stylistic division would suggest. For

96. 13 Kensington Palace Gardens. Here Gothic forms were applied to an essentially
Classical house from the middle years of the nineteenth century by Decimus Burton
with C. J. Richardson, strongly influenced by the owner, the Earl of Harrington. Nicknamed
'Millionaires' Row', Kensington Palace Gardens contained houses in many different and
contrasting styles: Classical, Gothic, Islamic and later, Queen Anne Revival.

both necessarily had to fulfil similar social needs, and made use of similar
domestic equipment and labour to do so. In any neighbourhood, the way
houses were run varied less than the way they looked; and the running of
houses in the Victorian period reached a fine, if seemingly elaborate, art. How
the Victorian house worked and the priorities it served are the subject of
Chapter 4.

🔲 FOUR 🔲

VICTORIAN PREOCCUPATIONS – HEALTH, PRIVACY AND SERVANTS

While other countries have contributed more to the art of painting, sculpture, music, or monumental architecture, the English have cultivated everything connected with daily life: they have made it an art to live in the right way.

S. E. Rasmussen, *London, the Unique City,* 1937

There was a wide range of stylistic possibilities in the Victorian period, but only rarely did they reflect a special view of the world. People living in the suburbs did not usually build their own houses, but took them on leases from a developer. They had little control over the external appearance. The expression of personal tastes had to be largely confined to the interior; and even then, fashion was not necessarily the first consideration. To the redoubtable Mrs J. E. Panton, author of *Suburban Residences and How to Circumvent Them,* choosing a house was a responsibility that had limitless ramifications for the family's comfort and welfare. Her priorities were health, privacy and keeping hold of good servants. When compared to the dwellings of all earlier times, the Victorian middling-sized house stands out for the elaboration of the behind-the-scenes services that catered to these requirements.

HEALTH

Health was a consideration even before you opened the garden gate. Suburbs, Mrs Panton believed, were 'not Paradise', but one undoubted benefit was fresher air than could be had in the town, with its smog and smuts. On the whole higher, breezier locations were preferred to low-lying ones, partly because 'bad air' was still regarded as infectious – although around London the heights of Highgate, Hampstead and Hornsey to the north, and Brixton Rise, Streatham, Dulwich and Norwood to the south, were held by the middle classes, while the most fashionable suburbs lay on the lower ground to the west (their aristocratic timbre being explained historically by nearness to

Buckingham Palace). Before settling on any area, Mrs Panton counselled that the prospective householder should inquire about the local authority and, most important of all, discover if the optional 'Infectious Diseases Act' was in force. If the local authority was not on the ball, who knew what latitude would be allowed to local butchers in the purveyance of not quite fresh meat, and so forth? It would also be as well to investigate the soil of the neighbourhood. 'I do not believe clay is or even can be fit for anyone to reside upon, and nothing anyone can say will cause me to alter my opinion,' wrote Mrs Panton, who had lived for twelve years in various suburbs before embarking on the book.

... Dearly as I loved Shortlands the clay there was always to be reckoned with, and made a long reckoning too, when all was told, for though roses flourished magnificently children didn't, and coughs and colds were 'the only wear' once autumn began to spread the leaves and winter came up to finish the little business, clad in the usual garments of fog and mist, changed at times to other more 'seasonable' ones of frost and snow.

Chalk was to be avoided by anyone rheumatic. Deciduous trees were to be viewed with suspicion as encouraging damp through wet leaves, although pines were regarded as healthy.

Of course, there were other practical questions to be settled in choosing your suburb. The most pressing was transport. A writer in the *Illustrated London News* of 23 August 1884 deplored the expansion of London, eating up the green fields around:

Year by year, almost month by month, the rural scenery of four English shires, Middlesex, Surrey, Kent, and Essex, is swallowed up by the Metropolitan Octopus, the huge congeries of more than half a million closely built houses, thrusting out of its town buildings with insidious pretensions to suburban pleasantness along the main roads of the Home Counties, north and south, east and west, north-west, north-east, south-west and south-east, absorbing the quiet old villages and hamlets, encroaching on their public 'Greens', devouring private parks and gardens, transforming the verdant hills and meadows into hideous brickfields, and subsequently into a labyrinth of gravelled roads with similar rows of petty villa-dwellings, or streets not much unlike those of any other modern English town.

But for the people who first took houses in the burgeoning suburbs, unlike those who followed them – by which time a further wave had pushed the urban boundary still further out – the sprawl had the advantage that their property might be on the very edge of open countryside. The art was to be sufficiently far out to have the benefit of views over the fields, yet not so distant from the centre that it was impossible to get in. It also required fine judgement on the part of the developer, who, as in the early development of Kelvinside on the west side of Glasgow, might be left with houses he could not let if he tried to extend his lines of communication too far. The problem of isolation was not as great as it had been two centuries earlier, when John Verney (later Lord Fermanagh) journeyed daily from what is now the Redcliffe Gardens area of the Fulham Road, known as Little Chelsea, to his merchant's office in the City. Coming home across the fields from Chelsea proper was not for the faint-hearted: 'by land It Is unsafe for Rogues, and by water tis cold besides a good walke in ye dirt and darke (if not rain) from Greate to little Chelsey,' he wrote in 1680. But Victorian householders had a much lower threshold of tolerance.

As regards the house itself, healthful precautions had to be taken before moving in. 'A real new, clean house, where no one has ever died, or had scarlet fever, smallpox, or diphtheria' was naturally attractive, but it had the immense drawback that the sanitary arrangements had not been tested by use and the drains had to be taken on trust. 'What a happy day it will be', exclaimed J. Stevens Hellyer in *The Plumber and Sanitary Houses*, (1880)

when the hygiene of a dwelling-house, as well as the style of its architecture, shall receive its due consideration – when the three most essential and at the same time the most inexpensive things in the world shall be let freely into our homes: when *fresh air* shall be made to circulate, not only through every room and cupboard in the house, but through every waste-pipe, soil-pipe, and drain; when *light*, the revealer, shall be made to shine into every corner of a dwelling, to shame dirt and filth away; when *pure water* shall be made to flow through every draw-off cock in the house; and when the want of these hygienic essentials shall 'no more hurt nor destroy' in homes of peasant or king.

The last phrase – 'in homes of peasant or king' – pointed the moral that all classes of society were vulnerable from bad drains, as the premature death of the Prince Consort, possibly hastened by faulty drains, and an attack of typhoid suffered by the Prince of Wales in 1872 had demonstrated. Hygiene reformers campaigned for the principle that the best way to prevent the dreaded sewer gas seeping back into the house was to have pipes ventilated rather than bottled up tight, and placed on the outside of walls, where they were accessible, rather than inside, where only the smell signified leaks. Norman Shaw himself pioneered a kind of highly ventilated drainage system for his own house in Ellerdale Road, Hampstead, and had it published in the building press. It never caught on in that form, but it undoubtedly worked: after thirty years in service the old soil-pipe had to be removed, and Shaw had a section from the middle of it cut out and brought into his dining-room, where it stood for some days to demonstrate that 'it had no smell and was quite clean inside'.

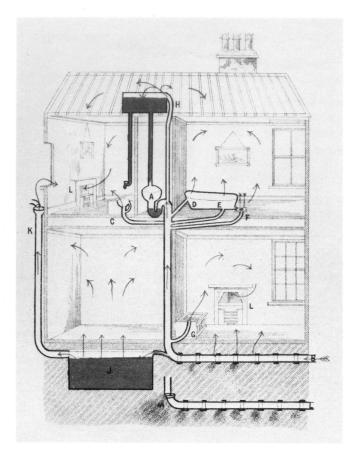

97. Illustration from *Dangers to Health* by T. Pridgin Teale (1878), showing a 'house with
every sanitary arrangement faulty'. The defects are: A, water-closet in
the centre of the house; B, a house drain under the floor of the room; C, the waste-pipe
of the washbasin untrapped and passing into soil pipe of water-closet, thus allowing a
direct channel for sewer gas to be drawn by fires into the house; D, overflow pipe
of bath untrapped and passing into soil pipe; E, waste pipe of bath ditto; F, save-all tray
below traps untrapped and passing into soil pipe; G, kitchen sink untrapped and
passing into soil pipe; H, water-closet cistern with overflow into soil pipe
of water-closet thus ventilating the drain into the roof, polluting the air of the house,
and polluting the water in the cistern; J, rain-water tank under floor, with overflow
into drain; K, fall pipe conducting foul air from the tank fouled by drain gas,
and delivering it just below a window; M, drain under house with uncemented joints leaking;
also a defective junction of vertical soil pipe with horizontal drain;
the drain laid without a proper fall.

The success of the hygiene reformers led to the adoption of rigid by-laws governing the drains of new houses. They embodied a standard of sanitation unknown in the eighteenth century, although the architect C. H. B. Quennell and his wife Marjorie believed that they eventually led to an ossification of practices which prevented the introduction of simplified and improved American methods (the 'one-pipe' as opposed to the 'two-pipe' system).[39]

It was also essential that adequate arrangements were made for the sewage once it had left the house. Only in 1865 did London acquire its system of drainage through sewers (the civil engineer responsible, Sir Joseph Bazalgette,

98. Illustration to *Dangers to Health*, showing 'How people drink sewage'.
The unemptied cess-pool has become full and overflowed, and the sewage is seeping through the ground into the well. The Victorians were newly conscious of hygiene and made health a high priority in building or choosing houses.

has a monument on the Victoria Embankment). Until then the usual method of disposing of sewage was into a cess-pool; for a long time it was illegal to have it discharged into a drain. The cess-pool might be in the back yard, so that when the men came to empty it at night they had to walk through the house bearing their unsavoury burden. Or it might be under the house itself, and perhaps forgotten until it overflowed. Contaminated water was a cause of cholera. Where drinking water came from a spring — as it usually did in country areas – there was always the danger of sewage seeping through the ground from the cess-pool to the water supply; water might also become tainted if the overflow of the domestic cistern was connected to the pipe from the water-closet. However, the provision of sewers was not the end of the drainage problem, because the sewers probably discharged into a stream or river, creating fresh (or rather distinctly unfresh) dangers there. 'The sewage of London from the main drainage is forming a great bank in the Thames,' wrote J. J. Stevenson in 1880.[40] For country houses he recommended an open, fenced tank near the kitchen garden, whence the sewage could be pumped by a hose to whichever vegetables would benefit most.

By the time Mrs Panton was writing, all new houses had water-closets. They were common, but perhaps not as common as one would think, in the mid nineteenth century; about 1850, according to Mayhew, 65.86 per cent of houses in the rich London parish of St James, Westminster, had them, while there were 45.99 per cent in the middle-class parish of St Anne, Soho, and just 10.06 per cent in the poor one of St George, Southwark. Primitive arrangements for this necessity of life are found in castles from the Norman period onwards; small overhanging rooms reached through passages in the thickness of the wall, furnished with a stone ledge in which the hole or holes would have been surrounded by a wooden seat. There was a sheer drop to the ground or, later, the moat (which was also, it should be remembered, used for breeding fish). From the late Middle Ages, the most common provision was a privy comprising a shed with a seat fixed above a pit dug in the ground, located at the other end of the garden or yard from the house. January's young wife May retired to one to read the note from her lover, Damyan, in Chaucer's *The Merchant's Tale*. It was probably little different from that belonging to the Norfolk parson and diarist the Reverend James Woodforde (1740–1803), which he called 'Jericho'. For the rich, however, water-flushed appliances were known from the 1590s, when Sir John Harington published a system in *The Metamorphosis of Ajax* (a punning title, since the Elizabethan word for privy was 'jakes'). This consisted simply of a receptacle with a plug that could be flushed with water as required. It allowed for no disconnecting trap to prevent smells or gas filtering back from the drain.

An S-bend pipe that provided a seal of water below the basin was incorporated in the water-closet patented by the London watchmaker, Alexander Cumming, in 1775. Shortly afterwards Joseph Bramah, a cabinet-maker, patented another type of closet, also water-cleansed, which had a flap trap at the bottom operated by a pull-up handle at the side. Water flushed for the time that the handle was raised. Encased in mahogany, Bramah's closet formed the basis of the kind

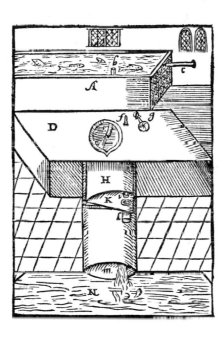

A. the Cesterne.
B. the litle washer.
C. the wast pipe.
D. the seate boord.
E. the pipe that comes from the Cesterne.
F. the Screw.
G. the Scallop shell to couer it when it is shut downe.
H. the stoole pot.
I. the stopple.
K. the current.
L. the sluce.
M.N. the vault into which it falles: alwayes remember that ( ) at noone and at night, emptie it, and leaue it halfe a foote deepe in fayre water. And this being well done, and orderly kept, your worst priuie may be as sweet as your best chamber. But to conclude all this in a few wordes, it is but a standing close stoole easilie emptyed. And by the like reason (other formes and proportions obserued) all other places of your house may be kept sweet.

99. Diagram of a water-flushed privy, from Sir John Harington's *The Metamorphosis of Ajax* (1596).
Providing the water tank at the bottom was changed at noon and at night,
'your worst privie may be as sweet as your best chamber'.

most preferred in the nineteenth century, and still to be found in some old houses. A gentlemen's WC to the right of the front door – regarded as the one point in the house a gentleman might be expected always to find by himself – was an unwritten law of Victorian country-house planning, while it was generally accepted that the minimum number of WC's, even in a small house, was three: one for family of each sex and one for the servants.

By itself, without other improvements in plumbing, bringing the water-closet inside the house was by no means wholly an advantage – quite the reverse. Moreover, Andrew Saint's researches have shown that a less sophisticated pan closet (operated by a tip-up pan at the bottom) was often specified for servants' quarters.[41] This was a false economy, because the pan closet was by no means as hygienic, yet would necessarily be placed near the kitchen and scullery areas where food was prepared, with the consequent spread of germs and disease. The wash-out closet developed in the 1880s, which prefigured the modern variety, was also not wholly satisfactory, but was later refined. Early this century, the celebrated Scottish architect Sir Robert Lorimer designed a special version – rather lower and flatter than usual – for Shanks, and named it the Remirol: his own name spelled backwards.

Mrs Panton, as we have seen, did not believe in taking a new house: better one where one knew a good family had lived a few years without harm. But if, notwithstanding, a new house were selected, it was best to install a caretaker ('even with her grimy self and her still more grimy goods and bronchial family') to keep the fires lit for a solid month before moving in. Thorough ventilation was as much a principle for the house as for the drains; but equally a constant war had to be fought against draughts. Thick curtains for the windows on each side of the doors were necessary if a bedroom were to be kept at 60°. A temperature of about 60° to, some thought, 64° was regarded as right for all rooms by nineteenth-century writers, although doubtless not all attained this ideal, and halls and passages, of which there were many to be negotiated on the way to bed, were a good deal colder.

In the 1850s and 1860s, fireplaces became considerably more efficient as the innovations of Count Rumford, first put forward in the late eighteenth century, were finally adopted. Count Rumford had been one of the more picturesque figures of his time. Born in Massachusetts as plain Benjamin Thompson, he married at the age of nineteen a rich New Hampshire spinster, several years his senior, and through her met the British colonial Governor, John Wentworth, for whom he became a spy. Subsequently he served as a soldier of fortune, while at the same time pursuing the scientific research for which he was made a Fellow of the Royal Society in London at only twenty-seven years old. His title was awarded for reorganizing the Bavarian army and ridding the countryside around Munich of 'tramps, beggars, vagrants, smugglers and defrauders of the customs', whom he put into workhouses as cheap labour to make goods for the army.[42] We are concerned here with the fourth of a series of essays he published in London in 1796. It was called 'Of Chimney Fireplaces, with Proposals for Improving them to Save Fuel...' Rumford had previously been researching into the action of fire with a view to its industrial application; but the filth of London persuaded him to tackle the domestic fireplace. As he wrote:

The enormous waste of fuel may be estimated by the vast dark cloud which continually hangs over this great metropolis, and frequently overshadows the whole

100. Count Rumford warming himself in front of one of the improved grates that bore his name. The Count showed that smaller fireplaces, with non-heat-absorbent sides and a narrow neck, were more efficient than the old, four-foot-wide variety.

country, far and wide; for this dense cloud is certainly composed almost entirely of *unconsumed coal*, which having stolen wings from the innumerable fires of this great city has escaped by the Chimnies, and continues to sail about in the air, till having lost the heat which gave it volatility, it falls in a dry shower of extremely fine black dust to the ground, obscuring the atmosphere in its descent, and frequently changing the brightest day into more than Egyptian darkness.[43]

Before Rumford's ideas were adopted, fireplaces had generally been four feet wide, with the grate, sides and back cast in metal, usually iron. Those designed by the Adam brothers and made at the Carron works, for instance, were often very attractive. But these metal fireplaces were highly inefficient. When the fire was lit, the metal absorbed heat and became very hot; Rumford showed that it was far better for the back and sides to be made of a material that did not absorb heat so well, because they would then reflect it out into the room. Further, the size of the fire could be reduced. And the shape of the flue was also at fault. Previously the whole of the upper part of the fireplace was left open to the chimney. Rumford, however, made the throat comparatively narrow by introducing a step and shelf at the back of the flue, which had the additional benefit of improving the draught.

Although Rumford took some of his ideas from Benjamin Franklin, and Franklin himself had not been entirely original, he pushed his theories with unprecedented energy and zeal. He worked throughout England improving fireplaces and became quite rich as a result (although he never took out a patent on his 'stove'). He and his fireplaces were also caricatured widely. Yet in 1865 Frederick Edwards junior, author of *Our Domestic Fire-Places*, still found it necessary to proselytize Rumford's principles in the face of opposition from ironmongers and the commercial emporia. When Rumford's ideas did become general, however, they had implications for design as well as efficiency. The smaller grate was often framed in an arch-shaped opening, and the surround could be decorated with pretty ceramic tiles. Fireplaces of this kind were made by the thousand in the late nineteenth century.

But movements in taste are unpredictable. Just as the Rumford fireplace was being widely adopted, some romantics looked back to much older and less scientific kinds of fire. They favoured a wide rectangular opening, burning logs. This was the medieval practice (except perhaps in the hall, where the central fireplace persisted into the sixteenth century), although such fireplaces could also still be found in some old-fashioned cottages in country districts; in *Old English Household Life* (1925), Gertrude Jekyll illustrates a fireplace big enough for two 'old folk' to sit inside it, either side of the fire (thus forming an ingle-nook, as revived by Shaw and Nesfield in the 1860s – see Chapter 3). The logs would be lifted off the hearth by two great firedogs or andirons, the design of which underwent a revival at the hands of Shaw, Nesfield, Burges and others. These log-burning fires were most suitable for country houses and were usually confined to the principal rooms; the bedrooms had conventional grates. During the Queen Anne Revival there was a nostalgic return to the old hob grate of the eighteenth century, but in looks only. All fireplaces were provided with fenders in iron (Gothic Revival) or brass (Queen Anne) as a necessary precaution for ladies wearing long dresses.

Central heating by hot water, hot air or steam was never more than a back-up to open fires in the nineteenth century. One suspects that its real benefit was to take the chill off the long, icy corridors of large country mansions, rather than to warm the main rooms. In any case the intestinal knots of pipes that constituted the early radiators (known as 'coils') were hidden behind pretty wickerwork or brass grilles in the best rooms, which must have considerably reduced their effectiveness. The problem was not, as one might think, that the pipes were not hot – Victorian boilers were extremely wasteful, but given the money, it was certainly possible to make the water hot enough – but that there were not enough coils to do the job unaided. The first central-heating systems seem to have been introduced about 1800. By the 1830s heating by hot water was sufficiently a reality to arouse vociferous opposition; I am grateful to Andrew Saint for drawing my attention to this bombastic objection from one hearty contributor to Loudon's *Architectural Magazine*:

It is earnestly to be hoped that the hot-water mania may never expel our ancient, cheerful, and wholesome open hearth from our dwellings; if so, we may expect to see the ruddy English cheek supplanted by the bleached and kiln-dried aspect of our Continental neighbours.

As ever, Mrs Panton was alert to the potential dangers of central heating or any other form of plumbing involving heavy cast-iron pipes and boilers. In severe weather such pipes and even boilers were liable to burst. In outside pipes this was merely an inconvenience (although one that could pose a threat to health – Mrs Panton noted that frozen pipes could serve to accumulate foetid water unless vigorously flushed and disinfected after the thaw). The bursting of pipes and boilers inside the house, should the heating for whatever reason not be on, presented a still more immediate danger. Cast-iron pipes can explode, sending sections of pipe half-way across a large room – although it is impossible not to suspect Mrs Panton of a certain dramatic heightening in her account of the long frost of early 1895:

No less than three boilers burst in one week in the place where I was staying; one resulted in the death of the servant and total blindness for the only child of the house; one in the death of three children, while the third maimed the cook for life.

Following in the wake of central heating came other amenities of life, such as (in the Edwardian period) heated towel rails. Although it was only large country houses that could afford their own laundry, most middle-class households preferring to send their washing out, airing cupboards were a desirable innovation. As Mrs Panton commented characteristically: 'Damp clothes may kill or maim a person for life.'

PRIVACY (AND DECORATION)

Mrs Panton's preoccupation with privacy was all the greater because she was writing about the kind of houses in which privacy, whether from neighbours or more particularly from servants, was not always easy to obtain. But even Robert Kerr, in *The Gentleman's House* of 1864, valued privacy so highly that he placed it number one in his list of qualities by which the worth of a gentleman's house could be tested:

> How objectionable it is we need scarcely say when a thin partition transmits the sounds of the Scullery or Coal-cellar to the Dining-room or Study; or when a Kitchen window in summer weather forms a trap to catch the conversation at the casement of the Drawing-room; or when a Kitchen doorway in the Vestibule or Staircase exposes to the view of everyone the dresser or the cooking-range, or fills the house with unwelcome odours.

Georgian householders of whatever rank had generally lived, in the most literal sense, on top of their servants, since the service quarters were in the basement. One argument for the sprawling Victorian service wing was to separate it more effectually from the main house. Also, in the Georgian period class demarcation was not as rigid as it was to become in Victorian England; and Georgian servants were likely to have had a more personal relationship with the family they served than their Victorian equivalents, who were supposed to be soundless and, ideally, invisible. But perhaps the greatest difference was in the Victorian concept of the home. While the Victorian squire shouldered a public role as a duty, his belief in the moral values of the family made him think of his fireside as inviolable. The Baroque notion (never wholly adopted in England) of the great gentleman being at all times exposed to the public gaze would have seemed an anathema. Queen Victoria's impenetrable seclusion in widowhood was seen as a justification.

This attitude to the home had its influence on both planning and decoration. As the purpose of rooms became more rigidly defined, rooms multiplied in number with the result that there was always an inner sanctum into which guests did not penetrate. With an increasing emphasis on family rather than social use, cosiness became a virtue. Robert Edis in particular advocated 'home-like' values in *Decoration and Furniture of Town Houses* (1881).

101. Colonel Robert Edis's own London dining-room, from his book
Decoration and Furniture of Town Houses (1881). He advocated 'home-like' values.
Note the curtains in front of the fireplace.

Kerr's other requirements were comfort ('in no other country but our own is this element of comfort fully understood'), convenience, spaciousness, compactness, light and air, salubrity, aspect and prospect, cheerfulness, elegance, importance and ornament. Of these, aspect and prospect had to be determined before the house was even planned. In a paper specifically on 'A Small Country House', Kerr described the ideal site as having the main road from which it was approached on the north, an open prospect on the south, and some form of shelter from the wind to the east. There might also be a view to the west, in which case the south lawn could sweep round on this side too, since 'the sunset, as a matter of prospect, was always of extreme value for a lawn in England'. As for the rooms, those which looked east were pleasant in the morning, but those which looked west were the reverse of pleasant in the evening, when there was glare from the sun. South-facing rooms 'had the hot sun upon them from noonday until several hours afterwards, and in hot weather the sunshine was very sultry'. South-westerly rooms were likely to be even more sultry, as well as 'exposed to the windy and rainy quarter'. The south-east aspect was therefore the most desirable. As a result of all these considerations, the entrance should be on the north, the 'offices' on north or east, the dining-room (which was used in the evenings) by no means on the west, the drawing-room south or south-east with a good view – avoiding the boisterous wet winds from the west.

But in the town or inner suburbs such refinements could not always be applied. A terraced house has only two aspects, front and back, and for people who rented houses there was always an element of putting up with what could be had. We have seen that it was to these home-makers that Mrs Panton addressed herself in particular, since self-expression inside the house had to some extent to compensate for lack of opportunity outside. Fortunately, a house of which Mrs Panton would probably have approved has been preserved in all the glory of its Victorian decoration: 18 Stafford Terrace, Kensington, the home of the *Punch* illustrator Linley Sambourne and his wife. These dark, lush rooms, with their deep-fringed chairs, elaborately flounced lampshades and embossed wallpapers, date from shortly after 1874, the year of the Sambournes' marriage – and about twenty years before Mrs Panton was writing. Middle-class taste changed less rapidly than that of the more fickle rich, and the Sambournes were more typically middle-class than one might think. Although Sambourne followed an artistic career and chose to live near, if not too near, the artists of Melbury Road, the money for the house came from his wife's family, and parental influence seems to have guided them towards the conservatism of stucco rather than the flamboyance of red brick and terracotta. Also, Sambourne preferred to present himself as a hard-riding, cigar-smoking,

102. 18 Stafford Terrace, Kensington, the home of the *Punch* cartoonist Linley Sambourne
and his wife. Built as part of a speculative terrace, the Sambournes took it in 1874,
the year of their marriage, and the decoration has remained virtually unchanged ever since.

103. The staircase at 18 Stafford Terrace, with stained glass on the landing for privacy.
The patterned wallpaper extends to the underside of the stairs.
Beneath the window there is a fish tank.

imperial-bearded squire rather than a Bohemian, and he parodied aesthetes such as Oscar Wilde in his caricatures.

Except for a few years at the end of his life, Sambourne did not progress beyond the not highly rewarded position of Second Cartoon. It may have been for this reason that after 1874 virtually no part of the house was redecorated during his lifetime. By good luck it was left more or less untouched by his successors. In recent years, its preservation is due to the Countess of Rosse, mother of Lord Snowdon and a founder of the Victorian Society, who has given it to the Greater London Council to be administered by the Victorian Society.

The hall at 18 Stafford Terrace is exactly like that which Mrs Panton recommends: the floor laid with encaustic tiles against muddy boots, a small fireplace (with a velvet valence), the walls lined not with original paintings but photographs of works of art. The photographs reflect Sambourne's professional interest in photography (working against deadlines he was not able to draw from models but used an enormous photographic collection instead). But equally Mrs Panton was to recommend 'good autotypes and Burne-Jones's photographs from Mr Hollyer of 9 Pembroke Square'. Lady Rosse remembers what it was like to arrive as a child when the Sambournes lived there:

> The heavy scent of rich Havana cigars was mingled with lavender water, so popular with the gentlemen of that day. Then came the sounds of the ticking of innumerable clocks, the trickle of the landing water fountains, and from the drawing-room strains of Schumann on the piano; my grandmother was a good pianist.

Those evocative smells and sounds have now gone, but not the visual shock as one exchanges a bright white stucco porch (white was in fact probably not the Victorian colour) for dark greens and maroon, patterned wallpaper spreading over dado, walls, ceiling and the underside of the staircase, and elaborate plaster cornices and ceiling roses. The last item was a point on which Mrs Panton would have fallen out with the Sambournes: she reiterated an aversion to ceiling roses; but at Stafford Terrace they concealed ventilator grilles for the gas lights. Although decorated in dark colours, the hall is made darker still by being lit only by a stained glass window over the stairs – to give privacy in a London house.

Following usual practice, the front room on the ground floor of 18 Stafford Terrace was the dining-room, with the morning room behind, overlooking the modest garden (but again with windows filled with stained glass). A mid-Victorian dining-room would normally have been 'characterized by the massive appearance of its furniture, and the rightness of its hangings', as recommended in *The Lady's Country Companion*.[44] But the Sambournes' dining-room was rather lighter in style; the sideboard, with its painted panels, is similar in form to one designed by Charles Eastlake and illustrated in his *Hints on Household Taste* of 1872. The walls were hung with Morris and Company's 'Pomegranate' paper – Morris's papers were two or three times more expensive than others, but the superiority of the design was generally recognized – although the dado and frieze are different both in colour and pattern. A cornice shelf supports a row of blue and white plates and vases. There is an octagonal rather than the conventional long table, prefiguring Mrs Panton's taste – she disliked long tables, which left the father, at the head, with his back to the fire but in full range of the draught whistling under the door from the cold hall. Many middle-class families used the dining-room as a family sitting-room as well as for meals, leaving the drawing-room upstairs for guests.

Meals in the 1870s still lasted a long time in some households, since the new method of serving dishes in a succession of courses had yet to overtake the old one of putting everything on the table at the same time. Under the earlier system, the table was already charged with food – the soup and hot dishes rapidly cooling – when the party entered the dining-room. According to menu cards surviving among the papers of Mary Yorke of Forthampton Court in Gloucestershire, which list both the dishes and the places that were to be set on the table, her five guests at a dinner of 1803 could contemplate, before they began: (at the head of the table) fish, (then clockwise) calf's head pudding, chicken, patties, (in front of Mrs Yorke) 'peas soup', a sirloin of beef, mutton 'stakes' with 'harico beans', ham and 'Dutch balls'. Guests were expected to help themselves from the dish in front of them and then offer it to the neighbours. If they wanted something on the other side of the table, they had to ask for it to be passed or have a servant bring it round. Wine 'in the china cooler' was in the centre of the table. The first course consumed, the debris was cleared and the table again laid with richer, more elaborately prepared fare – partridges, cheese cakes, 'spinage', trifle with 'Dauphin cream and upright biscuits round the edge', duck, cherry tart, artichoke bottoms, and 'mange with current juice in it'. Dessert – probably served with no cloth (unless the table was very good) – consisted of tea and coffee, buttered rolls, cake and 'a few of the preserved strawberries'.

A more elaborate feast began another evening at four o'clock. Wine was again in the centre. At the head were 'soles from London', then 'Palates' (tongues), 'whole turned round potatoes balls', fowl 'stuffed with trufles and morells', patties, (in front of Mrs Yorke) soup and sauté venison, then pork 'stakes', 'compost of venison not too high', and 'three little puddings green plum white'. Second course: beside the wine was orange posset and a basket of biscuits; at the head of the table pheasant, then a 'green apricot tart taken out of the copper shape', 'garden things in a covered dish', 'mange white' (blancmange), 'tabby ocre pudding', red cabbage and 'custard with apple sauce upon it, clear, froth over and salamandered'. Dessert was much the same as before, with the provision: 'Coffee poured out in the room but not sent in till some bread and butter is ready to come in with it. The muffins and cake to be sent in with the tea.'[45]

But at least by the 1890s, when for some reason Linley Sambourne started to pay attention to food in his diaries, habits had changed, and a dinner party at Stafford Terrace was served in the now standard manner, with one dish following another. *Service à la russe*, as this presentation was called, had the advantage of being quicker (it came to be accepted that dinner should not last more than an hour, whereas in 1784 François de la Rochefoucauld had complained that in England this wearisome experience might last from four to five hours), and it held out great hopes of a more sophisticated cuisine, no sauces could be offered under the previous regime, since they would have congealed as they sat on the table. Nevertheless, the old system held sway in some middle-class households until the end of the nineteenth century.

'Home dinner. Very good. They did not stay so late as usual,' Sambourne noted in his diary for 31 May 1895. 'Took some carbonate of soda at 12.15 when going to Bed. All went off well.' On that occasion the meal had started rather late, because he did not get home until 8.35, after a day trip to Calais. Usually it was hoped that the 'home dinners' would start about 8.00. The octagonal table usually limited the numbers to eight, although occasionally there were a couple more – in which case Sambourne's son, Roy, would sit by himself at a side table or even in the next room. The Sambournes usually hired a waiter or waitress, if possible the Royal Academy waiter, because it was of course always preferable to have someone you knew. On 13 March 1897, when Luke Fildes and his wife were in the party, 'a strange waitress muddled the wine'.

Sambourne took to recording the seating plan of his dinners, but for the exceptionally grand dinner for twelve on 25 July 1899, he was moved to write down the menu as well. They began with caviare and Château-d'Yquem 1881, which was followed by consommé and champagne. Surprisingly perhaps, he served 'Léoville 1875' – a claret – with the 'Filet de Soules à la Reine', although it stayed in the glass for the noisettes of tongue with mushrooms which came next. With the leg of lamb with peas and green beans came a burgundy. Then there was salad, and after that raspberry purée and fruit salad. The last dish was a savoury, with the special treat of Courvoisier 1851. However much

Sambourne enjoyed his home dinners, they do not seem to have taken place more than two or three times a year; it is clear from the diaries that most of the dinners he went to took place in clubs, but he does not say what Mrs Sambourne did on those evenings.

At Stafford Terrace there is no door in the opening through to the morning room, but on either side is a heavy velvet portière curtain hung from a brass pole. Elsewhere there are such curtains even where there are doors. Mrs Panton was a devotee of the portière curtain. Its heavy folds were a protection against the detested draughts, of course; but more than that, they were part of the armoury of privacy.

Anyone who has passed by a vista of open bedroom doors, left open when the owners have, at the sound of the gong, rushed downstairs to meals in too great a hurry to put their rooms tidy, will not need to have impressed upon them the fact that it is absolutely necessary to decency to have *portières* which fall into place behind the person who leaves his or her bedroom door open . . .

Portières could not be hung inside the bathroom, but one should be provided for the outside: 'it prevents sudden surprises'. But on this subject, as on others, opinions differed. All writers professed an abhorrence of 'dust traps', in the same way that all politicians claim to be in favour of democracy. It was on these grounds that Edis found portières objectionable – although today one would probably not call his own rooms (shown on page 185), which must have been, incidentally, among the best examples of the Queen Anne Revival, easy to clean.

On the first floor at 18 Stafford Terrace is the drawing-room, L-shaped and stretching the full depth of the house, so that it is lit from both ends. Kerr wrote: 'We live in the era of *Omnium Gatherum*; all the world's a museum, and men and women are its students.' The Sambournes' furniture is so eclectic that it looks at first sight as though it may have been collected over many years. Antiques were for the first time beginning slowly to come into vogue, and certainly the furniture here is in a variety of different styles – Sheraton, French eighteenth-century, neo-Gothic, Chinese lacquer, Victorian mahogany. But in fact it is nearly all reproduction, and bought quickly, since an inventory of 1877 indicates that almost everything was in place by that date. The house filled up within a few years. From the start a man of Sambourne's stout build would have had to take care as he edged between armchairs and cabinets, palm stands and bronzes. The walls are tightly packed with pictures – so tightly that when it was decided, quite soon after the room was first decorated, to change the paper, only a few strips were put on: none was hung behind the pictures,

104. 18 Stafford Terrace: the drawing-room on the first floor. The pictures are so tightly packed
that, when the wallpaper was changed, only thin strips for the narrow gaps
between the frames were put up.

because the frames almost touch. On the subject of drawing-room pictures,
Mrs Loudon casually recommended: 'A Claude or two, some of Guido's
exquisite female heads, and one of Raphael's Madonnas, would be very suitable;
but no pictures should be admitted unless its subject were pleasing.'[46] By 'a
Claude or two' she probably meant good copies after the originals, for, in
paintings as in furniture, little trouble was taken to distinguish between
reproductions and the genuine article before the end of the century.

The drawing-room contains the piano and, at one end, Sambourne's easel and drawing equipment – he was not grand enough to have a studio house, and in any case there were no models to be routed away from his wife. There is no doubt that the room is over-furnished, but it would be wrong to think that the arrangement is arbitrary. It was more a question of carefully contrived informality. 'As one chief use of it is as a conversation-room,' Stevenson wrote of the drawing-room, 'it should be planned to favour the forming of the company into separate groups.'[47] This remained the ruling principle into the Edwardian period, and a number of floor-plans survive from large turn-of-the-century country houses showing exactly where each piece of furniture was to be placed. Before about 1810, most houses were, by contrast, furnished in severe formality, with the furniture placed against the walls and only moved forward, probably by a servant, for use. John Cornforth has described the influences that encouraged a less formal look; they included the Grecian dress of the Regency (a lady could recline in a Grecian dress but not in the full skirts of the mid eighteenth century) and the growing appreciation of delicious, deeply buttoned upholstery.[48]

One of the few changes in 18 Stafford Terrace was the replacement of gas by electricity for lighting some time in the 1890s. Ceiling roses-cum-ventilators in the drawing-room indicate that it originally had gasoliers; but these were not replaced by electroliers, as electric chandeliers were called, and the room is lit by a number of table lamps scattered on tables and shelves. There was a difference in approach here from the dining-room, for it was recognized that the latter required strong light, while something subtler and – as Edis thought – 'less damaging to all works of art' was called for in the drawing-room.

At Newnham Grange, the childhood home of Gwen Raverat, which she described in *Period Piece*, there was a kind of hierarchy of lighting before electric light was installed: the bedrooms, nursery and passages had 'hissing, unshaded gas burners', the dining-room candles and the drawing-room an oil lamp (the latter perhaps because it was good for reading, since her father was a fellow of Trinity and Professor of Astronomy). 'Light the revealer' was not welcomed unequivocally; electricity, which became increasingly general after 1890, was at first disliked as too glaring for the complexion by some ladies – and much the same had been said of gas. But to designers the electric bulb had the immense advantage that it could be pointed in any direction, not just upwards like the gas flame. This freedom came just in time for the flamboyant decorative style of Art Nouveau – although it was only with Art Deco in the 1930s, its effects relying less on ornamental holders than on the qualities of light itself, that its nature was fully exploited. Town houses, which could be supplied by a power company, and large country houses, which could generate their own, were the first to benefit from electricity. Country cottagers went on lighting themselves to bed with candles in wax or tallow, or even rush lights, well into the twentieth century.

A conventional town house, arranged on the vertical principle that prevailed in England, allowed little room for flexibility. But in the country, where space was not at a premium, it was possible to be more expansive. Country houses could have more rooms, arranged in more ways; and as we have seen, they spread. Yet much of the multiplication, one suspects, was only an elaboration of the idea of conversational groups. This is the impression given by John Loudon's *Encyclopaedia*, one part of which paints a charming picture of mid-Victorian country life. The function of rooms cannot always be taken at face value. 'When there is company in the house,' writes the contributor

the library would be the morning sitting-room for the gentlemen, who might here read the papers and new publications, write and answer letters; and thus, with a stroll round the garden or farm, and a look into the stables and kennels, employ the time till luncheon, after which some would join the ladies in an excursion on horseback, while others rode with their host to see some improvements on the farm or estate.

Sportsmen would naturally be off hunting or shooting in the right seasons, while in their absence the

ladies would occupy the drawing-room or saloon, and there amuse themselves, some with needlework, others with a book or a drawing, others with writing or music, till they met the gentlemen at luncheon.

After luncheon, they might have a ride or a 'carriage airing' with the gentlemen, or pay calls with the lady of the house. Alternatively the whole party might venture forth in a carriage excursion, or walk in the park and gardens, or visit the schools and cottages in the village. But the day did not really begin until the afternoon, when it was possible to discuss, preferably with a member of the opposite sex, about all those things you had been doing during the day.

After luncheon, and in summer evenings, the doors of the living-rooms would be thrown open; and on the return of the party, they would, probably, arrange themselves in groups in each of the rooms. Thus, in the library, a gentleman may, perhaps, be referring to a book, while he explains something to the ladies with whom he had conversed during the morning ride. In the saloon a lady is, perhaps, playing a lively air, while the young ladies and some of the gentlemen are lounging about the room engaged in playful conversation. In the drawing-room would most likely be another group, some sitting upon a couch while others stood round the table collecting their work, books, or drawings, before they retire to dress; and all talking over the place or people they had visited in the morning.[49]

But then Loudon imagines this delightful scene breaking up as the bell rings for dinner and the ladies hurry off to their rooms, with the men slowly following.

Would they have taken a bath before dinner? To Loudon a bathroom was 'a cheap and useful luxury', which many people would have already regarded as indispensable in the perfect villa. 'A room of moderate size would contain the warm and shower baths' – although there would also be an old-style cold bath, often found in eighteenth-century country houses, in an ornamental building near the stream in the park. The practice of bathing in this country is reputed to have been brought back by the Crusaders from the East. Elizabethan London was provided with public baths known as 'bagnios' and 'hummums', although these were discredited by the overtones sometimes also associated with the saunas and massage parlours of today. The 'stews', in Shakespearian argot, were not pre-eminent for their cleanliness. When the Greek Revival turned educated interest to the practices of the ancients, however, public baths enjoyed a new vogue; and so did the habit of bathing within your own house. William Weddell, the connoisseur and patron of Robert Adam at Newby Hall, bathed in an Egyptian sarcophagus he had collected (he even died in a bath in London). The cold bath in the park, of which there is a famous example at Rousham (it is shaded by trees to ensure that it really was cold), was Roman in inspiration. But the plumbed-in bathroom Loudon recommended, with hot and cold water arriving through pipes, was a rarity before the mid nineteenth century. A report in the *Builder* of 8 December 1849 recorded that most first-rate new buildings had baths, even if 'the use of them among the middle class is not so general as might be'. But speculative houses in the suburbs were still on the whole built without baths. By now the inspiration was less Ancient Rome than the United States, where 'a bathroom is part of every modern dwelling, and *no one will occupy a house without one*'; and the habit of bathing was seen as a moral duty, not a recondite pleasure. The next thirty years witnessed a gradual improvement. When the *Builder* again looked at the question on 1 November 1879, new houses of £100 a year rent generally had baths and, 'in some of the fresh suburban neighbourhoods', even the not particularly fashionable ones like Paddington, Shepherd's Bush and Brixton, they were supplied to houses of £50 a year rent. 'There is no doubt it pays the builder to do so, for in most dwellings there is some dressing-room, or small room in a wing, where a hot and cold bath can be placed, and respectable tenants will pay 5 *l.* or 10 *l.* extra rent in a moderate-sized house to secure the

105. The cold bath at Rousham. In the eighteenth century, bathing was
particularly associated with the practices of the Ancient World.

benefit.' But this state of provision applied only to new houses. Very few £100
a year houses built in the pre-bath 1820s and 1830s, albeit in otherwise highly
salubrious neighbourhoods such as St John's Wood, Bayswater, Notting Hill
and Brompton, had them; and even the £200 to £300 a year houses of
Westbourne Terrace and Cleveland Square were often without. By the time
Mrs Panton was writing, bathrooms were to be found 'in the quite small
houses which are only meant for such a humble individual as the ordinary city
clerk'. Even the humble but houseproud Pooter in George and Weedon

106. Mr Pooter in *The Diary of a Nobody* taking a bath, having painted it with red enamel paint. The bath is filled by a geyser.

Grossmith's *The Diary of a Nobody* had one, the bath being enamel and filled with hot water from a gas geyser. Finding that the enamel was chipped, Pooter enlivened the bath by painting it red, and of course the paint dissolved when he ran 'a bath as hot as I could bear it' on suffering from a chill. The bath was in fact only one of the objects of Pooter's craze for red enamel paint. Along with the coal scuttle and the worn-out binding of the family Shakespeare, inter alia, he painted the wash-stand in the servant's bedroom – for The Laurels (otherwise 12 Brickfield Terrace, Holloway) did not have plumbed-in wash-basins in the bedrooms, at least not for the one servant.

If rich houses did not have bathrooms in the 1870s, it was not only blinkered conservatism; snobbery played a part too. Before piped hot water, hot water had to be brought up from the kitchen in jugs by the maids. Some wealthy people continued to feel that, if they wanted hot water, they liked to ring for it – a view to which Oscar Wilde subscribed in criticizing the wash-basins in the bedrooms of the Savoy Hotel. Thus there persisted an aristocratic belief

107. Luxurious bath from the late 1890s, from Kinloch Castle, a shooting lodge on the Isle of
Rhum. Water is controlled by two sets of dials, so that water in a variety of sprays
and waves could arrive from above and below simultaneously.

that bathrooms were 'only for servants', and this may explain why the Edwardian country house Minterne Magna, in Dorset, had no bathrooms on the main bedroom corridor (although the architect, Leonard Stokes, sensibly laid pipes in case they needed them later). However, this stand was unusual; in 1870 large country houses could be expected to have one bathroom to every three or so bedrooms. The novelist and poet Thomas Hardy, during his spell as a young man in an architect's office, took an interest in the subject. An entry in his architectural notebook for 28 April 1871 is headed 'Bath Room and Water Service of Dwellings': 'The less carving and woodwork the better – the bath standing by itself. It sh^d always have a light hinged flap or cover.'

When Lord Digby, the owner of Minterne Magna, took a bath, he would have had a portable bath brought to his bedroom; the water could never have been very hot, and the system depended on having plenty of servants. Taking a bath in the bedroom was a messy business, if vigorous splashing were involved: Mrs Panton recommended clearing furniture, taking up rugs, laying cork floors and putting up waterproof dados. Perhaps an advantage of the slipper bath – a form of bath shaped like a boot, which covered the legs – was that more of the water was kept inside. But there were not always large quantities of water to splash with: sponge baths and hip baths, in which the bather either crouched or sat, were designed for the use of little water and much sponging. In working-class families, the practice was not to bath in the bedroom but in front of the kitchen range, where the water was heated. This continued in quite a large number of households until the Second World War. It was a primitive arrangement, but is sometimes remembered with affection as a friendly family ritual. However, nothing could have offended more against Mrs Panton's ideal of privacy.

SERVANTS

Writing about the suburbs, Mrs Panton was especially concerned with what came to be called the 'servant question' – that is, the shortage of servants. Part of the attraction of the suburbs was that they tended to be one-class neighbourhoods, so that Victorian families – more supercilious in this respect than their Georgian forbears – were not thrown into contact with unsavoury elements, or the poor. Conversely this had its awkward side in an age when anyone seeking to struggle above the threshold of gentility – even the impoverished Micawbers or the lowly Pooters – had to have at least one servant, however overworked or badly trained. Georgian developments allowed for a mix of classes and in the country there were always plenty of labourers' or tenant farmers' daughters who wanted to become maids. But no pool of labour existed in the suburbs. The houses were not big enough to allow many servants to live in; and if they did live in, they were probably lonely, for there were relatively few other servants about and therefore little of the servant camaraderie that could be found both in big country houses and in towns. Towns also offered more to do on a night off. And servants who did not live in but came daily were reluctant to make the journey out, their homes being usually in the inner cities.

Complaining about servants, however, was nothing new to the nineteenth century. In the eighteenth century the criticism had been that, coming from the country or even doubling as farm labourers, servants were sometimes awkward and rustic. Both Defoe (in *Everybody's Business is Nobody's Business* and *The Behaviour of Servants Inquir'd Into*) and Swift (in *Directions to Servants*) focused robustly on possible sexual misdoings. Swift was in his highest vein of satire on this point. 'Never,' he advised the waiting maid

allow [my lord] the smallest liberty, not the squeezing of your hand, unless he puts a guinea into it; so by degrees make him pay accordingly for every new attempt, doubling upon him in proportion to the concession you allow, and always struggling, and threatening to cry out, or tell your lady, although you receive his money; five guineas for handling your breasts is a cheap pennyworth, although you seem to resist with all your might; but never allow him the last favour under a hundred guineas or a settlement of twenty pounds a year for life.

Defoe thought that country girls were liable to pick up loose morals in factories, and then move on to the towns to go into service – an interesting observation, since factories were later regarded as a major threat to the supply of good servants. For it was the relative independence of working in munitions and other factories during the First World War that, to many girls, seemed preferable to the lack of personal freedom entailed by service, and so brought the servant crisis to a head.

But whether you expressed cynicism about servants' morals as Swift did, or showed an intrusive degree of protectiveness towards them as later writers and employers were to do, it was, until the twentieth century, recognized by everybody that it was extremely difficult to do without servants. A glance at the 1881 census returns for Kensington shows how well-off, middle-class households were managed. Southwell Gardens, for instance, was almost entirely inhabited by lawyers and their families. At No. 1 lived Henry Giffard, a forty-two-year-old barrister, and his wife and son. They employed a butler, cook, nurse, three housemaids and page. At No. 2 was Jane Young, a widow of independent means, and her two daughters; they had a married butler, cook, lady's maid, housemaid and under housemaid. A few doors along at No. 5, Herbert Norman, another barrister, and his wife were rather unusual in keeping three men servants – butler, footman and coachman – as well as cook, lady's maid, housemaid and kitchen-maid. But at No. 7, Archibald Milman, who was second clerk assistant at the House of Commons, not only had four daughters but swelled the female numbers below stairs by employing a governess and a nurse. Here there were altogether six servants, only the footman being male. Near by in Cromwell Road the houses are rather bigger and the households correspondingly more affluent. A bright young lawyer called Henry Ince – only thirty-one years old but already a QC – lived at No. 98, supporting a household of twenty people: wife, seven daughters, son, sister-in-law, governess and eight servants. However, the Earl and Countess of Dunmore at No. 107 Cromwell Road had a larger staff (governess, butler, lady's maid, nurse, two nurserymaids, two housemaids, cook, kitchen-maid and page), and only three daughters. On the whole the most striking aspect of the figures – whatever the exact proportions – is the preponderance of women over men in most well-to-do Victorian establishments. John Inglis, a retired army officer in his early thirties who lived at 15 Grenville Place, was not wholly untypical. As well as his wife and four daughters, he had beneath his roof a cook, a lady's maid, two housemaids, a kitchen-maid and two nurses. The only other man in the house was the German butler.

When the employment of servants was at its height, in the middle years of the nineteenth century, no fewer than one in three of all girls between the ages of fifteen and twenty was in domestic service. The total did not reach its zenith until as late as 1891, when 1,549,502 servants were employed. As the numbers in service grew, so did the service wing.

The ideal service wing was to be found in big country houses, because only a very big wing could accommodate all the different functions that went on behind the green baize door and keep them separate. An idea of the Victorian expansion can be gleaned from Lanhydrock (Fig. 13, overleaf). The house had been growing since the seventeenth century and half of it had been rebuilt after a fire in 1881. Before the fire there were some seventeen rooms on the ground floor; after the reconstruction there were about thirty-one, most of the additions having been in the servants' wing.[50] The work was done by the obscure architect Richard Coad for the equally obscure peer Lord Robartes, and took place only a year or so after the publication of J. J. Stevenson's book on *House Architecture*. However, Stevenson is not a wholly appropriate guide, since his ideas were more advanced than those of either Coad or Lord Robartes – the latter sublimely ignoring the effects of the agricultural depression of the 1870s, which severely reduced the income of many landowners. 'I venture to doubt if a house should be planned as Mr Kerr recommends, so that the servants may shut themselves off from the family in a separate establishment,' wrote the liberal Stevenson. He believed that it was wrong and unproductive to treat servants as an inferior class. Coad, on the other hand, was more of Kerr's mind, and if you visit Lanhydrock today, expecting to see a large servants' wing as you walk down the drive, you will be struck by how much it has been put out of the way. You hardly see it from the entrance front, or from any of the other sides except that of the gentlemen's wing. The high regard for privacy – which was supposed to be as much the privacy of servants as of the family – would also have pleased Mrs Panton.

All Victorian writers were united on one principle regarding the servants' wing – that, in large houses, the rooms of the male staff under the butler should be separated as far as possible from those of the female staff under the housekeeper. The hub of the female side was the kitchen – at Lanhydrock, a tall two-storey room with an elaborately timbered roof. The height was not just medievalizing, but a necessary means of reducing the heat – there were windows in the roof to let out the steam. For kitchens were liable to become very hot and, since they, on the whole, lacked good ventilation, it is not surprising that cooks had a reputation both for bad temper and the imbibing of liquor. Roasting at Lanhydrock was done at a great open fire. The great roasts of Victorian days would either be spitted horizontally or would hang down vertically from a chain and revolve slowly in front of the flames. At Lanhydrock there was in addition a basket spit for the really big joints or whole animals; it could be moved up or down, or nearer or further away from the fire, by means of notches on the bars that supported it. Victorian spits were usually turned by a clockwork 'bottlejack' (at Lanhydrock by a device worked by hot air in the chimney) and the meat might be half enclosed in a metal 'hastener', which kept the back of the joint hot. For a long time cookery writers stressed the value of 'the taste of the fire'. Grilling, frying, boiling and baking were done at the range, which stood by a wall; really advanced kitchens, with perhaps a French chef, had ranges that stood centrally in the room and so could be got at from all sides. On top of the range were a series of hobs known as 'stewing stoves' and 'broiling stoves' and below were the ovens and hot closet. The latter was to keep the viands warm after cooking and to heat the plates. In smaller houses roasting was also done in front of the range: the fire was fitted

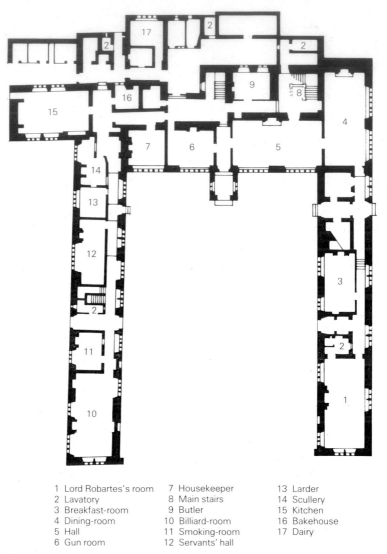

1 Lord Robartes's room	7 Housekeeper	13 Larder
2 Lavatory	8 Main stairs	14 Scullery
3 Breakfast-room	9 Butler	15 Kitchen
4 Dining-room	10 Billiard-room	16 Bakehouse
5 Hall	11 Smoking-room	17 Dairy
6 Gun room	12 Servants' hall	

(a)

FIG. 13 (a, b). Lanhydrock: (a) the plan of the house before the fire of 1881 contrasted with (b) the plan for the reconstruction of the house after the fire.

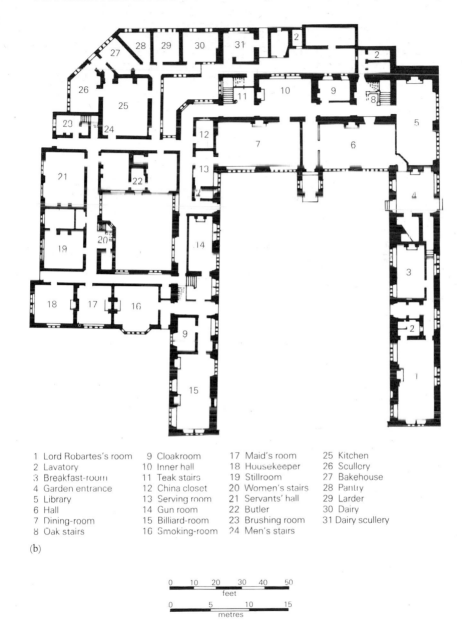

1 Lord Robartes's room	9 Cloakroom	17 Maid's room	25 Kitchen
2 Lavatory	10 Inner hall	18 Housekeeper	26 Scullery
3 Breakfast-room	11 Teak stairs	19 Stillroom	27 Bakehouse
4 Garden entrance	12 China closet	20 Women's stairs	28 Pantry
5 Library	13 Serving room	21 Servants' hall	29 Larder
6 Hall	14 Gun room	22 Butler	30 Dairy
7 Dining-room	15 Billiard-room	23 Brushing room	31 Dairy scullery
8 Oak stairs	16 Smoking-room	24 Men's stairs	

(b)

0 10 20 30 40 50
feet

0 5 10 15
metres

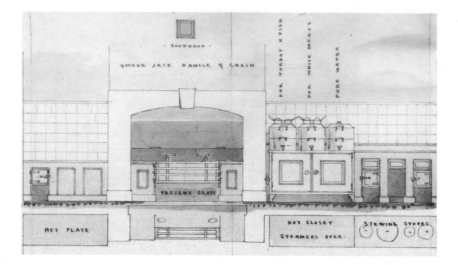

108. Cooking apparatus from an early-nineteenth-century kitchen at 56 Portland Place, London, by J. B. Papworth.

with an opening door so that meat could be turned in front of it. Next to the fire there was often a boiler, kept permanently full of hot water and fitted with a tap so that the water could be taken off as required. Before plumbed-in bathrooms, this was generally the principal source of hot water for the house.

The range grew in sophistication as the nineteenth century progressed. By the end of the century it was possible to control the heat from the fire by cranking it up, nearer the stewing stoves, or down, further away. Also, the size of the fire could be varied by a wall moved from side to side, making it bigger or smaller. But all ranges were enormously wasteful of fuel and, being kept burning all day, a major contribution to those smogs of which Rumford complained. (A distinguished doctor, Sir Frederick Treves, calculated that any square mile of air in a London fog contained six tons of soot.) In very modest dwellings the range was the focus of the whole house, since it was located in the parlour where the family lived. Its excess heat was therefore put to good use in heating the room. In the 1920s the range became very much more efficient with the invention of the Aga – where the heat was kept at an even

109. A simple vernacular kitchen from Thomas Carlyle's birthplace at Ecclefechan,
Dumfries and Galloway. Over the fire is a 'swee' or 'sway' – an iron bar
by means of which the girdle or the jelly pan could be moved nearer
or further away from the fire. There is no oven
in this three-room cottage built in 1791. The two coffeepots,
the teapot and the iron kettle by the fire, and the two candlesticks
on the mantlepiece, were all owned by Mrs Carlyle.

110. The kitchen at Carlyle's House in Cheyne Row, Chelsea.
The house was built in 1708 and water was pumped up from a well until the second
half of the nineteenth century. The cast-iron range was installed in 1852,
and twenty-five years later gas was brought in. The maidservant slept in the kitchen;
it was also to this room that Carlyle and guests such as Tennyson
would retreat to smoke a pipe up the chimney – to spare Mrs Carlyle's
feelings. The maid's feelings are not recorded.

temperature by means of a storage drum – by the blind Swedish physicist and
Nobel prize winner, Gustav Dalen. His aim was to simplify the controls for
the sake of other blind people like himself.

As well as the range and, possibly, open fire, and even perhaps a variety of
different hot closets and ovens (for pastry, for instance), the kitchen invariably
contained a long table for preparing meat and mixing ingredients. But it
probably did not contain a cold-water supply. That was in the scullery, where
there were sinks (of stone) and wooden plate-racks – and perhaps boilers for
meat, soup and vegetables, and steamers for meat, fish and vegetables,
according to Kerr. The scullery was where vegetables and fish were prepared

111. The serving-room at Lanhydrock, with a steel hot cupboard by Jeakes and Company of
Great Russell Street. The door was carefully arranged so that,
unless open to its maximum extent as shown here, it was impossible for the dinner guests
to see the behind-the-scenes preparations.

and the plates – quantities of them during a large house party – were washed
up by the unfortunate scullery-maid, her hands probably red from the caustic
soda. As Stevenson wrote, a major concern was 'to isolate the sinks and
connections with the drains, which might taint the atmosphere'. The scullery
always lay immediately off the kitchen; near the kitchen, too, were the larders
for meat, game, fish and pastry. It was best to have these near an entrance from
the outside, partly to give delivering tradesmen less opportunity to linger.

At Lanhydrock the kitchen was separated from the dining-room by a
corridor with two right-angled bends. This was deliberate – it was supposed to
keep noises and particularly the much disliked cooking smells out of the main
part of the house. Having made this journey, the dishes were set down in the
serving-room just outside the dining-room before being taken in. Here the
covers were taken off – if they had been removed in the kitchen the food

would have already become cold. Lanhydrock had the amenity of a splendid steel hot cupboard by Jeakes and Company of Great Russell Street, which was run off the main central-heating system (although other types could be heated by gas). 'But in most houses this is an unnecessary luxury,' commented Stevenson. The door into the dining-room was convenient for the sideboard therein, but so placed that guests at the dining-table could not see the behind-the-scenes preparations in the serving-room. The polite fiction was maintained that all the domestic arrangements of a large country house were achieved by magic.

Dinner at Lanhydrock was served *à la russe*, with menus written in French when there were guests. But the Robartes almost certainly had a female English cook – perhaps such as the old terror described in *Esther Waters* – rather than a male French chef, for French chefs were only found in the very grandest houses. The kitchen-maid who assisted her (there would also have been a scullery-maid) had to rise early and go to bed late. However, the advantage of her position was that, as Mrs Beeton explained, 'if she be fortunate enough to have over her a kind and clever cook she may very soon learn to perform various little duties connected with cooking operations, which may be of considerable service in fitting her for a more fortunate place'. For it was possible to move up the hierarchy that existed below stairs, and the nearer you got to the top, the pleasanter and less arduous life became. One can only pity a young girl like Esther Waters, starting out on her first place.

Lanhydrock must also have had a dairy-maid, because if we follow the passage round from the kitchen we come to the dairy and dairy scullery. The dairy-maid did not actually milk the cows – that was done by the cowman, who brought her the fresh milk twice a day. Dairies were desirable where they could be afforded because they ensured that the milk, cheese and, particularly, butter used in the house were in an edible condition; the butter bought in London, for instance, was quite often not. With their deliciously cool tiled or even marble walls, their scrupulously clean marble slabs on which to work, their marble dishes for cream, and wooden bowls, butter patters, butter moulds and tubs, country-house dairies must have been very alluring, especially when it was hot outside. The one at Lanhydrock had a marble slab in the centre and a slate shelf around the outside of the room; both were cooled by a rill of cold water. Mistresses often gave dairies special attention, since they were also somewhere for house guests to visit after luncheon. On the other hand, although the temperature was meant to be constant, they were liable to be cold in winter and letters sometimes speak of the difficulty of making butter when the milk had frozen over; but churning by means of a hand-operated butter worker was doubtless warming. ('The dairy-maid will find it advantageous in being at work on churning mornings by five o'clock,' commented Mrs Beeton.) Particular skill was required in thoroughly washing the butter in pure spring water to ensure it was entirely free of whey and so less likely to turn bad. It is noticeable from the Lanhydrock plan that the dairy scullery does not have a door through to the dairy – the dairy-maid had to go out into the passage and through another door before reaching the door to the dairy itself. This was because the dairy scullery was where the vessels used in the dairy were scalded, and the steam would have upset the temperature.

Another room associated with food was the still room, which had its still-room maid. Here jam, cakes and country cordials were made under the eye of the housekeeper (rather than the cook). At Lanhydrock it is next to the housekeeper's own room, which was generally something of a sanctum in view of the housekeeper's importance as head of the female staff, and because the more expensive stores were locked away there, only to be issued on request. So tight a rein was kept in some households that the stores were only given out by the mistress herself. Mrs Loudon, who imagined that the fictitious *ingénue* receiving the advice of *The Lady's Country Companion* would act as housekeeper herself (as was the case in more modest households), describes a housekeeper's room in some detail:

> you will find the store closet a most important place in the country, as it is necessary to lay in larger stores of all the common articles of daily consumption than are ever required in a town, where shops can be sent to on an emergency. Your housekeeper's room should therefore have ranges of cupboards and drawers all round the room, to contain the household linen, china, glass, pickles, preserves, and cakes, tea, coffee, sugar, and in short every article wanted by the family, a store of which is kept. There should be a bureau or desk with drawers beneath, to keep the account-books, receipts for bills, and other papers relating to housekeeping; and on one side of the fireplace you may have a cupboard with iron doors enclosing a range of charcoal stoves, and a small oven for making any dishes in French cookery, or any cakes or preserves that you may take a fancy to do yourself, with the assistance of your maid, apart from the observation of the other servants.

The reason for having cooking equipment for elegant dishes here was that some ladies enjoyed a little cooking but would have suffered a severe loss of caste to have worked in the kitchen, where cooking was for need rather than pleasure.

> . . . In one part you can have a cupboard to open with folding doors like a wardrobe, for keeping tea and sugar and similar articles. There should be shelves in this, on which should stand numerous tin canisters marked with the names of the different articles

they contain. In the upper part should be a shelf suspended by cords passing through holes bored in the corners, for loaves of sugar, or any similar articles likely to be attacked by mice. The common tea should be kept in a chest lined with lead, which may stand in the lower part of the closet, and the finer kinds should be kept in canisters. A bag of raw coffee may also stand on the lower shelf of the closet; but after the coffee is ground it should be kept in a canister, and as far apart from the tea as possible, as, if it is near it, it will give the tea an unpleasant taste.[51]

There might be a coffee mill, although usually this was best in the kitchen.

A similar cupboard to that described was to be set aside for soap and candles. Somewhere would also be needed for canisters of currants and so on for cakes and puddings, and for boxes of almonds and raisins for dessert. 'Sage and other herbs I have found keep best in powder, after they have been dried in an oven.' Since the young mistress-housekeeper lived some way from a town and had therefore to remember everything that was wanted when she sent there, a slate for shopping lists was a good thing.

Under the housekeeper's charge came the housemaids, and in big households such as Lanhydrock the juniors would have been supervised by a head housemaid as well. Their day began with sweeping, polishing, dusting and making up grates in the house – these young girls having to carry heavy coal scuttles for the purpose. It continued with the taking up of hot water for the family when it arose, emptying chamber-pots, washing and possibly scalding them, and making beds; then after luncheon, with a change out of the black dress and white apron into a cotton frock, sewing and mending before laying the table for dinner. The housemaids did not go off duty until taking up a final can of hot water for the bedrooms and putting warming-pans and hot-water bottles, as required, in the beds.

Perhaps because it was only a partial rebuilding rather than a completely new house, Lanhydrock is not a perfect example of the separation of the sexes: in some houses the two halves of the servants' wing were completely segregated, meeting neatly in the middle, so as to speak, at the servants' hall. The butler's pantry and sitting-room were on the top side of the internal service courtyard, near the serving-room; and the brushing-room, for brushing down muddy clothes (particularly after hunting), was on the other side of the passage, by the men's stairs. One of the butler's duties was to take care of the silver, which is why the safe is within his little domain. But the fact that this section for the men servants is no larger reflects the declining use of footmen as the century wore on. Even in the eighteenth century, when they served a purpose, running behind carriages or running with messages, footmen were regarded as an extravagance. They never had as much to do as the poor overworked housemaids, being prized for their size they ate a great deal, and they were likely to flirt. They were largely symbols of prestige, and – as waste came to be seen as one of the great domestic evils in the Victorian period – even such people as could afford them decided to do without them, with the exception of the ultra-smart. But the butler and the valet, or 'gentleman's gentleman', were not so easily dispensed with. Many households also kept a lad to carry coal, chop firewood, clean knives and forks, polish boots and devil for the butler.

It is difficult not to believe that in elaborate houses such as Lanhydrock the life below stairs was not to some degree governed by Parkinson's Law, work expanding in proportion to the number of servants. Efficiency was seen to lie in specialization, so that each servant had some different, well-defined task of his or her own. This required a large number of servants, and once you had them it was always necessary to find something for them to do, or they would become restive and squabble. Also, when everyone was a specialist, any one servant was reluctant to do another servant's work, even when there happened to be no other servant to do it, because that would have been an infringement of dignity. This was summed up in the phrase 'it is not my place'. Even at the level of the suburban residences circumvented by Mrs Panton, it was important to engage a good general servant who could cook, rather than call the same servant the cook and expect her to do a little housework as well. Once called a cook, 'she will cook, but she will not for one moment step out of her province to do anything else whatever'. Moreover, running a large house was as complicated in terms of personalities as running an office or factory today. Where twenty or thirty people were bottled up together seeing each other day in and day out, quarrels were bound to develop, as Stevenson stressed. Such was Dearman Birchall's experience at Bowden Hall in Gloucestershire. As he wrote in his diary for 16 October 1876:

Considered the servant problem. Mrs Newsholm had said that Sandy having left she would not mind coming back. Margaret said Mrs Newsholm was conscientious and well disposed but prejudiced and inclined to listen to tales. Mrs N. said that Sandy's language was shameful and unfit for young girls to hear and he neither could nor did work, leaving all to the footmen to do. Ann said for long servants had set one another against the place. Even Keen was unsettled the first year he was here, and told her he had heard tales enough to induce him to leave ten times. Tothill, although a good worker, had never been a friend of the family and never lost an opportunity of saying and hinting and insinuating things against us, and there was no love lost between Tothill and me. He was very ungrateful, Mrs Newsholm did not think Emily exactly put her in her right place in reference to underlings, and especially the housemaid whom she sometimes took into the store-room.[52]

Bowden was not a particularly large establishment and the possibilities of strife must have been greater in the really large households. Some thought that the answer was to keep your servants as busy as possible by finding yet more work for them to do, perhaps by having more guests to stay and therefore larger dinners. This in turn was likely to entail more expensive equipment, which then had to be used – and so the cycle went on.

It was on account of the principle of specialization that both owners and servants regarded big service wings as ideal in the middle years of the nineteenth century. Only towards the end of the century did owners and their architects start looking for ways to cut down, and even then that process was regarded as peculiarly difficult. The inflexibility of mid-Victorian arrangements can be seen from the plan of a row of houses designed by Kerr for the Grosvenor Estate in London in 1864. The basement contains nearly all the rooms we have seen at Lanhydrock – kitchen, scullery, pantry, larder, storeroom, butler's pantry and safe, beer store, cleaning place, wine cellar, housekeeper's room, stillroom, laundry, servants' hall, men's room and coal vaults. There was a stable and carriage house in the mews at the back, with accommodation for the coachmen and stable-boys on the first floor. But it was all crammed into a far smaller space than was available in a spreading country house, and – especially as the servants' rooms were in a dark basement – it must have been much more unpleasant to work in. The difficulty of cutting down is illustrated by Kerr's criticisms of Woodheyes Park near Manchester, designed by Horace Jones, architect of Tower Bridge and Billingsgate and Smithfield Markets in London, in 1859:

> The service-door in the Dining-room, in respect of its being so closely opposite the Kitchen-door, cannot be commended: if the Passage were wider and the Kitchen-door five or six feet off, with a small service-dresser intervening, convenience would have been better secured; and it may be noted that parsimony of space in such a passageway is especially to be avoided. The position of the Drawing-room door, so very near 'the way out' is unfortunate; as also that of the Dining-room so closely opposite to it. The Kitchen-vapours, to all appearance, must be troublesome. The Morning-room is a welcome feature; but the door and fireplace do not agree in position. The Cloak-room is well worth noting; but it ought rather to have been at the Entrance-end of the Hall if possible. The Back-Stair is not . . . a stair for Bedroom service, but merely an access to the Servants'-rooms.[53]

FIG. 14. Plan of the basement of a house by Kerr on the Grosvenor Estate in London. It illustrates how most of the servants' rooms of a country house could be crammed into the below-stairs region of a large London house.

BASEMENT.

1	Rear vaults for coal and dust	14	Beer
2	Laundry	15	Safe
3	Men's room	16	Wine cellar
4	Bed	17	Open area for light
5	Area	18	Storeroom
6	Stillroom	19	Larder
7	Servants' hall	20	Backstair lift
8	Cleaning place	21	Open area
9	Housemaid's closet	22	Scullery
10	Butler's pantry	23	Pantry
11	Passage	24	Kitchen
12	Housekeeper's room	25	Porch
13	Bedroom	26	Front vaults

```
0    10   20   30   40    50
         feet
0         5         10        15
         metres
```

FILLONGLEY VICARAGE, WARWICKSHIRE

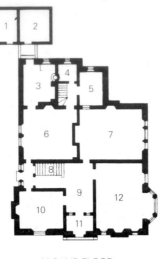

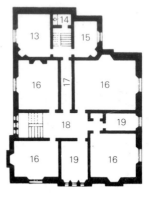

GROUND FLOOR   FIRST FLOOR

1 Coals	11 Porch
2 Larder	12 Drawing-room
3 Scullery	13 Servants' room
4 Pantry	14 WC
5 Butler's pantry	15 Bathroom
6 Kitchen	16 Bedroom
7 Dining-room	17 Passage
8 Staircase	18 Staircase landing
9 Hall	19 Dressing-room
10 Study	

(a)

FIG. 15 (a, b). Plans of (a) Fillongley Vicarage in Warwickshire and
(b) Woodheyes Park near Manchester. The architect, Robert Kerr, who was
the author of *The Gentleman's House*, thought Fillongley Vicarage
a good plan for a small house. The dining-room and drawing-room face south;
the kitchen was as much cut off from the rest as could be expected;
but Kerr criticized Woodheyes Park because the kitchen door was
too near the drawing-room and the drawing-room door was too near the front door.

More successful, however, was Fillongley Vicarage in Warwickshire, a quite
modest house by a Mr Murray. Kerr particularly commended the provision of
a back staircase although the house was small; his only criticisms concerned

WOODHEYES PARK, near MANCHESTER

GROUND FLOOR   FIRST FLOOR

1 Stable	12 Hall and staircase
2 Carriage house	13 Cloakroom
3 Harness	14 WC
4 Yard	15 Drawing-room
5 Pantry	16 Morning-room
6 Larder	17 Men servants' rooms
7 Scullery	18 Servants' rooms
8 Dining-room	19 Bedroom
9 Passage	20 Dressing-room
10 Kitchen	21 Staircase
11 Porch	22 Bathroom

(b)

the WC – one he thought was too few and in any case it was badly placed, among the servants' rooms. With its kitchen, scullery, pantry, butler's pantry, larder and coal store, the vicarage represented about the maximum degree of compression consistent with middle-class habits and expectations.

It was difficult to reduce the servants' rooms because it was impossible to cut down beyond a certain stage on the things that had to be done by servants.

The fewer the servants, the harder they worked. Even Mrs Beeton took pity on the maid of all work who was the only servant of the one-servant household. Her life of drudgery is reflected in the diary of Hannah Cullwick. The entry for Saturday, 14 July 1860, is representative of the whole dreary document:

> Opened the shutters & lighted the kitchen fire. Shook my sooty things in the dusthole & emptied the soot there. Swept & dusted the rooms & the hall. Laid the hearth & got breakfast up. Clean'd 2 pairs of boots. Made the beds & emptied the slops. Clean'd & wash'd the breakfast things up. Clean'd the plate; clean'd the knives & got dinner up. Clean'd away. Clean'd the kitchen up; unpack'd a hamper. Took two chickens to Mrs Brewer's & brought the message back. Made a tart & pick's & gutted two ducks & roasted them. Clean'd the steps & flags on my knees. Blackleaded the scraper in front of the house; clean'd the street flags too on my knees. Wash'd up in the scullery. Clean'd the pantry on my knees & scour'd the tables. Scrubbed the flags around the house & clean'd the window sills. Got tea at 9 for the master & Mrs Warwick in my dirt, but Ann carried it up. Clean'd the privy & passage & scullery floor on my knees. Wash'd the dog & clean'd the sinks down. Put the supper ready for Ann to take up, for I was too dirty & tired to go upstairs. Wash'd in a bath & to bed without feeling any the worse for yesterday [when she had gone to a play].[54]

The next day she records: 'Felt a little stiff this morning but nothing to speak of. I found one or two bruises on my knees but that was all.' Emotionally Hannah Cullwick was not a typical servant, since she could have taken better places if she had wished, but chose not to because of her bizarre relationship with the littérateur and connoisseur of low women, Alfred Munby, for whom the diaries were written. They both took a perverse pleasure in her degradation and she would lick his boots and cover herself in black lead to emphasize it still further. But her work was the same as that undertaken by a great mass of less complicated women, some of whom had the talent and opportunity to better themselves and ease their load but many of whom did not.

The life of a servant in a suburban house, even if not a maid of all work, was 'an extremely dull one', Mrs Panton conceded – 'despite the delirious joy of the tradesman's daily calls'. She continued:

> The routine is everlasting, the relaxations few, and the changes still fewer. In many households a friend to tea is a crime; an unexpected holiday an impossibility; while the days follow each other in a wearisome routine which would tell on the nerves of anyone even far more highly educated than is the orthodox maid-servant.

No wonder young girls stopped going into service as soon as other opportunities for employment gave them the chance to do something else. Mrs Panton urged mistresses to be more considerate, to give their maids the occasional concert or theatre ticket. Yet it was the same Mrs Panton who wrote, in another book, of maids' bedrooms:

I should like myself to give each maid a really pretty room... but, alas! it is impossible. No sooner is the room put nice than something happens to destroy its beauty; and I really believe servants only feel happy if their rooms are allowed in some measure to resemble the homes of their youth, and to be merely places where they lie down to sleep as heavily as they can.[55]

Attitudes, and with attitudes conditions, only altered when the shortage of labour began to bite, and change came too late to save the system. After a decade of near panic among domestic writers, the answer was found to lie in the vacuum cleaners, gas stoves and food-mixers that would help the mistress cope with a less formal way of life. The mistress began to share in the work of the house herself. And if that mistress lived in the suburbs she probably found it took the awful weight of how to find and keep servants off her mind.

◧ FIVE ◨

FROM THE HOUSE BEAUTIFUL TO THE SUBURB SALUBRIOUS

Instead of studying the five orders of architecture, we had far better study the five orders of Englishmen.

C. F. A. Voysey, 'Ideas in Things', in T. Raffles Davison, ed.,
The Arts Connected with Building, 1909

When the German architect Hermann Muthesius wrote his account of domestic architecture in Britain, *Das englische Haus*, at the turn of the century, he observed an 'enormous increase in house-building in England during the past ten or twenty years'. Muthesius had been sent by the German government as a special attaché to their embassy in London to report on this achievement, and he investigated every aspect of the subject with Germanic thoroughness. English middle-class life was regarded as having reached a state of advancement that should be emulated elsewhere in Europe – largely because the English lived in houses rather than flats as on the Continent. This was held to be 'in every way a higher form of life'.

The English house had evolved over centuries and Muthesius believed that, by the early twentieth century, it had reached a kind of perfection. It embodied all the best of what had gone before: the sensitivity to materials and location of the vernacular; the compactness of the villa; the freedom of the Picturesque; the efficiency and hygiene of the modern domestic machine. Of nineteenth-century architects, the one awarded by far the fullest treatment was Norman Shaw. Not for his enormous Baroque country houses like Bryanston in Dorset: Muthesius regretted Shaw's having fallen back on the stylistic language of the past. The work Muthesius most admired was, by contrast, Bedford Park, where 'small' houses were combined with a pleasant, semi-rural environment, and represented a type that could be applied on a fairly large scale. It signified 'neither more nor less than the starting-point of the smaller modern house, which immediately spread from there over the whole country'. Typical of later developments was the Webb estate at Purley, near Croydon, laid out from 1888 by the estate agent, William Webb. There was a village green and a smithy, and for a time geese were kept. With houses standing on broad, winding roads lined with trees and flowers, residents 'not only had the enjoyment of their own premises in desirable seclusion', wrote Webb, 'but . . . it may appear as though they are in one large garden of which their own holding is a part'.

112. Tower House and the lawn tennis grounds at Bedford Park in 1882.
The first garden suburb was famous for its communal life.

By 1914 a flood of books had appeared on the smaller house, particularly the smaller house in the country. It was a genre that seemed particularly well adapted to modern requirements and as such excited the attention of the best young architects of the time. It made its own demands on an architect's ingenuity, to be sure; designing a smaller house was in many ways regarded as more difficult than designing a large one. But an agreeable practice could be sustained by such work, and private clients were likely to be more amenable to innovation and experiment than public bodies.

One of the achievements of Bedford Park was that it helped relax the formality of suburban social life. Almost from the start it was a consciously 'artistic' suburb, one of the communal buildings being the Art School by E. J. May. The other leading institution was the tennis club, where men and women of all ages could meet together informally and perhaps try their hand at what was still a newly invented game. Tennis was to become an important middle-class activity. It responded to the growing interest in healthy exercise, which Muthesius saw as 'the only lasting antidote to the depressing influence of the English climate'. In the 1890s Sir George Sitwell told his most unsporting daughter, Edith, that 'there is nothing a man likes so much as a girl who is good at the parallel bars'.

The traditional field sports of hunting and shooting were expensive, required early training and involved an elaborate social ritual. But tennis and golf – golf being the other growing game of the time – were less extravagant, and therefore better suited to middle-class pockets and consciences. The clubs devoted to them were an asset to social life and even, in some quarters, an index of social status. Their importance was in no way diminished by the fact that the gardens of most houses had room for a private tennis court. 'The possession of a tennis ground has become such an imperative social necessity,' wrote the *Spectator*, as early as 26 July 1884, 'that every wretched little garden-plot is pressed into the service, and courts are religiously traced out in half the meagre back-gardens of the suburbs of London, even though the available space is little bigger than a billiard-table.' It was always necessary to arrange tournaments, to meet friends and perhaps even to find future partners in both senses of the word.

Communities of smaller country houses grew up wherever a good golf-course was made. The resort of Gullane in Lothian depended on the Muirfield Links, and here Lutyens built Greywalls for the aristocratic sportsman Alfred Lyttelton. Golf in Scotland was of longer standing and on many courses (not Muirfield) more democratic than south of the border. In England, exclusive seaside developments catered for dedicated players. The course at Aldeburgh in Suffolk was laid out in the 1880s by the Garrett family, who also developed a small suburb. Several of the houses were designed by Horace Field, the architect of the thatched clubhouse. In Cornwall, the presence of an interesting group of Edwardian houses at Trebetherick is explained by the St Enedoc's Golf Course. Sir John Betjeman's father built a house here in the 1920s; it was designed by another regular visitor, the architect Robert Atkinson.

Among Lutyens's many commissions were two for golf clubhouses, at Knebworth and at Renishaw, where the Lyttons and the Sitwells respectively were exploiting the new enthusiasm. At Walton Heath, Surrey, he built the Dormy House in 1906 as a residential annexe to the clubhouse, and at Walton-on-the-Hill a house called Chussex which overlooked the course.

More energetic forms of exercise were also coming into vogue. Some houses had fives or squash courts, while Parker and Unwin's Hilltop at Caterham in

1. Semi-rural, before the Town Invasion.   2. Some of the Invaders.   3. Outposts of the Attack.   4. In the Workshops.
5. The Growing Town.   6. Cricket-Field at West Kensington.   7. Workmen's Dwellings.   8. Lawn Tennis Club.

GROWING LONDON : SKETCHES IN THE WESTERN SUBURBS.

113. Nature tamed – wild woodland gives way to a new suburb complete with tennis courts,
shown here at Barons Court, West London, in 1884.

114. Physical exercise making its impact on the living rooms of the house.
At Hilltop, Caterham, the client W. E. Steers was a devotee of ju-jitsu
and made his gymnasium, decorated with forest scenes, the largest room in the house.

Surrey possessed a gymnasium decorated with murals of forest scenes –
presumably as a setting for the noble savage exercising therein. A gentleman's
dressing-room would probably be large enough for him to swing an Indian
club, and Swedish exercises – for which an institute was established in London
– attracted adherents in increasing numbers. The novelty of many Edwardian
sports, games and ways of exercise – including bicycling – was that ladies took
part. Their mothers had been restricted by conventions of dress to archery and
croquet, which were decorous and showed them to advantage. The cause of
dress reform was helped by the need for looser clothes for sports – although
these clothes would of course still seem restrictive today.

Fresh air and sunshine were as important inside the house as out. As the
architect Arnold Mitchell wrote in 1904, 'we cannot open our British homes
too generously to the sun's light and heat'. Muthesius was astonished by the
'English hankering for fresh air', which was 'shared by all classes'. He thought
it would have seemed excessive to his fellow countrymen. The English slept
with the window open – 'even in winter they open sash windows about an
inch at the top and sometimes at the bottom too'.

One reason for this obsession was the fear of tuberculosis. Although it was not yet known that the disease was carried in milk, the discovery had been made that it could be held at bay and even cured by quantities of pure air. This was an additional incentive for living outside the fogs of London, Manchester or Leeds, particularly when bringing up children. Once in the country, full advantage was taken of the fresh air by means of open-air sleeping balconies, large french windows opening on to terraces, and verandahs (the last were also useful for tennis parties). If they did not think it positively harmful, the mid-Victorians were as indifferent to fresh air as, apparently, to the warming effects of the sun on their rooms. It is not unusual for mid-nineteenth-century houses – such as Philip Webb's famous Red House, built for Morris – to face north. By contrast, Edwardian houses were nearly always oriented towards the south. To ensure the maximum entry of sunlight, a plan type known as the 'butterfly' or 'sun-trap' was evolved, after a hint from the ever-resourceful Norman Shaw at Chesters, in Northumberland. To this house Shaw added a great curving colonnade. The colonnade wall had no windows, but it suggested a development to Shaw's eccentric pupil E. S. Prior – a former high-jump blue at Cambridge. He built The Barn, Exmouth, 1895–7, with a canted front, and followed this

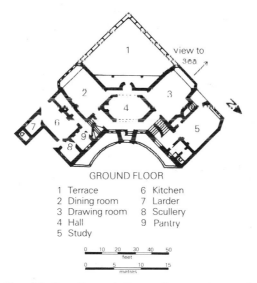

GROUND FLOOR

1 Terrace   6 Kitchen
2 Dining room   7 Larder
3 Drawing room   8 Scullery
4 Hall   9 Pantry
5 Study

FIG. 16. Plan of the Barn, Exmouth, Devon, of 1895–7. An example of the Arts and Crafts 'butterfly' or 'sun-trap' plan whereby the facades were curved to let as much fresh air and sunlight as possible into the house. Butterfly-plan houses were particularly suitable for the seaside.

comparatively small (but, because of Prior's unorthodox building methods, expensive) house with the much larger Home Place, Holt, in Norfolk, of 1903–5. The Barn no longer has its original thatched roof – although Prior covered it with an 'incombustible solution', it burnt in 1905. This type of plan appealed to radical architects. Describing his double sun-trap plan (producing an X-shaped house) for Happisburgh Manor, Norfolk, Detmar Blow said that it 'originated with my friend Mr Ernest Gimson who sent the little butterfly device on a postcard'.

Butterfly-plan houses were for the most part near the coast, where the owners could additionally benefit from the bracing air. Other attractions of the seaside were that it offered the best golf – on links courses – and there were opportunities for sailing. Exclusive resorts of large houses, like Frinton in Essex, took the lead in desirability from the popular Victorian seaside towns. At Rye the architect and dedicated sportsman Reginald Blomfield built himself a small cliff-side house from which to hunt and play cricket; there he knew Henry James, who had taken the lease of Lamb House – a little Georgian box with a walled garden – in 1897. Further along the south coast, another writer, H. G. Wells, had what he called 'a bright and comfortable pseudo-cottage' at Sandgate in Kent, designed by C. F. A. Voysey. He called it Spade House, having insisted that Voysey's favourite cut-out heart motif on the shutters was turned upside-down.

Some of the best-known smaller houses are by Voysey, who built little else. Voysey, C. R. Mackintosh and M. H. Baillie Scott – the other two also having been much involved with smaller houses – have been hailed as the 'pioneers of the Modern Movement', and indeed their influence on the Continent was enormous. Muthesius admired them enthusiastically, although he slightly feared the effect of their mannerisms on less brilliant followers. Voysey was a Puritan and advanced social thinker. His houses, with their white walls and low ceilings, were deliberately based on cottages rather than mansions. All the furniture, wallpaper and fittings – down to the door-knocker – was specially designed by the architect to achieve a harmonious whole. On the scrubbed oak chairs there was little in the way of upholstery or cushions: bodily luxury took second place to the moral uplift of the inhabitants. This outlook had less in common with Norman Shaw than with his contemporary, Philip Webb. But whereas Webb's work was never published in magazines, Voysey's regularly appeared in the *Studio* – a general magazine of art and decoration which would have influenced the taste of artistic clients. Hence the propagation of his characteristic roughcast and cottagey look throughout Britain down to the Second World War.

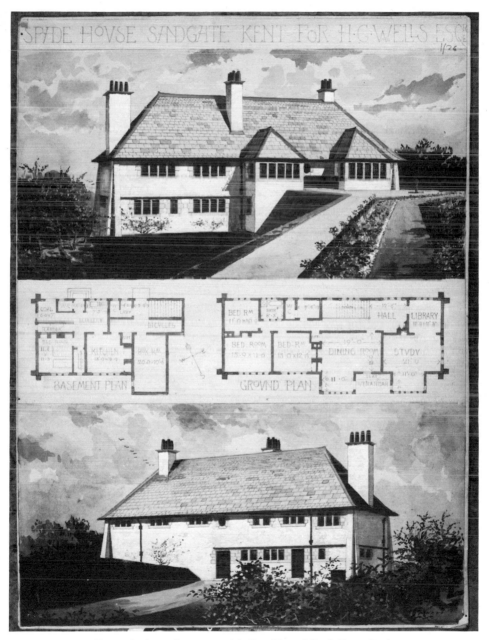

115. Progressive house for a progressive client. Voysey's Spade House, Sandgate,
for H. G. Wells, 1899.

Voysey helped to inspire continental Art Nouveau; but it was a movement that he and all his English contemporaries deplored. Only in Scotland did the style of sinuous lines and the whiplash curve take root, and even there to no lasting effect. C. R. Mackintosh was in many ways Voysey's Scottish equivalent – both were difficult, crochety characters. Aspects of Mackintosh's style might be called Art Nouveau – although the exteriors of his houses were in a stylized rendering of the Scottish vernacular, with harling, crowstepped gables and small windows. The interiors had some of the Art Nouveau's insistent linear qualities but with the rigid discipline of straight lines rather than curves. The famous Mackintosh chairs, which have straight, very tall backs, share the exaggeration of Art Nouveau. However, Mackintosh's inspiration came not from Vienna (where he was widely acclaimed) but from Japan. In this he was virtually alone among British architects; it can be seen in his free-flowing spaces, his use of screens, grid patterns and wood, and his love of the colour black.

116. An Arts and Crafts interior where every surface is decorated.
Design for the dining-room at Birkby Lodge, Huddersfield, 1901.
The architect, Edgar Wood, was a Morris admirer, who practised in Manchester.

All these themes can be seen at the Hill House, Helensburgh, a substantial villa built for the publisher W. W. Blackie. Here the principal reception rooms were entirely designed and furnished in Mackintosh's daring, extreme, manner; but it has recently been discovered that the family retained their comfortable Victorian furniture of a previous house for the dining-room and some of the bedrooms — a refuge for when the high art and high-backed chairs became too much.

Like Mackintosh and to some extent Voysey, Baillie Scott succeeded in giving his houses a distinctive look both inside and out; his work was altogether more comfortable and prettier in the use of colours. It depended on built-in furniture, exposed woodwork and the use of simplified natural patterns on fabrics and wall panels. The effect of the patterns was not so obsessive as in a William Morris interior, but was relieved with areas of white wall. He invented the cosy image of the Tudor half-timbered interior, which quickly came to seem almost elemental in its appeal to the hearts of English home makers. He

117. The hall at Everdene, 1905, by M. H. Baillie Scott.
Of the plan of this house, he wrote that 'the claims of romance
seem to meet most happily economical limitations'.

also introduced to the smaller houses Norman Shaw's concept of the multi-purpose hall, which combined entrance hall, staircase hall, living-room and even dining-room (the dining-table being set in an alcove). The modern architect 'looks back on the houses of the past,' wrote Baillie Scott in *Houses and Gardens.*

. . . And his first step is to revive the hall, but to revive it with a difference. It is to be a room where the family can meet together – a general gathering-place with its large fireplace and ample floor space. It must no longer be a passage . . . Whether it is called hall, houseplace, or living-room, some such apartment is a necessary feature as a focus to the plan of the house.

Scott further recommended that rooms

which do not demand a strict division from the hall should be divided from it by folding or sliding doors, or even by curtains, so that they share in its spaciousness and appear rather as recesses than rooms claiming a separate individuality.

This flexibility had already been successfully adopted in American houses, notably those by Stanford White.

The great attraction of the living hall – yet another name for this room – was that, by amalgamating a number of rooms, it was a way of making comparatively modest houses seem spacious. One may debate whether, in larger houses, the living hall was much used, since there was probably also a sitting-room or drawing-room. In practice its role was probably more that of the second sitting-room that it replaced, and which was necessary in large families as a place of escape for members who wished to be by themselves or to entertain friends without disturbing everyone else. (As late as 1926, in a book called *The Smaller House of To-Day*, Gordon Allen wrote that a second sitting-room was desirable on grounds of privacy: 'among other difficulties,' should there be only one sitting-room, was 'entertaining casual visitors who are not wanted in the family circle'.) Even so, it implied a greater informality in the way the family lived and entertained than the Edwardian norm. Because of its ambiguous character, sportsmen in muddy clothes could stand there with a cup of tea or a whisky and soda before going up to change – something that would not have been acceptable in the drawing-room.

Striking though Voysey, Mackintosh and Baillie Scott seem to us, their stylistic purism was not popular with the majority of middle-class clients. Most people's ideal was an unostentatious, soundly constructed house, which openly displayed its affinities with the past, and was quite probably intended as a setting both for antique furniture and for the not very innovative codes of Edwardian social life. They required at least one formal drawing-room to receive calls, and a conventional hall through which to process arm in arm to the dining-room when there was a party for dinner. What went out, in comparison to the larger houses of the previous generation, were billiard-

rooms and ballrooms, while the library, study and smoking-room tended to
merge into one all-purpose male room – sometimes called the den, after the
American pattern. Where there was no second drawing-room, morning-room
or boudoir, the drawing-room was generally renamed the sitting-room, living-
room or, in some cases, parlour.

As regards style, Norman Shaw and Ernest George had already established
the ground rules for domestic architects of the next generation, many of whom
they had personally trained. There were two possibilities. On the one hand,
from the old-fashioned vernacular of the Home Counties could be taken
hipped roofs, tile-hanging, leaded lights and a little half-timbering (not too
much). Houses of this kind were asymmetrical. On the other hand, a more
formal manner was offered by red brick, sash windows, quoins and a dashing
Baroque doorcase on the front elevation. These elements derived from the
early eighteenth century, and sometimes Edwardian Classical houses look
deceptively like their models – although the reduction in ceiling heights could
cause a change in the proportion of the windows, especially on the upper
storey. Also, the plan was different because of the Edwardian need for a service
wing for arrangements which would have been accommodated in the basement
of the Georgian equivalent.

Though the neo-vernacular and neo-Georgian types derived from widely
differing stock, the elements could be crossed from one to the other, and a
number of architects, particularly in the 1890s, deliberately blurred the
divisions. After 1905 attitudes hardened and the more formal neo-Georgian
style took the lead. With a King George once more on the throne after 1911,
neo-Georgian seemed doubly right. As Lawrence Weaver remarked: 'in our
Georgian day our mental attitude accords closely with that of our Georgian
forefathers'.[56]

By the early twentieth century both neo-vernacular and neo-Georgian had
become so deeply ingrained that many architects thought less about how a
house looked than how it was made. The real excitement of building came
from working to the highest standards with traditional materials and enjoying
the colours and textures that they provide. Long-neglected crafts like lead-
working for rainwater heads, flashing beneath windows and garden tanks was
revived, the speciality of the architect F. W. Troup. Apart from size, this was
the principal difference between the younger generation's work and that of
Shaw and George. It became important that buildings should look as though
they naturally belonged to the place they were built. Above all they should
never obtrude. Muthesius was forcibly struck by the reticence of the English
character as he saw it:

118. Bishopbarns, Walter Brierley's own house in York. Here the elaborate brickwork
was derived from Tudor examples; elsewhere he worked equally happily in neo-Georgian style.

The Englishman builds his house for himself alone ... he even avoids attracting
attention to his house by means of striking design or architectonic extravagance, just as
he would be loth to appear personally eccentric by wearing a fantastic suit.

In some quarters this point of view lasted until well after the Second World
War. 'Let us avoid being extreme, even if it does pay in these vulgar days to be
sensational,' urged Sir Giles Scott in 1933; 'let us beware of too much
machinery, and let us aim at quality rather than novelty . . .'[57]
Although based in London, architects such as Mervyn Macartney,
C. H. B. Quennell, Halsey Ricardo, Gerald Horsley, Arnold Mitchell, R. Weir
Schultz and Ernest Newton were keenly aware of local traditions. Prior and
the early Detmar Blow went to the length of trying to build only from
materials found on the site. Outside London there were regional practices of
strong local character – Bedford and Kitson in Leeds, Bateman and Bateman in
Birmingham, W. H. Brierley in York, C. E. Mallows in Bedford, R. S. Lorimer

and John Kinross in Edinburgh, and Harold Faulkner in Farnham. Guy Dawber moved to Moreton-in-Marsh after working as Ernest George's clerk of works at Batsford Park, and Ernest and Sidney Barnsley and Ernest Gimson established themselves in a Cotswold village to live simply and practise rural crafts and building.

It was a time of much talent in architecture, with a figure of genius appearing in Edwin Lutyens. Muthesius saw Lutyens as in love with the past, even as a slightly dangerous and subversive nostalgic. But to English contemporaries he appeared the man who revitalized the architectural content of the smaller house. This he did by using the conventional elements of neo-vernacular and neo-Georgian, but injecting ingredients of his own – especially a dazzling sense of geometry – to make them very much more exciting. He did indeed have a knack for playing with motifs from the past, as Muthesius said; but the German did not describe the extraordinary mental agility with which he composed three-dimensional shapes or his sophistication in making flat patterns by, for instance, the skilful placing of windows in a facade. Architecturally there is so much going on in a Lutyens house that often those who know it only from photographs are surprised when first visiting one that it is often quite small – the thrill of the design would lead you to expect a very much larger building. Sometimes Lutyens was reticent in style, sometimes he chose to go for big effects – whichever the case his houses always command attention, if only from the way he made the most unexpected things seem natural, even inevitable.

Lutyens came from Surrey, the county that meant more than any other to the development of the smaller Edwardian house. Its lanes were full of vernacular farmhouses and cottages which could be sketched and quarried for details; it was also already a favourite haunt of businessman house-builders who could reach the City by train. Such people did not wish to rival the aristocracy by surrounding themselves by landed estates – farming was in any case less profitable than it had been before 1870. In Surrey it was indeed the areas least suited to agriculture that became most prized for their wild beauty and rural charm. Today perhaps the best way to see the county is by helicopter, since its houses – hidden away among pine woods – are invisible equally from the road and from each other. In Surrey Lutyens built his first houses. From the Surrey vernacular he derived the deep roofs – sweeping around corners and meeting at angles – that are one of the hallmarks of his early style.

In 1890 he met the gardener and craftswoman Gertrude Jekyll, with whom he established an immediate sympathy. The house which he built for her six years later at Munstead Wood shows how she had restrained his playful nature

119. Munstead Hut, Surrey, sketch design by Edwin Lutyens, 1892. A romantic evocation
of a Surrey cottage where the great gardener, Gertrude Jekyll, lived in simplicity
before building the more famous Munstead Wood.

and taught him to look at the example of Philip Webb. Miss Jekyll herself
described the house in what should be regarded as a classic statement of Arts
and Crafts ideals:

... it is designed and built in the thorough and honest spirit of the good work of old
days, and the body of it . . . has, as it were, taken to itself the soul of a more ancient
dwelling place. The house is not in any way a copy of any old building, though it
embodies the general characteristics of the older structures of its own district.

Everything about it is strong and serviceable, and looks and feels as if it would wear
and endure for ever.[58]

It was built by an old-fashioned country builder, who seasoned his own wood,
chose it with the architect, and shaped it by hand with side-axe and adze.
Thereafter Lutyens and Gertrude Jekyll worked together on numerous houses
and gardens, Lutyens providing the architectural framework for Jekyll's
planting. This planting was a refinement of the traditional English cottage
garden. By Lutyens and others (notably Reginald Blomfield), the old formal
traditions of garden design were rediscovered as a means of uniting the house

and the landscape immediately surrounding it. Jekyll furthered Lutyens's career by introducing him to her gardening contacts, some of whom wanted houses. She also put him in the way of Edward Hudson, proprietor of the newly founded magazine *Country Life*, which at once began to champion his work with a tenacity unknown before in English publishing. Hudson, in turn, commissioned three of Lutyens's finest houses – Deanery Gardens at Sonning, in Berkshire, the remodelling of Lindisfarne Castle, off the Northumberland coast, and Plumpton Place in Sussex – as well as the neo-English Renaissance ('Wrenaissance' as Lutyens called it) former *Country Life* office in Covent Garden.

By the turn of the century Lutyens was playing the vernacular and Classical styles against each other with such sophistication that it is impossible to give some buildings a stylistic label. An example of this is Homewood in Hertfordshire, the house he built for his mother-in-law, the dowager Lady Lytton, in 1900. The duality remained with him all his life; but at Heathcote, outside Ilkley – a villa for a cotton broker – he rose to the intellectual challenge of the Classical orders, which he described as 'the high game'. In a less monumental manner, The Salutation in Sandwich, Kent – built for two bachelor brothers in 1911 – is a dazzlingly suave yet restrained reinterpretation of the old Georgian ideal and it was much emulated.

Two years earlier he had begun the stone-built Castle Drogo in Devon, which, although much reduced from the original design by the time it was finished in 1935, is still enormous. The client, Julius Drewe of the Home and Colonial Stores, wanted a real castle, flung up on a promontory and built as the medieval castle masons would have done. 'God keep the Feudal and preserve all that is best in it,' wrote Lutyens to his wife, while personally sympathizing with clients who preferred smaller houses. The sharply cut granite surfaces gave Lutyens a supreme opportunity to allow his geometrical imagination, as well as his inborn romanticism, free rein.

Obviously few could hope to rival the extravagance of Castle Drogo. By contrast the house that held most for Lutyens's many imitators was the earlier Middlefield in Cambridgeshire, a Classical building that was somewhat smaller than The Salutation. It had been commissioned by a Trinity Hall don in 1908, and the design was basically Georgian, interpreted with a supreme sense of geometry. An exaggeratedly low roof sweeps down on either side of the entrance front, in the centre of which is a Baroque doorcase; through the roof rise three magnificently tall chimneys. Two small wings come forward either side to form a courtyard. Seen from either front or back it looks immensely grand; but from the side it reveals itself as being relatively small. It is only one

120. The Salutation, Sandwich, by Edwin Lutyens, 1911. The most compact and formal design
by England's greatest domestic architect.

121. Middlefield, near Cambridge, the beau ideal of the Edwardian 'small country house', by Edwin Lutyens, 1908.

room deep, the hall having been turned into an entrance corridor. It was a clever plan, and one that was to be repeated all over the country as a solution to one of the great challenges of early-twentieth-century house building: how to give an imposing front to a relatively modest country house.

The majestic chimney-stacks at Middlefield were indicative of what Muthesius, as a German, saw as the pleasant irrationality of the English in their love of open fires. Since the climate did not require a more efficient method of heating, the fireplace survived as 'the domestic altar before which, daily and hourly, [the Englishman] sacrifices to the household gods'. Every room, including the bathroom, was expected to have one. The need for the flues to emerge in impressive chimney-stacks on the skyline allowed little freedom in the grouping of rooms. Furthermore, internal doors had to be placed so as not to create draughts between them and the fire. The smaller house looked deceptively simple, but to achieve that simplicity required the ingenuity of a specialized mind. In 1906 Leonard Stokes commented on students at the Architectural Association designing projects for small country houses – a type that had defeated many a full-grown architect. Muthesius was not unaware of the problems: 'The mutual positions of the fireplace, door and window,' he wrote of the drawing-room, 'are again the most important considerations in the specific design . . . and to meet every need would involve the planner in a web of difficulties from which even the most astute could only extricate himself with a compromise.'

Even a bedroom required the most elaborate consideration:

When designing the bedroom it is important to establish the position of the bed or beds . . . The English bed always stands with the head against the wall and the long sides jutting into the room clear of the wall. It is also an acknowledged rule in England that the bed must be so placed that the occupant does not face the window, for he would find it extremely disagreeable to be dazzled on waking. Yet this rule, which must seem a matter of course for every bedroom in the world, is very often broken in England. In England there seems often to be no alternative to placing the bed with the foot towards the window, since one of the walls lying at right-angles to the window is taken up by the fireplace and the other by the door into the dressing-room. There is no great harm in this position if the windows are closed by light-proof shutters at night. Some people also prefer it for another reason: it is a certain guarantee that the occupant of the bed will not be exposed to the draught.

122. Sir George Bullough's bedroom at Kinloch Castle on the Isle of Rhum. The Edwardian bedroom embodied more functional niceties than meet the eye.

Yet there can be no doubt that the only proper position for the bed is with the head against a side wall and the plan of the room must without fail provide for this. This having been established, English opinion further requires the left side of the bed in double bedrooms near the window. The reason for this is that the conjugal bedroom in England is always used as a dressing-room by the woman and the furniture that she needs for her toilette, such as wash-stand, dressing-table and wardrobe, stand next to the window. As we shall see, the dressing-table, indeed, stands right in the window. The woman therefore takes the side of the bed nearest to her part of the room and since by ancient custom the woman sleeps on the man's left, the bed must stand with its left-hand half on the window side . . . The door into the man's dressing-room is in the wall nearest to the right-hand side of the bed.

For the rest, the relative positions of the doors, windows and fireplace are subject to the general principles that we have already mentioned. A sharp lookout is kept, however, to ensure that the door opens with its back towards the bed and not the other way, for the desire to avoid embarrassing situations is specially apposite here. The modern English custom whereby a maid takes an early cup of tea to the couple's bedside before they rise makes the point clearly enough.

If, all these requirements having been met, the English were self-satisfied with the state of their domestic architecture in the years before the outbreak of the First World War, it was not perhaps without reason.

New House or Old?

But there was another aspect to Edwardian domestic architecture that should have sounded a warning note in the profession. A number of people did not want a new house at all but something with all the mystery and romance of age; the manor-house came to the fore after a long period of neglect. During the eighteenth and nineteenth centuries many stone-built late-medieval or Renaissance houses – especially those in the once-prosperous sheep-rearing counties that had subsequently become poor, remote and unfashionable – had fallen from their gentlemanly status and were in use as farmhouses. Frequently they were dilapidated and in poor structural condition. They might be surrounded with duckponds and cowsheds, and their halls with fine timbered roofs might be divided up into smaller compartments. Dorset in particular had many examples. Towards the end of the nineteenth century, however, there appeared a breed of enterprising new owner prepared to buy such buildings and take them in hand. They restored or, as they would have preferred to say, 'repaired' with sensitivity, respecting the fabric of the old work. Where additions had to be made, they were done with scholarship, and the greatest care was taken not to disturb the mellow harmony of the building as it stood. Architects were employed, but the impetus generally came from the owner himself; the approach was that of Ruskin and Morris and the Society for the Protection of Ancient Buildings (founded in 1877), and it often went with the collecting of oak and Queen Anne furniture for the rooms that had been restored. Gardening, particularly topiary, was also important.

Alfred Cart de Lafontaine, who bought Athelhampton in 1891, was an early romantic restorer. His work is described in Charles Latham's *In English Homes* (introduced and edited by H. Avray Tipping) of 1908: 'To have saved from destruction this rare specimen of a Gothic age, to have carefully brought it back to a semblance of its ancient self, to have collected so large a number of apt and excellent pieces of genuinely old furniture has been a triumph of patient endeavour and enlightened taste.' It was an ideal. Avray Tipping, who was himself an architect, restored three houses in Monmouthshire; another 'collector' of old houses was Col. F. B. de Sales La Terrière. Other turn-of-the-century restorations include Lytes Cary in Somerset; Avebury and Great Chalford in Wiltshire; Sandford Orcas, Chantmarle and Cranborne in Dorset; and Hidcote in Gloucestershire. Lutyens restored Lindisfarne on Holy Island off the Northumberland coast for Edward Hudson, the proprietor of *Country Life* – a magazine which was doing much to promote these values. In 1902 Rudyard Kipling bought Bateman's, a not markedly distinguished but old, weathered and irresistible house in Sussex (illustrated on the cover). It is dated 1634. 'We had seen an advertisement of her, and we reached her down an enlarged rabbit-hole of a lane,' Kipling wrote in *Something of Myself*.

At very first sight the Committee of Ways and Means [Mrs Kipling and himself] said: 'That's her! The Only She! Make an honest woman of her – quick!' We entered and felt her Spirit – her *Feng Shui* – to be good. We went through every room and found no shadow of ancient regrets, stifled miseries, nor any menace though the 'new' end of her was three hundred years old.

However, Kipling was not one to live wholly in the past or anything like it; he arrived in his Locomobile and had electricity generated by a turbine designed with the advice of his friend Sir William Willcocks, who had previously dammed the Nile at Aswan.

Indeed it is interesting that, with his go-ahead ideas, he should have fallen in love with Bateman's, but it was the perfect image of England – the kind of image, perhaps, that would inspire men in the outposts of the Empire to do stirring deeds.

And the image has endured. Bateman's and the other Edwardian romantic restorations (one must also include, supremely, Sissinghurst from the inter-war period) represent an ideal that is still potent today. Under the hand of a gifted owner, the past is brought into harmony with the present; and depending as it does on the passing effects of time on walls, on furniture and in the garden, the result is all the more beautiful for being transient. It is one of the great achievements of the English House.

Since the Edwardian period many of those seeking to acquire a gentlemanly house have preferred not to build from new.

THE TWENTIES

After the war several years passed before building work returned to its former level of activity. Materials, particularly timber, were in short supply and the cost of building had more than doubled. Despite this, clients seemed to want much the same sort of house as before, and they were able to get it. Coleton Fishacre in Devon, built by Lutyens's former assistant Oswald P. Milne, is an example – reticent, well-crafted, built of local materials on a modified butterfly plan.

The effects of post war shortages can be seen in a simplification of the bold profiles and complex shapes of the Edwardians. This corresponded with a change in taste in favour of less elaborate decoration and furnishings.

A detailed fictional case-study of a house built in 1924–5, when house building had only recently resumed, is found in *The Honeywood File*. This epistolary novel by H. B. Cresswell, an architect turned writer, was serialized in the *Architects' Journal* and has been in print almost continuously since. The client is a financier, Sir Leslie Brash, the tyro architect a promising but inexperienced young man, James Spinlove. He is just out of one of the newly popular architectural schools, but is quite content to build the brick-and-tile Honeywood Grange in Surrey in a continuation of the Edwardian manner. The question of style is taken for granted in the correspondence, and occupies a small part compared to the financial and administrative difficulties of getting the house built. Obstacles to be negotiated, apart from the feather-brained Lady Brash, are an interfering district surveyor – symbol of the increasing power of bureaucracy – and the machinations of the rejected jerry-builder, Nibnose and Rasper. Time and again the situation is saved by the intervention of Grigblay the builder, himself an Edwardian survival, who resents Spinlove's affectation of a 'sham medieval' roof-line to give the appearance of age. Budgets for houses like Honeywood were generally tighter after the war, and the architect's difficulties are in part a reflection of this. On one memorable, and

123. The National Trust's most modern historic house, Coleton Fishacre,
on the south Devon coast. Built for the second-generation hotel and opera impresario
Rupert D'Oyly-Carte by Oswald Milne, an assistant of Lutyens,
who used a more up-to-date 'jazz modern' when working for the same client at Claridges.

fatal, occasion Brash is more inclined to listen to a friend in the City who
suggested a way of saving a few pounds than to his professional adviser.

If a difference began to emerge in smaller houses after the war, it was that
the framework of architectural styles seemed to become slightly unhinged.
While the broad stylistic divisions of neo-vernacular and neo-Georgian still
held good, each was practised with a heightened self-consciousness which
amounted at times to self-parody. Signs of this could be seen before the war,
when young architects like Alwyn Ball and A. Winter Rose (both of whom
were killed in action), Oliver Hill, Clough William Ellis and H. S. Goodhart-
Rendel had refined the accepted styles in a spirit of affectionate mockery –

which was in some ways the architectural parallel of Rupert Brooke's *Grantchester*. After the war they became the leaders of the profession in the domestic sphere, replacing Lutyens and his generation.

Oliver Hill is of particular interest as a practitioner of all the styles of the time. Immediately after the war he built the wildly romantic and expressionist house, Cour, in Argyllshire, which was stone-built and drew on elements of Scottish fortified houses. This is perhaps an exceptional house in his *oeuvre*, built in a serious Arts and Crafts spirit. By contrast, the exaggerated folksiness of Croyde in Devon, a thatched seaside house for two lady playwrights, dramatizes the local vernacular. At Woodhouse Copse, Surrey, can be seen irregular elm boards and a clever use of other textures on a rambling plan – it is a dream cottage almost too good to be true. His later addition to Higher Traine in Devon is described by Sir Nikolaus Pevsner as 'somewhat crazy'. Hill's neo-Georgian, seen in two houses at Aldeburgh, owed much to Lutyens but introduced a period element of streamlining. Maryland in Surrey he built in a Spanish folk-style, in tune with the growing taste for the Mediterranean. There may even be influences from Normandy in 41 Chelsea Square, one of his several fashionable London houses which pioneered the 'Vogue Regency' style of interiors with luxurious mirrored bathrooms. We shall see later his suave adoption of the Moderne.

The historiography of 1920s houses owes much to Sir Osbert Lancaster for his invention of terms like 'Wimbledon Transitional', and above all 'Pseudish' – a combination of Swedish, Spanish and neo-Georgian. A master of this style was Philip Hepworth, an architect working somewhat in Hill's shadow. In Bishop's Avenue, Hampstead, he built three houses with characteristic green-tiled roofs and white walls, although the composition of the largest of them, Eliot House, of 1925, is derived with little alteration from Lutyens's Middlefield.

Both as man and architect, Oliver Hill was an original. But his houses, various though they were, occupy a curiously central position in the period. At either fringe were hints of fantasy. Neo-vernacular finds an extreme in the work of Blunden Shadbolt and Ernest Trobridge. The former, who worked largely around Crawley in Surrey, specialized in the re-use of old tiles and timbers, creating new houses to twentieth-century plans which nevertheless looked as though they had been standing for several hundred years. Roof-ridges sagged, walls were out of true, moss grew on the tiles (which were probably taken from old barns and carefully moved so that the patina would not be disturbed). It was the kind of work that often met with objections from the district surveyor, who frowned upon 'wibbly-wobbly' architecture which

124 and 125. Extremes of the inter-war architectural spectrum in two Surrey houses by Oliver Hill: *above*, Woodhouse Copse, Holmbury St Mary, 1924, and, *below*, Holthanger, Wentworth, 1935.

126. Stage set of the English house ideal: homespun, lived-in, open to the garden,
with a tennis racket casually thrown down on a friendly old chair,
at Oliver Hill's Merryfield House, Witney, Oxfordshire, 1927.

looked as though it was about to fall down. Builders like the honest Grigblay in *The Honeywood File* were sometimes baffled, too. The *locus classicus* of the Shadbolt style is P. A. Barron's *The House Desirable* of 1929, which records numerous examples seen by the author – who, typically, was an enthusiastic motorist and therefore by no means medieval in life-style – on motor-car rambles around the Surrey and Sussex lanes. Barron describes the difficulties involved:

Work such as this [he wrote of Shadbolt's Smuggler's Way in Hampshire, now demolished] needs a great deal of supervision, for everything has to be done in an unusual manner. Workmen have to be trained to forget all their conventional ideas. At first it seems to them that they are being asked to do everything as badly as possible. Instead of laying perfectly even courses of bricks of uniform colour, they have to use bricks which do not match, and to lay them crookedly, 'any which way', as I have heard them say. Chipped bricks, or broken bricks, which they have been taught to discard, must be built in with the sound ones. Timbers which are crooked, and so weatherworn that they look unsound, are chosen especially for prominent positions, and nice, clean wood, smooth and straight, is only used in places where it cannot be seen. To men who have never before seen work of this class, such methods are heartbreaking; but, as a rule, when they have begun to realize the architect is not mad but has a definite object in view, they show keen interest in the extraordinary tasks they are asked to perform. The work is difficult, and therefore engrossing. As I once heard a man say: 'It's a sight harder to do things wrong than to do them right.'

Shadbolt's house at the Ideal Home Exhibition of 1924, which was visited by George V, was re-erected as Monk's Rest in Pinner.

Pinner was also the centre of Trobridge's practice, which was for the most part concerned with small suburban houses of high individuality. They are very irregular and are crowded with vernacular motifs, unless they are disguised as castles. Their architectural density in some ways recalls the Regency *cottage orné*. The architect also pioneered a form of building using unseasoned elm to help with the post-war housing shortage, which met with some recognition from the Ministry of Works.

Shadbolt and Trobridge were not alone: Amyas Phillips, an antique dealer, built a large seaside house for Lord Moyne called Bailiffscourt, near Littlehampton, Sussex, between 1929 and 1931. Again it incorporated old windows, doors and ceilings, most of which came either from Hitchin, Phillips's own town, or Somerset, where he had recently spent his honeymoon.

But not all the further reaches of the neo-vernacular were so extreme. Imrie and Angell, for instance, also used old materials, but their houses in Esher and Weybridge and elsewhere are calmer and more genuinely craftsmanlike and comfortable. Thatch – scarcely a traditional feature of Surrey – was a recurrent motif both in their work and in that of many others.

127. Monk's Rest, Pinner, 1926, built by the neo-vernacular specialist, Blunden Shadbolt,
from old materials taken from a ruined house at Horley.

The taste owes something to the Edwardian sensitivity to the texture of materials. It also reflects the change that, since the late nineteenth century, had come upon the Englishman's domestic ideal. Increasing numbers of people preferred old houses – especially half-timbered ones – to new. But they were not prepared to do without twentieth-century comforts, so the old houses were enlarged – sometimes sympathetically, often making the place an infinitely more romantic and 'perfect' embodiment of Tudor England than it had begun. Jerome K. Jerome made one of his characters in *They and I* (1909) say:

> This house that I have bought is not my heart's desire, but about it there are possibilities. We will put in lattice windows, and fuss-up the chimneys. Maybe we will let in a tablet over the door, with a date – 1553 always looks well: it is a picturesque figure, the old-fashioned five. By the time we have done with it – for all practical purposes – it will be a Tudor manor-house. I have always wanted an old Tudor manor-house.

The dilettante collector and decorator George Crawley had a genius for this work, having enlarged Crowhurst Place, Surrey, first for himself, then for Consuelo Vanderbilt, Duchess of Marlborough shortly before the First World War. He did the same at Old Surrey Hall in the 1920s. The National Trust's Stoneacre in Kent has 1920s wings made with old materials which could deceive visitors who are expecting to see a fifteenth-century yeoman's dwelling and nothing more. These were added by the writer and connoisseur of medieval art, Aymer Vallance, who bought the house with the intention of giving it to the Trust and wished to make it large enough to be taken by a tenant.

The nostalgic look of these different houses – it rarely went far indoors – typifies the deeply nationalistic sentiments of both architects and clients in the early twentieth century. However, architects made an exception to insularity in favour of America, where historical styles were handled with great sophistication. The majority of house-building clients did not want to break the conventions of good manners and reticence established by the Edwardians. The desire of a minority at the end of the 1920s for futuristic originality may be seen partly as another result of the unhinging effect of the war.

THE MODERN MOVEMENT

This desire for absolute novelty was inspired by French and German efforts to return to the first principles of architecture and start with a clean slate. Le

Corbusier's *Vers une architecture* was published in 1922 and its revolutionary reputation ran ahead of the English translation of 1927. 'The house is a machine for living in' was a striking phrase, although, as we have seen, the smaller Edwardian house was perfectly adapted in every detail to the life it was meant to support. More attractive were Corbusier's examples of a new visual style of white walls and flat roofs – a quixotic personal inversion of Classicism justified by portentous theorizing and supported by his instinctively good eye for composition. Corbusier actually admired the English domestic tradition greatly and some of his earliest designs were adapted from Baillie Scott. In the 1920s he told the young English architect Paul Paget that the English ought not to build in concrete as they had such good brick and understood how to use it, unlike the French.

In Germany there were a large number of smaller houses by architects like Guido Harbers and F. A. Breuhaus de Groot who worked in the tradition of Heinrich Tessenow, using traditional idioms with a relaxed freedom which may have been more influential than the adaptations of the white-box style. With the Weissenhofsiedlung, a small suburb at Stuttgart created for an exhibition in 1927, an international style emerged from the work of nine architects representing four countries. It was characterized by an exclusive reliance on pure geometric forms and machine-smooth textures; and acted as a focus of attention for the rest of the world.

Peter Behrens, the oldest architect represented at the Weissenhof and former employer of three others – Le Corbusier, Walter Gropius and Mies van der Rohe – designed New Ways, Northampton, in 1925 for the model train manufacturer Basset Lowke, a former patron of C. R. Mackintosh. It is a symmetrical, box-like house, with some decorative elements which were adopted for houses in Messrs Crittalls' model village at Silver End, Essex, by T. S. Tait in 1927. High and Over at Amersham, designed by Amyas Connell for Professor Bernard Ashmole in 1927 was closer to the continental models, although its Y-shaped plan is only an adaptation of the Edwardian butterfly.

By the end of the thirties 'Modern Movement' houses had advanced in sophistication from their faltering beginnings. They were a tiny proportion of the whole number of houses being built by private clients and were still regarded as eccentric and possibly 'bolshevik'. They appealed to the enthusiasm for light and air which had modified the design of Edwardian houses, and were able to satisfy it with their large windows (sometimes folding right back to the jambs or even winding down into the wall) and sun-roofs. Wells Coates and D. Pleydell Bouverie developed a prototype 'Sunspan' house for the Ideal Home Exhibition which was meant to catch as much of the precious health-

128. Le Château, Silver End, Essex, by Thomas Tait, 1927. A house for D. Crittall
in the modern garden suburb built for workers at the Crittall window factory,
and naturally employing their influential product.

giving rays as possible, and a number of houses were built to this pattern. The
healthy outdoor image of the Modern Movement house, looking at times
more like a piece of ocean liner come adrift, meant that it was favoured for the
seaside.

The Frinton Park Estate in Essex was developed from 1933 under the
supervision of Oliver Hill as an English Weissenhof where many architects
could contribute to a homogeneous holiday settlement. Nearly forty 'Modern'
houses were built but other styles were permitted and proved to be more
popular with buyers.

The distinguishing character of the Modern Movement amongst the styles
of its time was that to a number of architects it was not a style but a cause –
social and moral as well as architectural – which had to be fought for. To Hill,
Hepworth, Marshall Sisson and many other architects it was a style to be used
only when it suited the client and the occasion. Then it could be visually

129. Adling, Grayswood, Surrey, by Connell, Ward and Lucas, 1931.
The shock of modern constructivism heralding a decade of architectural uncertainty.

sophisticated and stylish without puritanical doubts and self-questionings, as at Hill's Joldwynds, Surrey, of 1933. The voluptuous curves of the front were set in the mature grounds of a Philip Webb house which had been disgracefully demolished, and it may be that his injured spirit combined with Hill's slapdash construction to bring about serious structural disorders within a short time. By 1939 the client, the barrister Wilfred Greene, had built himself another house next door – still modern, but with a pitched roof.

Among those dedicated to the cause of modernism, the firm of Connell, Ward and Lucas made use of vigorous cubic modelling in houses like Adling, Grayswood, Surrey, built for Sir Arthur Lowes Dickinson in 1931. The houses of Maxwell Fry have a more horizontal calm. Miramonte, Kingston, was built in 1936 for a property-dealing ex-bookie who asked for a double garage with chauffeur's flat above and 'the rest of the house to scale and don't stint it'. It was ironic that Fry and others saw the Modern Movement as the instrument of extensive social change, yet were compelled to work for the English middle classes (however unconventionally they had arrived at this status) for want of other opportunities.

If we are in search of a guide to take us through the rooms of a Modern Movement house, the Australian Raymond McGrath may stand as a latter-day Muthesius. In 1934 he published a revealing account of Modern domestic architecture in *Twentieth Century Houses* – a book which includes at the back 'A Note on Basic English' by C. K. Ogden and a chart of basic words (kitchens become 'cooking-rooms', dining-rooms 'rooms for meals'). Divisions between rooms had broken down along the lines of the Baillie Scott model – 'freer planning for freer living'. Now the Edwardian notion of the living hall found its full realization. McGrath regarded the living-room as the 'centre of the house', and in some of the most open plans it was 'a room for meals, library, music-room and workroom in one'. Again, the extent of open planning was partly a function of size, since larger houses still tended to have more rooms. Some houses had living-rooms which went up through two storeys – the split-level room did not arrive until after the Second World War – but little attention had been given to acoustics in living-rooms, although they were frequently used for music. In complete contrast to Muthesius, McGrath found that the design of the bedrooms had been neglected.

. . . In the last five or six years we have been dependent on France, America or Germany for developments in design. The tendency at present is to make the bedroom more of a living-room, sometimes with a writing-table and a small winter garden, and to have it planned wherever possible with a sleeping-terrace, dressing-room and bathroom as a self-dependent series ['suite' did not exist in Basic]. A bed which may be readily moved about is still the best, though it has to have a side table, reading-light and telephone.

Adjoining the bedroom was likely to be a sun-room or terrace – the emphasis was on sunshine as well as on sleeping out of doors, which had remained a cult since Edwardian days. There were no open fireplaces, only a central-heating system and gas or electric fires in the rooms.

No really large houses were created in the Modern Movement style, and even a 'rich man's house' like St Ann's Hill, Chertsey, in Surrey, designed by McGrath in 1935, has very few rooms. Its circular shape necessitated much built-in furniture. This was favoured by 'Modern' architects as an aid to achieving the desired sparseness of furnishing; it also helped to suppress the individual character of the owner. Sadly, McGrath's Rudderbar, designed for a site near Hanworth Airplane Field in 1932, was never built. It would have included an aircraft hangar, since the client was an airwoman about to attempt the record for the longest time spent above ground. She was to have dropped the first brick at the start of the flight, and to have come back to enter the house fully ready at the end of the flight. 'Why this did not come off is a long story,' McGrath comments.

Two of the best examples, distinguished like St Ann's Hill by their sensitive response to the landscape setting, were built by architects for their own families. Serge Chermayeff's Bentley Wood, Halland, Sussex, 1935, and Patrick Gwynne's The Homewood, Esher, Surrey, 1937, have a Japanese sense of contemplative repose in harmony with nature; this was to be one of the

130. The Homewood, Esher, by Patrick Gwynne and Wells Coates, 1939
A classic statement of the modern house in a landscape setting.

principal attractions of the Modern Movement to private clients after the Second World War.

The flat roof was a distinguishing feature of Modern Movement houses in the 1930s. Le Corbusier had advocated it for gardening and sunbathing, but in England it was usually more convenient to indulge these pastimes at ground level. It had, in fact, been used before 1914 in a number of houses by the Manchester architect Edgar Wood, to conform to his rectilinear 'Free Tudor' style. Neither he nor most of the thirties architects made full use of its chief advantage to the designer: the relative freedom of planning it allows. It seems rather to have been a piece of architectural sign-language, as Randall Phillips recognized:

If one desires to have a 'modern' house, a flat roof becomes an essential part of it. Certainly it gives the architect great flexibility in planning. Parts may project here, or rooms be placed there, without any difficulties in roofing. The house may be in a position where a flat roof becomes an admirable point of vantage – overlooking the sea or the river perhaps. But there is a lot to set against it. Neglecting any such argument that it is un-English, it is necessary to remember that a flat roof is not cheaper nor more speedily erected than a pitched roof; it lacks the latter's insulating air content, it involves problems concerning the placing and insulation of water tanks, and altogether it is far less suited to our climatic conditions. It needs to be particularly well laid, and, even then, is likely to give more trouble in maintenance than a pitched roof.[59]

The other Modern Movement article of faith was the use of new materials, but as Phillips explains, these were least appropriate in the domestic context:

We hear much about concrete, steel, plywood and synthetic materials, but when we come to consider what is actually being adopted in the building of houses today what do we find? First that concrete and steel are little used for individual houses . . . many houses in the 'modern' style may look as though they were built of concrete, but in point of fact they are built of brick rendered with cement.

Belief in architectural good manners often got the better of tolerance of the individualism which Modern Movement houses paradoxically expressed. Many of them were fiercely opposed by local residents and officials, leading in some cases to the forced adoption of more traditional materials.

Indeed, by the end of the 1930s many Modernists had returned to materials like brick, stone and weather-boarding while retaining the large windows and simple profiles of the International Style. McGrath's Carrygate, Galby, Leicester, was built for the furniture manufacturer Charles Keene in 1938, using old Tudor bricks. The Vicarage, Rock, Northumberland, was commissioned from Leslie Martin and Sadie Speaight in 1939 by Helen Sutherland, a notable collector of modern paintings. The composition of the garden front resembles a Ben Nicholson painting, but it is achieved with brick walls rising from a rough stone base, foreshadowing the style of London County Council housing developments under Martin's direction after the Second World War.

An even more prophetic house at the end of the thirties is the Sheiling, Jordans, Buckinghamshire, designed by Samuel and Harding. It has a shallow-pitched tiled roof and the end gable is filled with dark weatherboarding enclosed between the pale brick side walls, in which metal-framed windows are informally arranged. The sensible, reasonable and possibly rather dull compromise that it represented was to have an enormous appeal to individuals who commissioned smaller houses after the war. The gap between 'traditional' and 'modern' was now hardly recognizable.

THE FIFTIES AND AFTER

With the decline of domestic service and changed ideas about 'life-style' after the war, a new house seemed to many people in the 1950s, as prosperity gradually returned and restrictions on building were lifted, an attractive alternative to an unfashionable Victorian or Edwardian house.

To build in the 'modern' style required capital, because building societies would still not consider houses without certain traditional features like a pitched roof, but enough patrons existed to make the post-war period particularly rich in smaller houses which fulfilled some of the ideals of the 1930s. Like Voysey's patrons at the end of the nineteenth century, they were mostly members of the professional middle classes, with a tradition of patronizing the arts.

The variety of surface and texture noted as a development of the later 1930s became the leading feature of the 1950s 'Contemporary' style. Modern architecture emerged from its puritanical phase, and, where in previous centuries mouldings and ornament had created interest and variety, veneered surfaces of stone and wood were employed to give a natural feeling. The chief influences were the houses (going back to 1900) of Frank Lloyd Wright and the Chicago 'Prairie School', and more recent adaptations of Modernism in Scandinavia.

The use of indoor plants and the lure of tropical zones can be seen in Osbert Lancaster's characterization of the 'Jungle Jungle' style. As the satirist Michael Flanders put it in *At the Drop of a Hat* in 1958:

> We're terribly *House and Garden*
> Now at last we've got the chance;
> The garden's full of furniture
> And the house is full of plants.

The restraint of the 1930s was thrown overboard even by a veteran like Basil Ward (formerly of Connell, Ward and Lucas) in his house at Matson Ground, Windermere, of 1961. Sir Nikolaus Pevsner took a critical view: 'It is large and in its surfeit of motifs – glass, timber, boarding, a chimney-stack of slate, monopitch roofs and even sloping walls – a little too reminiscent of the villas of Cortina.'[60]

Pevsner greatly preferred Farnley Hey, near Huddersfield, West Yorkshire, by Peter Womersley, 1955. It returned to the Arts and Crafts liking for a double-height living hall, partly screened from a glazed sun-terrace by plants twining up a white-painted grille.

131. Farnley Hey, West Yorkshire, by Peter Womersley, 1955.
The 'contemporary' style was a reaction against austerity.

The proliferation of surfaces in different colours and textures was copied more cheaply in new materials like formica. Older houses were often transformed internally in the desire to give them the contemporary look, as demonstrated in the 1951 Festival of Britain South Bank Exhibition. In the age when domestic service declined sharply, the kitchen was often the focus of these attempts to make a new start.

The diversity of textures and the informal way in which they were composed provoked a reaction from a younger generation of architects. Known as the 'New Brutalists', they returned to the austerity of the 1930s, adding the rough textures of late Corbusier, notably exemplified in his Maisons Jaoul, Neuilly, Paris, 1952. The Brutalists looked for the cheapest and simplest solutions to building problems, sometimes disregarding traditional building skills. Their houses were intellectual and comfortless, like the example by Stirling and

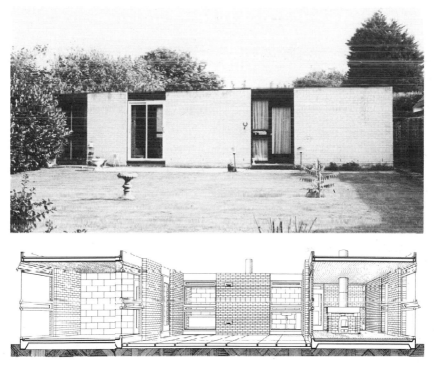

132. House in Baring Road, Cowes, by James Stirling and James Gowan, 1957.
Austerity returns as an architectural fashion.

Gowan in Baring Road, Cowes, Isle of Wight, 1957, with its brick, concrete and blockwork exposed on the inside. Their ideals were extremely influential in the 1960s in the field of public housing.

Many architects steered a middle course between the extremes of decorative and unforgiving surfaces. Patrick Gwynne moved on from the rectilinearity of his pre-war Homewood to a more sculptural approach. His house of the early

133. House at Shipton-under-Wychwood, Oxfordshire, by Stout and Litchfield, 1964. A striking house combining modern forms with vernacular materials.

1960s at Witley Park, Surrey, for Gerald Bentall, has a complex polygonal plan, in which the first floor is treated as a *piano nobile*.

Even more geometrically adventurous is the house at Shipton-under-Wychwood, Oxfordshire, by Stout and Litchfield, 1964. Rough windowless walls of Cotswold stone are raised at acute angles to carry a series of disjointed monopitch roofs, and the composition is reflected in an ornamental pool of Japanese inspiration. Like many houses of the post war Modern Movement, the plan opens up the interior space, but tries hard to exclude the outside world. Salt Hill, Grantchester, Cambridge, by Kenneth Capon of Architects' Co-Partnership, 1959, stands isolated in an open field, but still has a windowless entrance facade.

Houses of the 1960s were frequently of two storeys, the upper projecting and clad in wooden boards with a flat roof, derived from Alvar Aalto's own villa at Munkinnemi, Helsinki, 1936. An exception to this is the house at Christmas Common, Oxfordshire, by Lionel Brett, 1967, which revives the tower-house form of the Border country. Going further back into the supposed origins of the English house, another architect, Phillip Dowson, built an A-frame house at Monks Eleigh, Suffolk, 1959, in the manner of the legendary Tea Pot Hall (see page 26).

Not all 'modern' houses conform to the self-denying ordinances of intellectual architecture. The influence of Hollywood, its celluloid fantasies and its film-star luxury houses, has been seen in many English examples, although these are some way behind the extravagances of Los Angeles, or of England in the 1920s. One of the more remarkable is the Tukal, Beaulieu River, Hampshire, built by J. Seymour Harris in 1970. The house, whose name means 'hut on a marsh' in Ethiopian, is like a flying saucer lightly touched down in the New Forest. Most of the rooms are curved in shape, with panoramic windows. The description of the bedroom fittings, taken from recent particulars of sale, encapsulates the needs of the age:

... built-in fitment, incorporating bedhead, twin counter-balanced folding bedside tables, hi-fi radio, record-player and storage racks, secret cupboard with GPO intercom telephone, attack button linked to burglar-alarm system, built-in cupboards and shelves and storage drawers.

The novelty and excitement of the Modern Movement have been dissipated by its gradual adoption for all purposes since the war. Its principal rival for house-building over the same period has been the Georgian style, as might be expected from the concurrent predominantly Georgian taste in furnishing and decoration. Modernists were convinced that it would have to be ruled out on

134. The Tukal, Beaulieu, Hampshire, by J. Seymour-Harris, 1970.
A luxury house with overtones of science fiction.

grounds of cost, if not of taste, but H. Dalton Clifford, commenting on a five-
bay house in Bedford, built in 1953–4 by Sir Albert Richardson, begs to differ:
'This house cost no more than would a house of corresponding quality built in
the "contemporary" style, but it is safe to conjecture that its market value
would be higher now and in the years to come.' The house has mahogany sash
windows, cornices and panelled doors. It cost £6,000. As Dalton Clifford
remarks, 'it is of a quality usually reserved for banks and board rooms of city
companies. Its elegant refinement of detail makes one realize how much has
been lost owing to the invention of plywood and the wholesale acceptance of
the flush door.'[61]

Another architect who stood out for Classical standards was Raymond Erith,
already mentioned in Chapter 2. He practised from Dedham in Essex, where
in 1937 he had built his Great House in the High Street to look like a house of
the 1820s to all but the keenest eyes. In post-war work he returned to earlier
periods of Classicism for inspiration, touching on Italian Mannerism in the
President's Lodge at The Queen's College, Oxford, 1959.

In later years Erith was assisted by his partner, Quinlan Terry, who has
continued the practice since Erith's death in 1973. He believes that the small
Classical house is an ideal form for the late twentieth century.

135. Newfield, Ripon, West Yorkshire, by Quinlan Terry, 1982.
Palladianism revived and the villa returned to its original function as a working farm.

More and more people are finding that they have got a big house which they can't comfortably live in. It's either too cold in the winter or it's too big. They tend to cut down on their social life; on the other hand, they do like to have fourteen people round the dining-room table. But they don't like them staying the night quite so much.[62]

Newfield, near Ripon, Yorkshire, 1982, has a large kitchen/dining room for family use as one of the three main rooms which the Palladian villa plan provides. Terry describes his houses as 'little, grand houses – now a little grand house when compared to a Victorian house is a Georgian House'. From the relative seclusion of Bridlington in Humberside, Francis Johnson has been building large numbers of 'Yorkshire Georgian' houses since 1935.

The work of Erith and Terry should be seen in the context of a general questioning of the Modern Movement since the 1970s. There has been no equivalent in Britain to the exuberant Californian post-Modernism, nor to its East Coast intellectual counterpart. With greater profit, architects have returned to the traditions of the smaller house in England, particularly to houses built at the turn of the century. Lutyens has been restored to the popularity he once enjoyed among architects. His houses still serve well for present-day needs, and at Fulbrook, Surrey, Roderick Gradidge has shown how garages and a swimming pool can be sympathetically added to a house of the late 1890s.

Similar work is still in progress at Tancred's Ford, Surrey, a house of 1913 by Harold Faulkner.

A young architect, Robert Adam, has skilfully adapted the Victorian parsonage tradition in a small house at Easton, Hampshire, 1981, and his design for a Classical house in the Cathedral Close, Salisbury, promises to be an interesting fusion of Edwardian Classicism with earlier sources.

The nearest equivalent of a full Victorian revival house, reflecting a dominant taste of the 1970s, is Barly Splat, Liskeard, Cornwall, designed by Martin Johnson for the painter Graham Ovenden; most of the building work has been carried out by Ovenden himself using traditional methods and materials, including granite walls. The house is still in progress, and will include a room devoted to Lewis Carroll with stained glass by Peter Blake illustrating scenes from *Alice*. It is a worthy successor to the eccentric artists' houses of the late Victorian period.

The 'do-it-yourself' approach has been adopted by a small group of young designer-craftsmen who restore buildings, living and working on the site in a way which reflects the enthusiasm of early members of the SPAB mentioned in Chapter 1. Their dedication to authentic materials has yet to be applied to a completely new house.

At the time of writing, there is perhaps a greater variety of current styles in domestic architecture than at any time since the 1920s. The building of a new house in the 1980s is a demonstration of individualism and self confidence, and deserves to be given appropriate architectural form.

136. Barly Splat, Liskeard, Cornwall, by Martin Johnson, late 1970s.
An idiosyncratic Victorian revival house for the painter, Graham Ovenden.

◨ SIX ◧

EVERYMAN'S ENGLISH HOUSE

Let the architect with his sober plan
Build a residence for the average man.

W. H. Auden *Paul Bunyan*

Parallel to the history of houses built for individual requirements there is a history of houses not specially commissioned, but built by speculators, philanthropic societies and local and national governments either for sale, lease or rent. One of the continuing themes of the twentieth century is the way in which the standards chosen by the more fortunate few may be adapted for the many. 'Architectural taste . . . travels downwards' and so do architectural building types, so that ideas first tried out in isolation by private patrons and their architects can have widespread importance.

In Chapter 2, we traced the evolution of the villa form until the mid-Victorian search for eclectic novelty had left only an identity of name with the Classical prototype. The 1870s brought a house-building boom, and Bedford Park, mentioned at the beginning of the last chapter, was a manifestation of it. The unusual quality of Bedford Park was that it was designed by architects like E. W. Godwin and Norman Shaw, who were of high national standing. Their work may be contrasted with the simultaneous growth of small-scale 'artisan' housing, known as 'by-law housing' from its adherence to the minimum standards laid down in the Public Health Act of 1875. In the period from 1877 to 1880 there was a sudden growth in 'workmen's villas', which Sir John Summerson considered in 1948 'so familiar to all of us and so terrible in their familiarity'. They were usually built in terraces, but the individuality of the villa was emphasized in the bay windows and the ornamentation, creating a monotonous but restless pattern in the regimented streets.

The ornament, including such features as the flattened, stilted arch and the keystones with heads and dog-tooth mouldings which Summerson found so disagreeable, was an indication of the social superiority of these houses to earlier plain terraces. The relative simplicity of Bedford Park reflected another type of superiority higher up the social scale, which in turn worked its way downwards in the house-building boom of 1897–9.

This contrast helps to explain some of the tensions which have always existed between builders and developers on one hand, working in a free market and exploiting their customers' sensitivity to the language of social class expressed in architecture, and on the other hand architects and philanthropists seeking to impose a different and possibly unwelcome set of standards. Both types reinforced the English preference for the suburb, with its emphasis on 'class distinction and proper drains'.

The conflict can be traced in the antagonism between the 'by-law' house and the 'reformed workman's cottage' which developed at the time that Hermann Muthesius was writing *Das englische Haus* at the turn of the century. In 1901 Raymond Unwin planned a development of workmen's houses outside York for the manufacturer and reformer Joseph Rowntree. At New Earswick, as the place was called, Unwin tried out the principles of the 'small country house' on a reduced scale and introduced the large living hall to replace both the old living-room (where cooking also took place) and the parlour, which had become an important status symbol. Although it was kept only for special occasions, the parlour was furnished with the best things in the house, and presented an outward face of respectability towards the vicar's wife or any other critical visitor. It was therefore a standard feature of the by-law house, occupying the front room on the ground floor. The back living-room only had a small window, as there was also a back extension containing the scullery (the sole source of hot water) and, beyond it, a larder and lavatory entered from the outside. The stairs running up from a narrow hall received no natural light, as all the outside walls were needed to light the three bedrooms.

Unwin was determined to bring the benefits of light and air to the working man, and the large living hall could be lit from three sides and receive the sun all day long. The stairs rose from the middle of the house towards the front, with a three-light cottagey window on the entrance side. The most peculiar feature of these houses was the entry to the earth closet next to the front door which made what should have been discreet visits highly conspicuous. The latter feature was never repeated, but argument continued about the parlour. Unwin saw his large living-room in a nostalgic historical light, and in an up-to-date social context as a means of discouraging workmen from what he believed to be useless pretensions:

When mankind first took to living in houses these consisted of one room; perhaps the most important fact to be remembered in designing cottages is that the cottager still lives during the daytime in one room . . . However desirable a parlour may be, it cannot be said to be necessary to health or family life . . . There can be no doubt that until any cottage has been provided with a living-room large enough to be healthy, comfortable and convenient, it is worse than folly to take space from that living-room where it will be used every day and every hour, to form a parlour, where it will be used only once or twice a week.[63]

It is doubtful whether Unwin had asked many of the inhabitants for their views, but the non-parlour houses proved so unpopular in this respect that when Unwin came to supervise the building of houses for munitions workers at Gretna in 1915 they were given a specially wide frontage to allow for a parlour. As advisor to the wartime committee on housing chaired by Sir John Tudor Walters, MP, for the Local Government Board, Unwin gathered some of the arguments for the parlour:

The desire for a parlour . . . is remarkably widespread both among the urban and rural workers . . . It is the parlour which the majority desire.

Such witnesses state that the parlour is needed to enable the older members of the family to hold social intercourse with their friends without interruption from the children; that it is required in cases of sickness in the house . . . that it is needed for the youth of the family in order that they may meet their friends; that it is generally required for home lessons by the children of school age, or for similar work of study, serious reading or writing, on the part of any member of the family; that it is also needed for occasional visitors whom it may not be convenient to interview in the living-room.[64]

It was nonetheless considered that the minimum sizes for the living-room and scullery should not be changed, and that the parlour should be the first sacrifice to economy, as indeed it was in the early stages of the post-war housing campaign.

The external appearance of the house was also seen as an area for reform. The houses at Port Sunlight and Bournville, the principal prototypes of the Garden City in the 1890s, were designed by architects, but without the puritanical simplicity which became the identifying quality of public-sector housing in the twentieth century. Unwin wrote that cottages should have 'a simple dignity and beauty . . . which assuredly is necessary, not only to the proper growth of the gentler and finer instincts of men, but to the producing of that indefinable something which makes the difference between a mere shelter and a home'.[65] Simplicity should also have made for economy, although it needed materials of a more expensive quality than the speculative builder would have used. He understood how ornament and variety of texture distracts the eye from possible defects.

Unwin's demand for simplicity was followed in the schemes with which he was concerned in the years following New Earswick. They are almost a history of the Garden City movement itself. In 1903 he won the competition for the design of the first Garden City at Letchworth, Hertfordshire, and in 1905 he

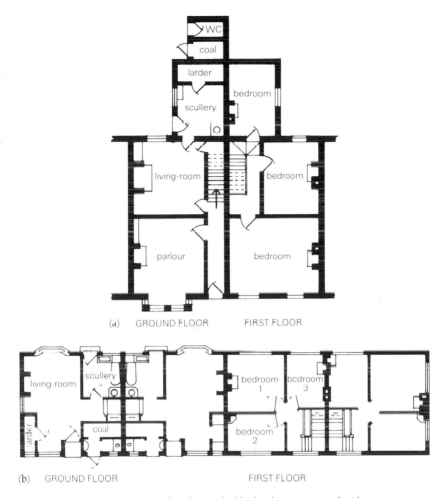

FIG. 17 (a, b). (a) Plan of a standard by-law house contrasted with
(b) an improved cottage plan by Parker and Unwin for New Earswick, York, 1902.

was invited to prepare a master-plan for Hampstead Garden Suburb. Both these projects were inspired by Ebenezer Howard's book *Tomorrow ; the Peaceful Path to Real Reform*, published in 1896 and later republished as *Garden Cities of Tomorrow*. Howard's premiss was that the Garden City, unlike the suburb, should be a self-contained, balanced community, and should include industry, business, administrative buildings and social centres. Unlike the large city, its growth would be limited and people would live reasonably near to their workplace. Howard's proposals were illustrated in diagrammatic form, and introduced a concept of organized zoning of housing, industry and public buildings in clear relation to each other.

Unwin interpreted the diagram, and added his own ingredients. He was particularly interested in the grouping of cottages to produce interesting corners and vistas, recalling the informality of vernacular villages, although actually set out on rather rigid lines. In a pamphlet, *Nothing Gained by Overcrowding* (1912), he contrasted the grid of by-law streets with his own layout of cottages to a lesser density, proving that the economy in making roads paid for the extra land involved. The best type of road from this point of view was the cul-de-sac leading off a through road. By getting exemption from the by-laws for roads at Letchworth and Hampstead, Unwin managed to achieve both variety and economy by suiting the width and construction of each road to the weight of traffic it was likely to carry. He also introduced a number of footpaths at the backs of houses, and some communal plots of grass in front, evoking some of the features of traditional villages.

The influence of Unwin's ideas is due to their clarity. They can easily be applied as a formula, and influenced the fifty or so Garden City schemes, mostly on a small scale, which were started before 1914. Among these, the cottage estates of the LCC at Totterdown Fields, Tooting, and White Hart Lane, Harringay, should be noted as the first housing of this kind by a municipal authority. Since 1893 the Council's architects had been building flats with a high quality of architectural design and accommodation in central London, but henceforth the official preference was for low-density housing developments on the fringe of the built-up area. The Old Oak Estate, Hammersmith, begun in 1911, is a demonstration of the ideas on grouping and the use of unfolding vistas found in Unwin's book *Town Planning in Practice* (1909). For this book, Charles Wade, later the owner of Snowshill Manor in the Cotswolds, had drawn a series of fairy-tale villages of the imagination based on Unwin's principles, and the success of Old Oak as a visual composition (under the direction of A. S. Soutar) is largely due to Wade's vision.

The position of official involvement in housing was altered by the First World War, and at each stage Unwin played his part. First there was the housing of munitions workers at Gretna, already mentioned, and at the Well Hall Estate, Eltham, Kent. This scheme, in which Unwin played no part, was perhaps the most architecturally distinguished of all. It contradicts several of Unwin's principles by having long unbroken rows of cottages, 'cottage flats' in

137. Eltham Well Hall Estate, Greenwich, by the Office of Works (Frank Baines), 1915.
Built for wartime munitions workers, this remains one of the finest early cottage estates.

some cases instead of conventional cottages, and by using an abundant variety
of building materials and textures. It was the creation of a young Office of
Works architect, Frank Baines. Unfortunately, for causes largely beyond
Baines's control, the Well Hall Estate was also very expensive, and so many of
its aesthetic lessons were ignored and Unwin's views dominated the Tudor
Walters Committee.

The Report of this Committee was published in the week of the Armistice
in 1918. On the day following the Armistice Lloyd George, the Prime Minister,
made his famous and often misquoted speech, in which he promised
'habitations fit for the heroes who have won the war'. He was not merely
prompted by gratitude. It became clear that as thousands of soldiers were
'demobbed', with revolution in the air all over Europe, some positive pledge
of improved standards of living in the future was needed to justify the political
status quo. The housing shortage was estimated at 500,000 in 1918, and likely

to grow at 100,000 a year. It was not merely the quantity but the quality of houses which had to be seen as a new start.

Only under these exceptional political circumstances would the reluctant officials of the Treasury have given way to the Tudor Walters Committee's demand that standards of space and construction should not be compromised, even though all possible economies were made. As Mark Swenarton writes, 'In the turbulent atmosphere of 1918 this seemed no more than common sense.'[66] The Housing Act of 1919 promised to assist the building of 500,000 houses. The recommendations of the Committee were codified in the *Manual on the Preparation of State-aided Housing Schemes*, published by the Local Government Board in April of the same year.

Thus in less than twenty years the ideas of the Garden City movement had become official policy. This is perhaps more important than the inevitable falling-short in the numbers of houses built (just under 176,000) and the decline in standards after the winter of 1920–21. The subsidized houses of this period are a familiar sight in all parts of the country. In pairs or short terraces, with hipped roofs, sash or casement windows and a simple projecting hood over the front door, they may be inviting or bleak according to the quality of the layout and landscaping. They evidently have sufficient appeal today for tenants to buy their freeholds, although having done so, they may then set about altering the appearance – changing the windows and painting the brickwork or covering it with 'stone-cladding'. Houses of this kind often look best in a small group at the edge of a village, with colour-washed roughcast and well-tended gardens.

The Garden City movement also transformed the character of private-enterprise housing. Numerically, this was much more important. Of the four million houses built between the wars, three quarters were independent of state aid. At Golders Green in north London an old country-style signpost stands at a road junction, reminding us that in 1901 it was still 'a place within three miles of Regent's Park where there are roses in the hedgerows and the larks are singing . . . a place almost unique in its rural character'. It was cut off from central London by the high ground of Hampstead and Highgate, and it was only the arrival of the electric Underground Railway in 1907 that began the transformation. The houses built there by speculative builders were prophetic. As Alan Jackson says, 'Half-timbered, tiled and gabled, and cottagey in appearance, the Golders Green houses set the trend for the next three decades

138. Typical semidetached houses at Mollison Way, Queensbury. Individuality and uniformity in unstable balance, but the commercial success of these houses cannot be denied.

of London suburban exteriors.'[67] And not only London, for the new style, adapted from Bedford Park and other architects' prototypes, was quickly disseminated through magazines like the *Illustrated Carpenter and Builder*, which had been founded in 1877 to popularize the 'workman's villa'. The new generation of suburban houses was calculated to appeal to freehold buyers. They were not unlike the cottages at Hampstead Garden Suburb, adjoining Golders Green. The back extension of the by-law house was abolished, so that all the rooms were better lit, and the rear living-room could open into the garden. The houses were in pairs (semidetached) or short terraces and some attempt at planting trees and gardens was made. In other respects, they appealed to the house-buyer's interest in individuality, which Unwin was anxious to suppress in his schemes. There was less sculpted ornament than on the by-law house, but instead there was a variety of texture based on neo-vernacular models from higher up the architectural and social scale.

A further common feature, after the Tudor Walters Report, was the adoption for private and public housing of a 70 ft (21 m) minimum distance between houses facing each other across a road. This gave suburbia its diffused character, incapable of really impressive architectural treatment. The reason for the rule was the Edwardian concern for sun and air which has already been emphasized. With the 70 ft distance the rooms of each house could receive direct sunlight even at midwinter. This convention was only dropped after 1973, to enable houses to be grouped closer together for architectural effect.

The inter-war period thus reinforced the pattern of suburban houses in settlements of low density, a pattern which derives directly from the moral attitude of the early Victorians. Their belief that uneventful family life in the suburb was the highest form of civilization was perpetuated, so that it was unnecessary for developers and councils to consider extensive provision of communal buildings and it would have been unpopular to place houses closer together or to build higher.

Both these alternatives appealed to the architectural profession, however. As we have seen, there had been a tension from the early days of the Garden City movement between how people wished to live and how architects thought that they ought to live.

This became more acute, especially in the 1930s, when architects expressed their revulsion at the aesthetic consequences of privately owned suburban houses and the social assumptions of suburbia of all kinds. In one sense, this merely perpetuated the professional architect's resentment at his redundancy in the process of speculative building. In addition, however, it reflected the architect's growing interest in shaping society on his own terms rather than merely fulfilling the commands of a patron. To the generation of architects that grew up after the First World War, this seemed their most useful task. The continental buildings of Gropius and Le Corbusier which they so much admired were a preview for the future, not merely in architectural style, but in systems of social organization.

Seen in these terms, the suburbs were wrong because they reflected the desire of the middle classes for houses which looked old and comfortable. To apply stained deal laths to a brick house to make it look Tudor seemed dishonest. 'It is also a very extravagant way of building; unnecessary money is being spent to escape from our own age. Surely this craving for the past is unhealthy.'[68] Suburbs were wrong because they encouraged people to stay at home rather than become 'active citizens'. They were wrong because they presented a dream of living in the country, but actually blighted and obscured the country. It was generally assumed by left-wing intellectuals that they would become 'the slums of tomorrow'.

The principal alternative was to build blocks of flats, occupying less land, under 'expert' aesthetic control, and making use of economies of scale in modern facilities. At Kensal House, London, 1936, Maxwell Fry provided a nursery school and social club/canteen. A contemporary promotional film shows the occupants gathering there last thing at night to drink tea or Ovaltine and discuss the international situation rather than hugging their own (gas) firesides.

A much larger development at Quarry Hill, Leeds, 1932–41, inspired by the Labour council leader, the Reverend Charles Jenkinson, and designed by R. A. H. Livett, more closely resembled the massive blocks of socialist Vienna. The 937 flats were served by the Garchey system of waste disposal, which provided the heating for the free communal laundry. Tennis courts, bowls, playground and mortuary chapel were among the other facilities. Owing to the structural failure of the Mopin system of steel construction, the flats were demolished in 1975, but like many others now in poor condition in English cities, they served an important short-term need for housing.

In the private sector, Dolphin Square, London, by Gordon Jeeves, 1935, introduced American scale and amenities, including a swimming pool and restaurant.

Flats were an attractive alternative to the traditional house for people without family ties, and architects believed that thoughtful planning, and the advantages of shared facilities, would overcome the deeply rooted English suspicion of them.

For those interested in the housing problem, the Second World War provided an opportunity for a new start. The bombs accomplished slum clearance much faster than the borough councils in their fight against vested interest. The frustrated enthusiasms of the inter-war period were channelled into government inquiries and reports which proposed much stricter control on the use of land and greater opportunities for public housing.

The plans for the County and City of London by Patrick Abercrombie (1943 and 1944) were important documents. Residential areas were to be thinned out to lower densities. Industry and housing were to be zoned separately and the type of attic or backyard workshop familiar since the Middle Ages officially discouraged in favour of larger factories on industrial estates. In continuation of the ideals of the 1930s, much housing was built in the form of flats, although these were seldom in tall 'tower' blocks as in the 1960s. The prevailing orthodoxy was 'mixed development', exemplified in the showpiece of the LCC Architects' Department, the Alton Estate at Roehampton, Surrey, 1952–8. It has now been widely demonstrated that this scheme was based on many false assumptions about preferred ways of living, and it remains to be seen whether the visual qualities of the architecture gain strength as they are absorbed into the perspective of history.

THE NEW TOWNS AND THE FUTURE

For the New Towns, which formed an integral part of Abercrombie's proposals for London and the Attlee government's national post-war plan, a more traditional approach to housing was adopted. Many of Ebenezer Howard's ideas were still influential: the New Towns should be far enough away from existing towns to achieve their own cultural identity; housing, industry and transport should be integrated, but clearly defined and separated; and the aesthetic consequences of individualism should be controlled by a master-plan.

New Towns were a focus of national enthusiasm. As E. W. Clarke, the engineer and surveyor for Peterlee, Durham, wrote:

No jerry builders will be permitted in Peterlee. This scum of the building trades will not be allowed to stake a claim in this town of ours. Their nefarious operations have been permitted long enough. Peterlee must be designed in all its phases by a modern and proven team of impartial experts and only the best is good enough.

Let us, therefore, close our eyes on the nineteenth-century degradation and squalor, and let us look with unseeing eyes on the sordid excrescence of the first decade of this century, let us blind ourselves to the septic and ugly building wens and ribbons perpetrated and planted on us between the wars, but let us open our eyes and look brightly forward and onward to the new town, the new living . . . Peterlee.[69]

At Peterlee the master-plan of the first 'impartial expert', Berthold Lubetkin, composed of large 'slabs' of flats, was rejected in favour of terraces of small houses; their austere design, and the intervention of the abstract painter Victor Pasmore, kept the traditional suburban aesthetic at bay.

In the ring of New Towns around London, Stevenage, Hertfordshire, and Harlow, Essex, were launched in the 1940s, and relied largely on terraced houses with occasional low-rise flats. Yellow brick and shallow pitched roofs

139. The Downs, Harlow New Town, Essex, late 1960s.
The welfare-state prescription for architecture and planning.

were the *lingua franca* of the 1950s – worthy but generally dull. The main innovation was the segregation of motor traffic, in over-reaction to the traffic difficulties of older towns.

Prefabrication had been seen as an important contribution to the post-war housing shortage, but little use was made of it in the New Towns. From 1944 onwards the government and various private contractors devised numerous prototypes of houses which could be delivered from factory to site and assembled in a few hours without using skilled building labour – 'prefabs'. Among them were the 'Airoh', 'Alcrete', 'Arrow', 'Airey', 'Acton', 'Arcon', 'Coventry', 'Portal', 'Tarran' and 'Uni-Seco' houses, all single-storey bungalows. The houses were popular because of their ingenious and economical planning, and their generally generous allocation of private garden. Although few are still inhabited, an Arcon house (rolled steel clad with corrugated asbestos) has

140. Arcon Mk V prefabricated house at Avoncroft Museum, Bromsgrove. This was one of the most successful of the many attempts to solve the post-war housing shortage with factory-made houses.

been re-erected at the Avoncroft Museum at Bromsgrove, a worthy companion of the prefabricated timber-framed houses of the Middle Ages which surround it.

In the period from the early New Towns to the present, housing has not ceased to be a contentious social and aesthetic issue. This is not least because so many mistakes have been made in both categories and have affected the lives of thousands of people.

The newest New Town, Milton Keynes, provides an opportunity for stock-taking in the middle 1980s. It affirms the dominance of the single-family house on its own plot of land, unshaken after centuries of evolution. It demonstrates the emergence of a new attitude to architectural style in the last ten years. The earliest housing at Milton Keynes, such as Bean Hill, 1975, was in the lightweight 'high-tech' style claimed by its supporters to be the

141. Housing at Bean Hill, Milton Keynes, by Foster Associates, 1975, modified in 1984 with the addition of a pitched roof.

142. Housing at Neath Hill, Milton Keynes, 1977, in the influential neo-vernacular manner.

architecture of the future. The Civic Centre at Milton Keynes has indeed been continued in a similar manner, but it has become clear that it is no longer popular for houses. Not only have subsequent housing developments adopted a vocabulary of brick and tile, but traditional features of design are now consciously sought for aesthetic and practical reasons. Compared to its Edwardian predecessors, the vernacular revival of the 1980s is often clumsy and financially constrained, but it does embody sound practical building methods for which future generations will be grateful. Meanwhile, the flat-roofed 'high-tech' flats and houses are being given pitched roofs to make them attractive to purchasers.

The political climate of the 1980s is unfavourable to New Town development, but Milton Keynes is proving successful in attracting growing industries, and the housing programme is going forward, adapted to the era of 'privatization'. Under a current scheme, it is possible to buy a share in a new house from the Development Corporation, and pay rent for the remaining share until a full purchase is made. It is also possible to buy a plot of land and build your own house, individually or with a group. This programme of 'self-build' is a logical answer to the economic problem of house ownership at its most basic level, and an extraordinary return to the practice of the wealthy peasant class of the Middle Ages. It has been pioneered over several years in the London borough of Lewisham by the veteran architect Walter Segal, who has provided a standard but variable design for timber houses; the scheme saves money through bulk orders of materials and the sharing of building skills. The process of building also assists the community spirit in a way that makes all other means seem artificial.

At Milton Keynes it is rare for architects to be involved in self-build schemes, although they are officially vetted by the corporation. As a result, the neo-vernacular style has now progressed to neo-Tudor, confounding all predictions about the development of architectural style.

Perhaps the most telling indication from Milton Keynes is the premium which has been placed on preserving older properties in the area. Houses of all periods and in all parts of the country have been found to be adaptable to modern living conditions. There was a major turning-point in the 1970s when local councils saw the logic of rehabilitating older properties instead of demolishing them, following a practice which has been current for many years among private house owners. The resultant gain is a gain not only in economic terms, but in the preservation of familiar scenes and the realization that, more than any other building type, houses tell us about the people of the past and give a sense of identity for the future.

NOTES

(Place of publication is London unless otherwise stated.)

1. Nikolaus Pevsner, *An Outline of European Architecture*, Harmondsworth, 1943; rev. ed., 1963, p. 15.
2. Geoffrey Keynes, ed., *The Letters of William Blake*, 1980, p. 23.
3. F. W. B. Charles, *Mediaeval Cruck Building and its Derivatives*, 1967, pp. 17–25.
4. ibid., p. 8.
5. C. F. Innocent, *The Development of English Building Construction*, Cambridge, 1916, p. 59.
6. R. T. Mason, *Framed Buildings of the Weald*, Horsham, 1969, p. 51.
7. A. R. Myers, *England in the Late Middle Ages*, Harmondsworth, 1952, p. 11.
8. William Harrison, *Description of England*, 1577; ed. 1921, pp. 118–19, 113.
9. Eric Sandon, *Suffolk Houses*, Woodbridge, 1977, p. 95.
10. Nikolaus Pevsner, *The Buildings of England: N. Somerset and Bristol*, Harmondsworth, 1958, p. 186.
11. Harrison, op. cit., pp. 191–2.
12. Quoted in G. M. Young, 'The Country House', in *The Legacy of England*, 1935.
13. Richard Carew, *The Survey of Cornwall*, ed. F. E. Halliday, 1969, p. 124.
14. Mary Sturge Gretton, *Burford, Past and Present*, 1945, p. 16.
15. Harrison, op. cit., pp. 114–15.
16. John Harvey, *Gothic England*, 1947, p. 47.
17. *The Journeys of Celia Fiennes*, ed. Christopher Morris, 1947, p. 202.
18. Richard Jefferies, *The Toilers of the Field*, 1892, pp. 71–2.
19. S. O. Addy, *The Evolution of the English House*, 1898, p. xvii.
20. James Lees-Milne, *The Age of Inigo Jones*, 1953, p. 216.
21. James Lees-Milne, *English Country Houses, Baroque*, 1970, p. 219.
22. J. H. Cheetham and John Piper, *Wiltshire, A Shell Guide*, 1968, p. 72.
23. Rudolf Wittkower, *Palladio and English Palladianism*, 1974, p. 90.
24. R. J. Mingay, *English Landed Society in the Eighteenth Century*, 1963, p. 18.
25. Marcus Binney, *Sir Robert Taylor*, 1984, p. 40.
26. 'C. R. Cockerell's Ichnographica Domestica', ed. John Harris, *Architectural History*, XIV, p. 10.
27. Pierre de la Ruffinière du Prey, *John Soane*, 1982, p. 295.

28. John Summerson, *The Life and Work of John Nash, Architect*, 1980, p. 41.

29. Christopher Hussey, *English Country Houses, Late Georgian*, 1958, p. 103.

30. James Lees-Milne, *Caves of Ice*, London, 1983 (in the diary for 1946).

31. William Cowper, 'Retirement', 1782.

32. John Summerson, *Georgian London*, 1945; rev. ed. Harmondsworth, 1978, p. 175.

33. G. M. Young, *Portrait of an Age*, 1953, p. 150.

34. John Summerson, 'The London Surburban Villa', *Architectural Review*, CIV, 1948, pp. 63–72.

35. John Martin Robinson, *Country Life*, 27 January 1983, p. 197.

36. David Watkin, *Thomas Hope and the Neo-Classical Idea*, 1968, p. 126.

37. T. C. Croker, *A Walk from London to Fulham*, 1860, pp. 190–91.

38. A. W. N. Pugin, *Contrasts*, 1836, pp. 30–31.

39. Marjorie and C. H. B. Quennell, *A History of Everyday Things*, vol. 4, pp. 101–2.

40. J. J. Stevenson, *House Architecture*, 1880, vol. 2, p. 275.

41. Andrew Saint, 'Heat, Light and Drains' (unpublished lecture).

42. His life and career are described by Sanborn C. Brown in *Benjamin Thompson, Count Rumford*, 1962.

43. Quoted ibid., p. 167.

44. Mrs. Loudon, *The Lady's Country Companion*, 1845.

45. These meals might be compared with the dining habits at Oakly Park near Ludlow, observed by the American Anna Maria Fay fifty years later. See John Cornforth, *English Interiors 1790–1848, The Quest for Comfort*, 1978, p. 20.

46. Mrs Loudon, ibid.

47. Stevenson, op. cit., p. 57.

48. Cornforth, op. cit.

49. J. C. Loudon, *An Encyclopaedia of Cottage, Farm and Villa Architecture*, 1836, p. 799.

50. Victorian Lanhydrock is described by John Cornforth in *Country Life*, 16 and 23 February 1978.

51. Mrs Loudon, op. cit.

52. Dearman Birchall, *The Diary of a Victorian Squire*, ed. David Verey, Gloucester, 1983, pp. 85–6.

53. Robert Kerr, *The Gentleman's House*, 1864, p. 466.

54. Hannah Cullwick, *The Diaries of Hannah Cullwick, Victorian Maidservant*, ed. Liz Stanley, 1984, p. 106.

55. J. E. Panton, *From Kitchen to Garret*, 1888, p. 152.

56. Lawrence Weaver, *Small Country Houses of Today*, vol. 2, 1919.

57. Quoted in Raymond McGrath, *Twentieth Century Houses*, 1934, p. 216.

58. Gertrude Jekyll, *Home and Garden*, 1901, p. 3.

59. R. Randall Phillips, *Houses for Moderate Means*, 4th ed., 1953, p. 8.

60. Nikolaus Pevsner, *The Buildings of England: Cumberland and Westmoreland*, Harmondsworth, 1967, p. 230.

61. H. Dalton Clifford, *New Houses for Moderate Means*, 1957, p. 109.

62. Quinlan Terry, interview with Clive Aslet, *The Times*, 3 August 1983.

63. Raymond Unwin, *Cottage Plans and Common Sense*, London, 1902 (Fabian Tract).

64. The Tudor Walters Report, Parliamentary Papers (Cd 9191), 1918, vii, paragraph 86.

65. Unwin, op. cit.

66. Mark Swenarton, *Homes Fit for Heroes*, 1981, p. 96.

67. Alan Jackson, *Semi–detached London*, 1973, p. 76.

68. Anthony Bertram, *Design*, Harmondsworth, 1938, p. 55.

69. E. W. Clarke, *Farewell Squalor*, 1946, quoted in J. B. Cullingworth, *Environmental Planning*, 1979, p. 73.

BIBLIOGRAPHY

(Place of publication is London unless otherwise stated)

GENERAL

Braun, Hugh, *The Story of the English House*, 1940.
Cave, Lyndon F., *The Smaller English House*, 1981.
The Country Seat, ed. by Howard Colvin and John Harris, 1970.
Cook, Olive, and Smith, Edwin, *The English House through Seven Centuries*, 1968.
Cooke, Robert, *West Country Houses*, Bristol, 1957.
Dutton, Ralph, *The English Country House*, 1949.
Fedden, Robin, and Kenworthy-Browne, John, *The Country House Guide*, 1979.
Gotch, J. A., *The Growth of the English House*, 1928.
Jordan, Robert Furneaux, *The English House*, 1959.
Lloyd, Nathaniel, *A History of the English House*, 1931 (reprinted 1975).
Oswald, Arthur, *Country Houses of Kent*, 1933
    Country Houses of Dorset, 1959.
Pevsner, Nikolaus, and others, *The Buildings of England* (all counties), Harmondsworth, 1951.
Potter, Margaret, and Alexander, *Houses*, 1948.
    Interiors, 1957.
Reid, Peter, *Burke's and Savill's Guide to Country Houses*: II, *Herefordshire, Shropshire, Warwickshire, Worcestershire*, 1980; III, *East Anglia* (with John Kenworthy-Browne, Michael Sayer and David Watkin), 1981.
Richards, J. M., *A Miniature History of the English House*, 1938.
Royal Commission on Historic Monuments, County Inventories, especially Cambridgeshire, Dorset and the town of Stamford.
Shell Guides (various counties).
Survey of London (41 vols. to date); 1900.
Turnor, Reginald, *The Smaller English House*, 1952.
Watkin, David, *English Architecture, A Concise History*, 1979.
Wrightson, P., ed., *The Small English House, A Catalogue of Books*, 1977.

CHAPTER I

Addy, S. O., *The Evolution of the English House*, 1898; 2nd ed. (revised John Summerson), 1933.

Barley, M. W., *The English Farmhouse and Cottage*, 1961.

Brunskill, R. W., *Illustrated Handbook of Vernacular Architecture*, 1970.

    Vernacular Architecture of the Lake Counties, 1974.

    Traditional Buildings of Britain, 1981.

    (with Alec Clifton-Taylor) *English Brickwork*, 1977.

Charles, F. W. B., *Mediaeval Cruck-building and its Derivatives*, 1967.

Clifton-Taylor, Alec, *The Pattern of English Building*, 1972.

    (with A. S. Ireson) *English Stone Building*, 1983.

Cook, Olive and Smith, Edwin, *English Cottages and Farmhouses*, 1954 and 1982.

Darley, Gillian, *The National Trust Book of the Farm*, 1981.

Harris, Richard, *Discovering Timber-framed Buildings*, Aylesbury, 1978.

    Timber-framed Buildings, 1980.

Harrison, William, *Elizabethan England* (introduction to *Holinshed's Chronicles*, 1577 and 1587, ed. by 'L. W.', introduction by F. J. Furnivall), 1921 (and earlier editions).

Harvey, John, *Gothic England*, 1947.

Hewett, Cecil A., *English Historic Carpentry*, 1980.

Hoskins, W. G., *The Making of the English Landscape*, Harmondsworth, 1973.

Innocent, C. F., *The Development of English Building Construction*, Cambridge, 1916; Newton Abbot, 1971.

Lloyd, Nathaniel, *A History of English Brickwork*, 1925; Woodbridge, 1983.

McCann, John, *Cob and Clay buildings*, Aylesbury, 1983.

Mason, R. T., *Framed Buildings of the Weald*, Horsham, 1969.

Mercer, Eric, *English Vernacular Houses*, 1975.

Oliver, Basil, *The Cottages of England*, 1929.

Oliver, Paul, *English Cottages and Small Farmhouses*, 1975.

Peate, Iorweth C., *The Welsh House*, Liverpool, 1944.

Sandon, Eric, *Suffolk Houses*, Woodbridge, 1977.

Smith, Peter, *Houses of the Welsh Countryside*, 1975.

Tipping, H. Avray, *English Homes*, Period I, Vol. 1, and Period II, Vol. 1, 1921 and 1924.

Wood, Margaret, *The English Medieval House*, 1983.

CHAPTER 2

Ackermann, James, *Palladio*, Harmondsworth, 1966.

Airs, Malcolm, *The Buildings of Britain: Tudor and Jacobean*, 1982.

Belcher, John, and Macartney, Mervyn, *Later Renaissance Architecture in England*, six parts, 1898–1901.

Binney, Marcus, *Sir Robert Taylor*, 1984.

Blomfield, Reginald, *A History of Renaissance Architecture in England 1500–1800*, 1891.

Campbell, Colen, ed., *Vitruvius Britannicus*, Vol. I, 1715, Vol. II, 1717, Vol. III, 1725, Vol. IV (ed. Badeslade and Rocque), 1739, Vols. V and VI (ed. Woolfe and Gandon), 1767 and 1771; reprinted in 3 vols. with *Guide to Vitruvius Britannicus*, New York, 1972.

Cornforth, John, and Hill, Oliver, *English Country Houses. Caroline*, 1966.

Colvin, Howard, *A Biographical Dictionary of British Architects 1600–1840*, 1978.

Crook, J. M., *The Greek Revival*, 1972.

Cruickshank, Dan and Wylde, Peter, *London: The Art of Georgian Building*, 1975.

Dyos, H. J., *Victorian Suburb, A Study of the Growth of Camberwell*, Leicester, 1961.

Field, Horace, and Bunney, Michael, *English Domestic Architecture of the 17th and 18th Centuries*, 1928.

Fiennes, Celia (ed. Christopher Morris), *The Journeys of Celia Fiennes*, 1949.
The Illustrated Journeys of Celia Fiennes, 1981.

Girouard, Mark, *Life in the English Country House*, Harmondsworth, 1980.
Robert Smythson and the Elizabethan Country House, 1983.

Gotch, J. Alfred, *Early Renaissance Architecture in England*, 1901.
The Growth of the English House, 1909.
The English Home from Charles I to George IV, 1918.

Gunther, R. T., *The Architecture of Sir Roger Pratt*, Oxford, 1928.

Gyfford, E., *Designs for Small Picturesque Cottages and Hunting Boxes*, 1807.

Harris, John, *Sir William Chambers*, 1970.
A Country House Index, 1979.
The Artist and the Country House, 1979.
The Palladians, 1981.
William Talman, Maverick Architect, 1982.

Hussey, Christopher, *English Country Houses: Early, Mid, and Late Georgian*, 1955–8.

Jourdain, Margaret, *The Work of William Kent*, 1948.

Kip, J., and Knyff, L., *Britannia Illustrata*, 1707; a selection was reprinted, ed. Harris, J. as *Die Hauser der Lords und Gentlemen*, Dortmund, 1982.

Lees-Milne, James, *Tudor Renaissance*, 1951.

The Age of Inigo Jones, 1953.

The Age of Adam, 1947.

Earls of Creation, 1962.

English Country Houses: Baroque, 1970.

Lugar, Robert, *Architectural Sketches*, 1805.

The Country Gentleman's Architect, 1807.

Villa Architecture, 1828.

Middleton, Charles, *Picturesque and Architectural Views for Cottages, Farm Houses and Country Villas*, 1793.

Morrice, Richard, *The Buildings of Britain: Stuart and Baroque*, 1983.

Muthesius, Stefan, *The English Terraced House*, 1982.

Olsen, Donald, *The Growth of Victorian London*, 1975.

Town Planning in London, the Eighteenth and Nineteenth Centuries, 1964; 2nd ed., 1982.

Palladio, Andrea, *I Quattro Libri dell'Architettura*, Venice, 1570.

The Four Books of Architecture of Andrea Palladio, translated and published by Isaac Ware, 1758; reprinted 1977.

Papworth, J. B., *Rural Residences*, 1818.

Plaw, John, *Ferme Ornée, or Rural Improvements*, 1795.

Rural Architecture, six editions 1785 to 1804.

Prey, Pierre de la R. du, *John Soane, the Making of an Architect*, 1982.

Ramsey, S. C., and Harvey, J. D. M., *Small Georgian Houses and their Details 1750–1820*; new edition with introduction by J. M. Richards, 1972.

Ramussen, Steen Eiler, *London, the Unique City*, 1937; new edition, Cambridge, Massachusetts, 1982.

Richardson, A. E., and Gill, C. L., *Regional Architecture of the West of England*, 1924.

Richardson, A. E., and Eberlin, H. D., *The Smaller English House of the Later Renaissance 1660–1830*, 1925.

Robinson, John Martin, *The Wyatts, an Architectural Dynasty*, Oxford, 1979.

Georgian Model Farms, Oxford, 1983.

Sitwell, Sacheverell, *British Architects and Craftsmen*, 1945.

Stroud, Dorothy, *Henry Holland*, 1950.

Henry Holland, 1966.

George Dance, 1971.

Sir John Soane, 1984.

Summerson, John, *Georgian London*, revised ed., Harmondsworth, 1978.
  The Classical Language of Architecture, 1983.
  John Nash, 1980.
  Sir John Soane, 1952.
  'The London suburban villa', *Architectural Review*, 104 (1948), 63–72.
  'The idea of the villa: the classical country house in eighteenth century England', *Journal of the Royal Society of Arts*, 107 (1959), 539–87.
  Architecture in Britain 1530–1830, Harmondsworth, 1970; 7th ed., 1983.
Turnor, Reginald, *The Smaller English House*, 1952.
Watkin, David, *Thomas Hope, 1769–1831, and the Neo-Classical Idea*, 1968.
  The English Vision, 1982.
  Athenian Stuart, 1982.
  The Building of Britain: Regency, 1982.
Wittkower, Rudolf, *Palladio and English Palladianism*, 1974.

CHAPTER 3

Bax, Basil Anthony, *The English Parsonage*, 1964.
Burton, Decimus, *View of the Rustic Village now Being Formed at Furze Hill on the Estate of I.L. Goldsmid Esqr. Brighton*, n.d.
Clark, Kenneth, *The Gothic Revival*, 1928.
Davis, Terence, *The Architecture of John Nash*, 1960.
  John Nash, The Prince Regent's Architect, 1966.
  The Gothic Taste, 1974.
Dearn, T. D. W., *Sketches in Architecture*, 1807.
Dixon, Roger, and Muthesius, Stefan, *Victorian Architecture*, 1978.
Eastlake, Charles, *A History of the Gothic Revival*, 1872; ed. J. Mordaunt Crook, 2nd ed., Leicester, 1978.
Elsam, Richard, *An Essay on Rural Architecture*, 1803.
Fiddes, V., and Rowan, A., *Mr. David Bryce 1803–1876. Exhibition Catalogue*, Edinburgh, 1973.
Fulford, Roger, *Royal Dukes*, 1933.
Girouard, Mark, *Robert Smythson and the Architecture of the Elizabethian Era*, 1966.
  Sweetness and Light, 1977.
  The Victorian Country House, Oxford, 1970.
Gloag, John, *Mr. Loudon's England*, 1970.
Gyfford, E., *Designs for Elegant Cottages and Small Villas*, 1806.

Halfpenny, John and William, *Chinese and Gothick Architecture Properly Ornamented*, 1752.

Rural Architecture in the Gothick Taste, 1750–52.

Honour, Hugh, *Horace Walpole*, 1957.

Chinoiserie, 1961.

Hunt, T. F., *Designs for Parsonage Houses, Alms Houses, etc.*, 1827.

Exemplars of Tudor Architecture Adapted to Modern Habitations, 1830.

Half a Dozen Hints on Picturesque Domestic Architecture, 1825.

Hussey, Christopher, *The Picturesque*, 1927.

Jones, Barbara, *Follies and Grottoes*, 1953.

Lethaby, W. R., *Philip Webb and His Work*, 1935.

Lewis, William S., *Horace Walpole*, 1961.

Loudon, J. C., *An Encyclopaedia of Cottage, Farm and Villa Architecture*, 1833.

Lugar, R., *Plans and Views of Buildings, Executed in England and Scotland, in the Castelated and Other Styles*, 1811.

Architectural Sketches for Cottages, Rural Dwellings, and Villas, 1805.

Villa Architecture, 1828.

Macaulay, James, *The Gothic Revival, 1745–1845*, 1975.

Malton, James, *An Essay on British Cottage Architecture*, 1798.

Nash, J., *The Mansions of England in the Olden Times*, from 1839.

Papworth, John Buonarotti, *Rural Residences*, 1818.

Piggott, Stuart, *William Stukeley*, Oxford, 1950.

Pugin, Augustus Welby, *Contrasts*, 1836.

The True Principles of Pointed or Christian Architecture, 1841.

Ricauti, T. J., *Rustic Architecture*, 1840.

Robinson, P. F., *Rural Architecture*, 1823.

Saint, Andrew, *Richard Norman Shaw*, 1976.

Summerson, John, *John Nash*, 1952.

Stanton, Phoebe, *Pugin*, 1971.

Stroud, Dorothy, *Capability Brown*, 1950.

Humphry Repton, 1962.

Watkin, David, *Thomas Hope 1769–1831 and the Neo-Classical Idea*, 1968.

The English Vision, 1982.

Walpole, Horace, *A Description of the Villa of Mr. Horace Walpole*, 1784.

Williams, Marjorie, *William Shenstone. A Chapter in Eighteenth Century Taste*, 1935.

Letters of William Shenstone, 1939.

Willis, Peter, *Charles Bridgeman and the English Landscape Garden*, 1977.

Wilson, Michael I., *William Kent*, 1984.

CHAPTER 4

Adamson, Gareth, *Machines at Home*, 1969.

Allen, Gordon, *The Cheap Cottage and Small House*, 1912.

Aslet, Clive, *The Last Country Houses*, 1982.

Mrs. Beeton's Book of Household Management (numerous editions).

Brown, Sanborn C., *Benjamin Thompson, Count Rumford*, 1962.

Cooper, Charles W., *Town and Country, or Forty Years in Service with the Aristocracy*, 1937.

Cullwick, Hannah, *The Diaries of Hannah Cullwick*, ed. Liz Stanley, 1983.

Eastlake, Charles L., *Hints on Household Taste*, 1872.

Edis, Col. Robert, *Decoration and Furniture of Town Houses*, 1881.

Edwards, Frederick, jun., *Our Domestic Fireplaces*, 1865.

Franklin, Jill, *The Gentlemen's Country House and its Plan 1835–1914*, 1981.

Gloag, John, *Design in Modern Life*, 1934.

Harrison, Molly, *The Kitchen in History Reading*, 1973.

Harington, Sir John, *A New Discourse of a Stale Subject, called the Metamorphosis of Ajax*, 1596.

Hellyer, S. Stevens, *The Plumber and Sanitary Houses*, 1877.

Horn, Pamela, *The Rise and Fall of the Victorian Servant*, Dublin, 1975

Jekyll, Gertrude, and Jones, Sydney R., *Old English Household Life*, 1939.

Kerr, Robert, *The Gentleman's House*, 1864.

Lanceley, William, *From Hall-Boy to House Steward*, 1925.

Lewis, Lesley, *The Private Life of a Country House, 1912–1939*, 1980.

Lockhead, M., *The Victorian Household*, 1964.

Loftie, Mrs, *The Dining-Room*, 1878.

Loudon, Mrs, *The Lady's Companion*, 1845.

Martin, Arthur, *The Small House*, 1909.

McBride, Theresa M., *The Domestic Revolution*, 1976.

McNeil, Ian, *Joseph Bramah*, 1972.

Megson, Barbara, *English Homes and Housekeeping 1700–1960*, 1968.

Panton, Jane Ellen, *From Kitchen to Garret*, 1888.

   Suburban Residences and How to Circumvent Them, 1816.

Peel, Dorothy Constance, *The Labour-saving House*, 1917.

Phillips, R. R., *The Servantless House*, 1923.

Quennell, Marjorie and C. H. B., *Everyday Things in England*, 5 vols., 1918–31.

Stanley, Liz, ed., *The Diaries of Hannah Cullwick*, 1983.

Stevenson, John J., *House Architecture*, 1880.

Teale, T. Pridgin, *Dangers to Health*, 1879.
Turner, E. S., *What the Butler Saw*, 1962.
Verey, David, *The Diary of a Victorian Squire*, Gloucester, 1983.

CHAPTERS 5 AND 6

Abercrombie, Patrick, ed. *The Book of the Modern House*, 1939.
Architectural Association, *Parker and Unwin*, 1980.
Aslet, Clive, *The Last Country Houses*, 1982.
Baillie Scott, M. H., *Houses and Gardens*, 1906.
Barron, P. A., *The House Desirable*, 1929.
Boulton, E. H. B., *Timber Buildings for the Country*, 1938.
Brandon Jones, John and others, *C. F. A. Voysey, Architect and Designer*, 1978.
Calabi, Donatella, *Architettura Domestica in Gran Bretagna 1890–1939*, Milan, 1982.
Carter, Ella, *Seaside Houses and Bungalows*, 1937.
Chatterton, Frederick, *Small Houses and Bungalows*, 1932.
Clifford, H. Dalton, *New Houses for Moderate Means*, 1957.
Cresswell, H. B., *The Honeywood File*, 1929.
    The Honeywood Settlement, 1930.
    Grig, 1942.
    Grig in Retirement, 1943.
Davey, Peter, *Arts and Crafts Architecture*, 1980.
Edwards, Arthur M., *The Design of Suburbia*, 1981.
Esher, Lionel, *A Broken Wave: the Rebuilding of England 1940–1980*, 1981.
Gradidge, Roderick, *Dream Houses*, 1980.
    Edwin Lutyens, Architect Laureate, 1981.
Gould, Jeremy, *Modern Houses in Britain 1919–1939*, 1977.
Hussey, Christopher, *The Life of Sir Edwin Lutyens*, 1950.
Hope, Alice, *Town Houses*, 1963.
Jackson, Alan A., *Semi-detached London*, 1973.
James, C. H., and Yerbury, F. R., *Modern English Houses and Interiors*, 1925.
Macartney, Mervyn, ed., *Recent Domestic Architecture*, 5 vols., 1905–   .
McGrath, Raymond, *Twentieth Century Houses*, 1934.
Macleod, Robert, *Charles Rennie Mackintosh*, 1968; new ed., 1983.
Muthesius, Hermann, *The English House*, edited by Dennis Sharp, 1979.
Oliver, Paul and others, *Dunroamin, The Suburban Semi and its Enemies*, 1981.

Pawley, Martin, *Architecture versus Housing*, 1971.
   The £1000 House, 1928.
Phillips, R. Randal, *Houses for Moderate Means*, 1936.
   The Modern English House, n.d.
   The Modern English Interior, n.d.
Richards, J. M., *Castles on the Ground*, 1946; new ed., 1973.
Robinson, John Martin, *The Latest Country Houses*, 1984.
Savage, Peter, *Lorimer and the Edinburgh Craft Designers*, Edinburgh, 1980.
Sparrow, W. Shaw, *The British Home of Today*, 1904.
Stamp, Gavin, *The English House*, 1980.
Swenarton, Mark, *Homes Fit for Heroes*, 1981.
Weaver, Lawrence, *The Country Life Book of Cottages*, 1913.
   Small Country Houses of Today, 2 vols., 1913 and 1919.
Wright, H. Myles, *Small Houses £500–£2,500*, 1937.
Yorke, F. R. S., *The Modern House in England*, 1937; 2nd ed., 1944.

INDEX

Page numbers of illustrations are given in **bold** type.
★indicates houses which are regularly open to the public.
†indicates houses which are owned by the National Trust.